THE
EVERYTHING®
EASY
VEGETARIAN
COOKBOOK

Welcome to the EVERYTHING® Series!

These handy, accessible books give you all you need to tackle a difficult project, gain a new hobby, comprehend a fascinating topic, prepare for an exam, or even brush up on something you learned back in school but have since forgotten.

You can choose to read an Everything® book from cover to cover or just pick out the information you want from our four useful boxes: e-questions, e-facts, e-alerts, and e-ssentials.

We give you everything you need to know on the subject, but throw in a lot of fun stuff along the way, too.

We now have more than 400 Everything® books in print, spanning such wide-ranging categories as weddings, pregnancy, cooking, music instruction, foreign language, crafts, pets, New Age, and so much more. When you're done reading them all, you can finally say you know Everything®!

QUESTION

Answers to
common questions

FACT

Important snippets
of information

ALERT

Urgent
warnings

ESSENTIAL

Quick
handy tips

PUBLISHER Karen Cooper

MANAGING EDITOR, EVERYTHING® SERIES Lisa Laing

COPY CHIEF Casey Ebert

ASSISTANT PRODUCTION EDITOR Alex Guarco

ACQUISITIONS EDITOR Lisa Laing

SENIOR DEVELOPMENT EDITOR Brett Palana-Shanahan

EVERYTHING® SERIES COVER DESIGNER Erin Alexander

Visit the entire Everything® series at *www.everything.com*

THE EVERYTHING®

EASY VEGETARIAN COOKBOOK

Jay Weinstein

Adamsmedia

Avon, Massachusetts

An Everything® Series Book.
Everything® and everything.com® are registered trademarks of F+W Media, Inc.

Published by
Adams Media, a division of F+W Media, Inc.
57 Littlefield Street, Avon, MA 02322. U.S.A.
www.adamsmedia.com

Contains material adapted and abridged from *The Everything® Vegetarian Cookbook* by
Jay Weinstein, copyright © 2002 by F+W Media, Inc., ISBN 10: 1-58062-640-8, ISBN 13: 978-
1-58062-640-8; *The Everything® Guide to Being Vegetarian* by Alexandra Greeley, copyright
© 2009 by F+W Media, Inc., ISBN 10: 1-60550-051-8, ISBN 13: 978-1-60550-051-5; and *The
Everything® Vegetarian Slow Cooker Cookbook* by Amy Snyder and Justin Snyder, copyright
© 2012 by F+W Media, Inc., ISBN 10: 1-4405-2858-6, ISBN 13: 978-1-4405-2858-3.

ISBN 10: 1-4405-8719-1
ISBN 13: 978-1-4405-8719-1
eISBN 10: 1-4405-8720-5
eISBN 13: 978-1-4405-8720-7

5656709I 4/15

Printed in the United States of America.

10   9   8   7   6   5   4   3   2   1

Always follow safety and commonsense cooking protocol while using kitchen utensils,
operating ovens and stoves, and handling uncooked food. If children are assisting in the
preparation of any recipe, they should always be supervised by an adult.

Many of the designations used by manufacturers and sellers to distinguish their products
are claimed as trademarks. Where those designations appear in this book and F+W Media,
Inc. was aware of a trademark claim, the designations have been printed with initial
capital letters.

Cover images © StockFood/Castilho, Rua; StockFood/Dinner, Allison; StockFood/Food
Image Source/Food Image Source; StockFood/Emap Esprit.
Photographs © iStockphoto.com.

This book is available at quantity discounts for bulk purchases.
For information, please call 1-800-289-0963.

Contents

Introduction

WITH MORE THAN 8 million vegetarians in the United States and even more of the population describing themselves as vegetarian-inclined, the necessity for meat-free cookbooks is on the rise. However, simply leaving the meat out of dishes is no longer enough for some conscientious consumers. Veganism, defined as avoiding all animal products, including dairy, eggs, honey, and meat, is also gaining in popularity. Even those who are not vegetarian or vegan may eat vegetarian one or two days per week. These people do so because of the health benefits provided by eating more nutrient-rich fruits and vegetables, instead of cholesterol- and fat-heavy meats and cheese. Many households must now accommodate meat eaters, vegetarians, and vegans alike. All of today's diet options mean the home cook needs to be flexible, and recipes must be adaptable.

Gone are the days when being a vegetarian or vegan meant the most exciting thing you ate was brown rice and plain tofu. These days, meat-free recipes are anything but boring because cooks aren't afraid to load them with flavor that comes from an array of herbs, spices, exotic ingredients, and more common ingredients that are now used in new and interesting ways. Vegetarian and vegan diets no longer make you think of everything you can't eat and instead open the door to all of the delicious foods you may have once ignored. The availability of mouthwatering meat-free recipes, the abundance of prepared vegetarian items in national grocery store chains and at restaurants, and the wealth of information about the health and environmental benefits of a humane diet mean that this way of eating is on the rise. Luckily, this book will arm you with 300 easy and delicious vegetarian recipes.

The Everything® Easy Vegetarian Cookbook features recipes for everyday meals and every appetite. Browse through each chapter and you will see recipes from Asia, India, Africa, Europe, and from just about every part of North America. Whether you're vegan, vegetarian, or a meat eater, these global recipes offer something for everyone. Even better, they can easily be altered to please a variety of taste buds. So, give vegetarian cooking a try, but remember to experiment, eat, and enjoy!

Note: Some recipes contain a VN symbol to indicate that the recipe is vegan. Veganism takes vegetarianism to the next level. The vegan recipes have no animal products at all—including dairy, honey, and ingredients derived from animal byproducts (such as gelatin).

CHAPTER 1

What Does "Vegetarian" Really Mean?

For anyone who has tuned into the national dialogues about the environment or about eating for good health, the term "vegetarian" must certainly be familiar. Even so, precisely what it means causes plenty of confusion. Some "vegetarians" continue to eat chicken; others include seafood. Still others exempt all meat and dairy products from their kitchen. So just what is a vegetarian?

Vegetarian 101

Vegetarians may come from any walk of life, from any educational background, from any culture, and from any age group. So the word "vegetarian" really describes a diverse group of people.

A vegetarian is usually defined as one who does not consume animal flesh, including fish and other seafood. Most people who refer to themselves as vegetarians do eat eggs and dairy products, and may still wear animal products such as fur, leather, and wool. Those who take their stance against cruelty to animals a step further and avoid all animal products, including meat, eggs, dairy, and honey, are called *vegans*. In many cases, this lifestyle choice does not apply only to food but is also reflected in their choice of clothing, makeup, and household products. In most cases, vegans try to live a 100 percent cruelty-free lifestyle.

FACT

Eating meat means wasting an essential resource—water. The average vegetarian diet takes 300 gallons of water per day to produce, while the average meat-filled diet takes more than 4,000 gallons of water to produce.

Vegetarianism and veganism are rapidly gaining in popularity across the United States, but the reason for going meat-free varies greatly from person to person. For some, the decision is reached after watching graphic footage of how animals are housed and then slaughtered on modern factory farms and in slaughterhouses. Some people realize that they can no longer contribute to the routine cruelty they've witnessed. The decision may be based on the many health benefits of choosing a meat-free diet or the desire to try to undo the environmental harm caused by the meat industry. For others, the decision may be based on religion, upbringing, or other personal factors.

Vegetarian Diets

Eating plants as food is basic to all vegetarians, but over time people have devised many different vegetarian categories to suit their various beliefs and lifestyles. For beginners, the distinctions may seem bewildering. Here is a brief overview of some of the most common categories:

- **Lacto-Ovo:** Perhaps the largest group, these vegetarians eat both dairy products and eggs, but no meat of any kind. Their food plan is broad and offers substantial choices to include greens, grains, fruits, and legumes, plus moderate amounts of nuts, dairy products, eggs, and plant oils, and in the smallest quantities, sweets.
- **Lacto:** This group omits eggs but does include all dairy products in a diet that otherwise resembles the lacto-ovo food plan.
- **Ovo:** These vegetarians include eggs but omit all dairy products in a diet that otherwise resembles the typical vegetarian one.
- **Vegan:** Following the strictest plant-based diet, a vegan excludes eating or using all animal meats or products, including all dairy, eggs, and honey. And a strict vegan will not wear anything made from silk, leather, or wool. They are careful to avoid eating any processed foods that may have required animal products in their manufacture, such as refined sugar. While the eating plan sounds restrictive, careful vegans plan their meals to include a wide range of nutrient-dense foods.
- **Flexitarian:** Whether you call this group flexitarian or semi-vegetarian, these people do include some meat in their diet. Some people may eat fish (pescatarian) but no red meat or poultry; for health reasons, this particular form of vegetarianism is increasingly popular. Some may eat poultry, but no red meat or fish. And others may limit their meat intake to an occasional meal. But to the active vegetarian community, flexitarians are just vegetarians in the making.
- **Macrobiotic:** While a macrobiotic diet is not strictly all vegetarian all the time—it may include seafood—it is plant based and prohibits the use of refined sugars, dairy products, and nightshade plants such as potatoes and tomatoes. The diet may have Greek roots, but it has an Asian pedigree: Its founder, a Japanese doctor, turned to Buddhist and Chinese principles to create a diet that includes many Asian foodstuffs, such as miso, tofu, tempeh, Asian greens, and sea vegetables.
- **Fruitarians:** As the word implies, this group eats mainly fresh raw fruit and nuts and seeds, including sprouts. Believers claim that their diet promotes good health, but because it lacks substantial protein sources, it

is not suitable for youngsters. Note that long-term fruitarians may lose a dramatic amount of weight.

- **Raw Foodists:** Most raw foodists are vegans, eating only fruits and vegetables—preferably organic—as they are found in their natural state. But occasionally, some raw foodists eat raw meat and eggs and drink certified raw milk and other certified raw dairy products.

Why Become a Vegetarian?

People turn to vegetarianism for many different and often compelling reasons. For some it's about health; for others it's about ending animal cruelty. And increasingly, vegetarianism appeals to an activist population concerned about environmental issues.

Health Reasons

With their increased worries about the growing incidence of chronic diseases, many Americans cite health as the reason for changing lifestyle and diet. According to the Centers for Disease Control and Prevention (CDC), the leading causes of death in the United States are cancer, diabetes, and heart disease, all of which account for about 1.7 million deaths annually. But the sad truth, say the experts at the American Heart Association, American Cancer Society, and others, is that many of these deaths would have been preventable if the patient had altered his or her diet to reduce consumption of saturated fats (animal fats) and had exercised regularly. Vegetarians, particularly vegans, can drastically reduce their fat intake.

Furthermore, research shows that vegetarians are less likely to become obese; to develop coronary heart disease, high blood pressure, or diabetes; or to suffer from certain cancers. Vegetarians may develop less osteoporosis, suffer less often from constipation, and develop fewer gallstones. It's easy to see why many people become vegetarians simply to feel better, stay slimmer, and to possibly live longer.

Cruelty to Animals

Imagine spending your entire life stuffed into a cramped shed or cage, with barely enough room to turn around, and being fed to grow so large your legs cannot withstand the weight of your body. The only escape from this suffering is when you are en route to being slaughtered using a cruel and outdated method that does not allow you to quickly escape the painful world in which you live, but often prolongs the agony. This is the life of millions of animals, such as chickens, cows, and pigs, on today's modern factory farms and in slaughterhouses. Most animals are not kept in the sunny pastures or on quaint family farms you see on television or in ads. Instead, they are treated as objects so that companies can maximize their profits at the expense of an animal's well-being. The conditions are no better for dairy cows and egg-laying hens. They, too, suffer on factory farms, and when they can no longer produce as expected are slaughtered.

QUESTION

Isn't cruelty to animals illegal?
While some federal laws exist to protect animals on factory farms, they are inadequate and often poorly enforced. Many industry standards that result in suffering, such as debeaking without painkillers and overcrowding animals, are not covered.

Several animal rights groups have released undercover video exposés that show what really happens to animals when people think no one else is looking. Visit PETA's website (*www.peta.org*) to watch video footage online and to learn more about these issues.

The only way to avoid contributing to the cruelty to animals described here is by not eating animals. Whether you are an animal activist or simply a pet owner, you may abstain from eating meat out of respect for an animal's life.

Environmentalism

Global warming, the greenhouse effect, and pollution all play a role in how concerned citizens view their shrinking and endangered natural resources. Many consumers now see a link between their health and the planet's health and are beginning to believe, for example, that supporting livestock on limited agricultural lands just for meat consumption is speeding up the destruction of land and water resources. That is particularly worrisome as populations grow and the demand for meat keeps pace with that growth.

ALERT

Farmed animals consume about 70 percent of the grains and cereals American farmers grow each year, an amount that could presumably feed nearly 9 billion people. In those terms, changing to a plant-based diet could make a positive environmental impact—and feed more people.

Religious Beliefs

Numerous religions—including some Buddhist sects, Jains, Hindus, and Seventh-day Adventists—support a plant-based diet, or at least recommend their believers embrace a vegetarian lifestyle. Other religions, such as Judaism and Islam, prohibit eating certain kinds of meat, specifically pork; Jews who keep kosher follow stricter meat-eating laws, for they are forbidden to consume specific animal or animal products or to eat certain fish and shellfish. And many Baha'is prefer following a vegetarian diet because they believe a plant-based diet is how future generations should eat.

A Growing Movement

Whether health or environmental concerns are propelling the movement forward remains unclear. But statistics show that increasing numbers of Americans and Europeans are switching to a plant-based diet—and many Asians already call themselves vegetarian. As evidence, the growth of vegetarian food items in supermarkets and vegetarian choices in school cafeterias support the notion that, for many consumers, this is a movement whose time has come.

ESSENTIAL

October 1 is World Vegetarian Day, and it begins the month-long series of parties and presentations of National Vegetarian Month, also known as Vegetarian Awareness Month. World Vegan Day occurs on November 1. For a comprehensive listing of what's going on and where, check out *www.vegetarianguides.co.uk*.

Vegetarian Nutrition

What do vegans eat? Where do vegetarians get their protein? Are you worried about becoming anemic? These are common questions many vegans and vegetarians face, but they are largely unfounded. Vegan and vegetarian diets are loaded with essential nutrients and, if done right, can be healthier than a diet full of meat and cheese. Like with any diet, the key is to choose healthful foods and limit your consumption of fatty, sugar- or sodium-heavy, and overly processed foods to a minimum. When choosing the healthiest foods the majority of the time, vegan and vegetarian diets can be full of protein, iron, calcium, and other vital nutrients.

Protein

Protein is a required nutrient for maintaining a healthy body. Luckily, many foods considered the staple of a meat-free diet are rich with protein, without containing any of the fat and cholesterol found in meat. The real protein powerhouse is the soybean. This powerful bean contains a whopping 28.62 grams of protein per cup. Soybeans are commonly used in mock meats and vegan dairy products, but they can also be cooked and prepared in other recipes, so getting your daily requirement of protein should not be a problem if soy is a part of your plan.

HEALTHY PROTEIN SOURCES	
Ingredient	Grams of Protein
Soybeans, boiled (1 cup)	28.62
Lentils, boiled (1 cup)	17.9
Pinto beans, boiled (1 cup)	15.4
Black beans, boiled (1 cup)	15.2
Chickpeas, boiled (1 cup)	14.5
Soymilk, unfortified (1 cup)	8.0
Roasted peanuts (1 ounce)	8.0
Spinach, boiled (1 cup)	7.6
Couscous, cooked (1 cup)	6.0
Broccoli, cooked (1 cup)	5.7
Whole-wheat bread (1 slice)	4.1

Source: USDA.gov

Another benefit to consuming plant-based proteins over animal proteins is that these ingredients typically contain fiber and complex carbohydrates that are not found in animal products. For example, lentils, which contain 17.9 grams of protein per cup, also contain 15.6 grams of fiber!

Iron

Anemia, which can be caused by iron deficiency, is a common concern of some new vegans and vegetarians. People worry that if they leave meat off their plate, they won't be able to reach the daily recommended intake. However, a study in the American Journal of Clinical Nutrition states that there is no significant difference in anemia levels between vegetarians and meat eaters. Vegetarian foods are loaded with iron, and according to the USDA National Nutrient Database for Standard Reference, some of the most iron-rich foods are vegetarian. Several cereals top the USDA's list, along with Cream of Wheat, soybeans, some canned beans, lentils, and more. Iron deficiency is a very real concern, but not more so for vegetarians and vegans than for meat eaters.

Calcium

Cows produce milk to nourish their young and provide all of the nutrients they need to grow strong, just as humans do. But no species drink the milk of another species—except humans. Humans consume cow's milk throughout their lifetime, even though it is the number one cause of food allergies in infants and children, and millions of people around the world suffer from lactose intolerance. Many plant-based foods are an alternative source of calcium that don't come with the health problems associated with drinking cow's milk. Many soymilks and brands of orange juice are fortified with calcium, but it is also found naturally in several items. Collard greens, rhubarb, spinach, and soybeans are just a few of the rich sources of plant-based calcium.

FACT

As with any diet, eating a variety of fresh and healthy foods is the key to optimal nutrition. Vegetarians should focus on consuming a variety of whole foods such as beans, nuts, whole grains, fruits, and vegetables. This, paired with supplements for any vitamins you may be missing, will put you one step closer to a healthier you.

Protein, iron, and calcium are just some of the nutrients you find naturally in vegan and vegetarian foods, but there are a couple that may be best consumed through a supplement or other method. For example, you may prefer to get your daily dose of vitamin D from basking in the sun, but you can also get it through items such as fortified soymilk. However, vitamin B_{12} is not found naturally in plant-based foods and must be obtained through a supplement such as a multivitamin. Just be sure to read the label and make sure it contains B_{12}.

Achieving the Switch

If you have decided that vegetarianism makes sense for you and your lifestyle, you may want to start in slowly, learning what you need to eat and trying out the various vegetarian options in your market. Veggies and fruits are one thing, but what about all those different tofu and soy products? How do they fit in?

Plan a week's worth of menus, basing your main dishes on ones you love, but switching out, say, the beef meatballs for vegetarian ones. Or if you are a chili head, why not create some really appealing meatless chilies, or for that meaty texture, add the taco-seasoned soy ground meat with plenty of beans and salsa for a satisfying entrée.

If cheese is your secret passion and you're a vegan, try any of the shredded or sliced soy cheeses in your favorite recipes. These soy products not only taste and look like meats and dairy cheese, they give nonvegetarians the sense that they can edge into their new diet without feeling deprived of their favorite foods. Even if you get derailed along the way, and keep a few meats and seafood in your menus, you will still feel you've made the great vegetarian leap.

Adapting Recipes for Your Vegetarian Diet

Adapting recipes for your vegan or vegetarian diet can be easy, healthy, and tasty. Some adaptations will include replacing an animal product with a cruelty-free alternative, but others will involve finding a new and exciting approach to food. Instead of always trying to find a way to make your dish taste as if it contains meat, dairy, or eggs, there are many ways for adding rich flavors.

Know Your Cooking Times

Faux meats and soy cheeses may offer flavors similar to animal products, but they are very different than the real thing. Many mock meats require a much shorter cooking time than animal flesh; conversely, vegan cheeses may take much longer to melt. When replacing the flesh or byproduct of an animal with a cruelty-free version, remember to read the package instructions and adjust your cooking times accordingly.

Some Techniques Should Be Avoided

When reading the packaging for many faux meats, you will also find that certain techniques for preparation should be avoided. Some brands of veggie hot dogs or sausages can be prepared on the open flame of a grill, but not all. Cooking on a grill may lead to an overly done and tough veggie dog. For others, baking in the oven may not lead to optimal results. Be sure to read the package instructions before proceeding.

Flavors Don't (Have to) Change

If you are replacing chicken flesh with a vegan product, such as Gardein Chick'n Scallopini, you can build the flavors in your recipe around it just as you would real chicken. The accompanying flavors in your recipe do not need to be adjusted just because you're ditching the meat. You can, however, take this opportunity to explore a diverse world of new flavors. A meal does not have to be centered around meat for the protein—beans, tempeh, and tofu are great alternatives that are rich in protein and will bring new tastes and textures to your cooking.

ESSENTIAL

Finding vegetarian and vegan versions of your favorite products is easier than ever before; just check out all of the options at your local grocery store or natural health food store. For any products that are hard to find in your area, try ordering online.

One of the best parts of trying a new diet is that you get to experiment with new recipes and foods! Ethnic cuisines such as Indian, Japanese, and

Middle Eastern can be more vegetarian friendly than traditional American fare because of the diverse proteins used in their recipes. Experiment with recipes from around the world to find your favorites, or experiment with "veganizing" your family's favorite recipes.

Where to Find Ingredients

Finding the ingredients to help you fuel your vegetarian or vegan diet is now easier than ever before. Many national grocery store chains carry popular mock meats, such as the Boca Burger and MorningStar Farms brands. Several even have health food sections that are stocked with vegan mayonnaise, tofu, and soymilk. Better yet, many of the products sitting in your cupboards right now might be "accidentally vegan." Popular items such as Bisquick, some Duncan Hines cake mixes, and even some flavors of Jell-O brand instant pudding are all vegan if you prepare them with vegan products. For those items that aren't quite as easy to find, try searching online for vegan retailers.

FACT

In addition to online vegan specialty stores that sell food products, there are a multitude of other resources online that will help with your transition to a vegetarian or vegan diet. Groups such as People for the Ethical Treatment of Animals (PETA) offer free vegetarian starter kits, recipes, lists of "accidentally vegan" food items, information on animal rights, and much more.

Staying Veg

Welcome to the world of vegetarianism meals. You've walked the path successfully, but now you ask yourself, Can I stick to the plan? Of course, but if you feel you need family support, ask for it. Treat yourself to vegetarian cookbooks like this one so that your mealtimes don't become routine and your food boring. And continue to learn about this new lifestyle, perhaps even monitoring any health or energy changes you note. That way, you'll feel positive about the choices you've made, and, perhaps, you may even inspire others, too.

Answering the Naysayers

Once you've started on the path, and friends and family see that you've changed how and what you eat, you may face criticism or teasing. As the Vegetarian Resource Group advises, point out to people that vegetarianism is becoming increasingly popular. Then add that eating a meat-free diet is a personal choice you've made for the following reason or reasons, then list them.

You might also win over others to your way of cooking, living, and eating by preparing delicious vegetarian meals, or at the very least, taking friends and family along when you eat at a vegetarian restaurant. They may be in for a real surprise, especially when they total up the bill and see how reasonable vegetarian food costs can be.

CHAPTER 2

Appetizers and Dips

Artichoke Dip

This recipe calls for serving this dip warm, but it is also delicious served cool.

INGREDIENTS | SERVES 8

2 (15-ounce) cans quartered artichoke hearts, drained and rinsed

1 medium red bell pepper, seeded and finely chopped

1 medium green bell pepper, seeded and finely chopped

3 cloves garlic, minced

2 cups mayonnaise

Ground white pepper to taste

1 pound grated Parmesan cheese

Preheat oven to 325°F. In a mixing bowl, mix all ingredients except ¼ pound Parmesan cheese. Spread into a 9" × 9" baking dish or 1½-quart casserole dish, sprinkle remaining Parmesan over the top, and bake 45 minutes until golden brown. Serve with crackers or bread.

Baba Ghanouj VN

Toast whole cumin seeds in a dry pan until they give off a slight smoke and brown slightly, about 2 minutes over medium heat. Pulverize them in a coffee grinder. If you are using powdered cumin, just give it a quick toast in a dry pan until it becomes highly fragrant, about 1 minute.

INGREDIENTS | SERVES 4

2 cloves garlic

1 whole medium eggplant, roasted 1 hour in a 400°F oven, cooled, pulp scooped out

1 tablespoon tahini

1½ teaspoons kosher salt

2–3 teaspoons toasted cumin powder

Juice of 2 medium lemons

¼ cup extra-virgin olive oil plus a little extra for garnish

¼ teaspoon freshly ground black pepper, or to taste

Paprika and chopped parsley for garnish

Pita bread for dipping

1. In a food processor, chop the garlic until it sticks to the walls of the processor bowl. Add eggplant pulp, tahini, salt, cumin, and half of the lemon juice. Process until smooth, gradually drizzling in the olive oil. Season to taste with black pepper, additional salt, and lemon if necessary.

2. Spread onto plates, and garnish with a drizzle of extra-virgin olive oil, a few drops of lemon, a dusting of paprika, and some chopped parsley. Serve with wedges of warm pita bread.

Curry Dip VN

If your raisins aren't especially soft, you can soak them in a little
warm water overnight. They'll plump right up!

INGREDIENTS | MAKES 2½ CUPS

1 teaspoon olive oil

½ cup finely chopped onion

½ medium jalapeño pepper, seeded and finely chopped (about 1 teaspoon)

2 teaspoons finely chopped red bell pepper

1 teaspoon Madras curry powder

1 teaspoon ground cumin

½ teaspoon ground coriander

½ teaspoon ground turmeric

Pinch of cayenne pepper

¼ teaspoon salt, plus more to taste

1 tablespoon very fresh, soft raisins

1½ cups soy mayonnaise

1 tablespoon chopped fresh cilantro

A few drops fresh lemon juice

Ground black pepper, to taste

1. Put the oil in a small skillet over medium heat. Add onions, jalapeño, and bell pepper; cook stirring occasionally until onion is translucent, about 5 minutes.

2. Add curry powder, cumin, coriander, turmeric, cayenne, and ¼ teaspoon salt. Cook 1 minute more until spices are very fragrant. Add raisins and about 1 tablespoon of water. Remove from heat.

3. Transfer to a food processor. Chop on high speed for 30 seconds; scrape down sides of bowl with a rubber spatula. Add soy mayo and cilantro; process 30 seconds more, until smooth and even. Adjust seasonings with lemon, salt, and black pepper.

What Is "Curry Powder"?

What you know as "curry powder" is actually a blend of spices, invented by the British to resemble one of the famous masalas (spice blends) of India. In addition to ground coriander, cumin, mustard seed, turmeric, and other spices, good Madras curry (such as Sun Brand) contains ground, dried curry (or "kari") leaves, which are a typical spice of southern and southwestern India. Most authentic Indian recipes call not for curry powder but a combination of spices (a masala) specifically designed for that dish.

Watercress Dip VN

This dip couldn't be easier to make and is so delicious your guests will be amazed.

INGREDIENTS | MAKES 1½ CUPS

1 bunch watercress, stems trimmed by 1", roughly chopped

1 cup soy mayonnaise

¼ teaspoon salt

¼ teaspoon ground black pepper

In a food processor, purée watercress until very fine, about 1 minute. Add mayonnaise; pulse to combine. Season with salt and pepper.

Chili-Cheese Dip

The perfect accompaniment for this dip is salty corn tortilla chips.

INGREDIENTS | SERVES 12

1 (15-ounce) can vegetarian chili

¼ cup diced onions

½ cup diced tomatoes

1 (8-ounce) package cream cheese or vegan cream cheese

1 cup Cheddar cheese or vegan Cheddar

1 teaspoon garlic powder

1. In a 4-quart slow cooker, place all ingredients.

2. Stir gently; cover and heat on low for 1 hour.

Vegetarian Chili

Most major grocery stores sell canned vegetarian chili. One of the easiest to find is Hormel's Vegetarian Chili with Beans, which contains textured vegetable protein instead of meat.

Vegan Spinach and Artichoke Dip

Serve with toasted pita points or slices of warm baguette.

INGREDIENTS | MAKES 4 CUPS

1 (15-ounce) can artichokes, drained and chopped

2 cups water

1 teaspoon lemon juice

1 tablespoon vegan margarine

1 cup thawed frozen spinach, chopped

8 ounces vegan cream cheese

16 ounces vegan sour cream

⅓ cup vegan Parmesan cheese

¼ teaspoon garlic powder

¼ teaspoon salt

1. In a 4-quart slow cooker, add all ingredients.
2. Cover and cook over low heat for 1 hour.

Red Garlic Mayonnaise (Rouille)

Roasted red peppers give this mayo a smoky and delicious flavor.

INGREDIENTS | MAKES 1½ CUPS

2 cloves garlic, chopped very fine

1 cup mayonnaise or soy mayo

1 small roasted red bell pepper, peeled and puréed

Salt, to taste

½ medium lemon

Pinch of cayenne

In a medium bowl, whisk together garlic, mayonnaise, and roasted pepper purée. Season with a pinch of salt, a squeeze of lemon, and cayenne.

Eggplant Caviar VN

Some people choose not to take the step of salting an eggplant and rinsing the extracted juices. If you do salt your eggplant slices, leave them for 10-20 minutes, then rinse and use it according to your recipe.

INGREDIENTS | SERVES 4

1 large eggplant
2 tablespoons olive oil
1 large onion, finely chopped
3 cloves garlic, finely chopped
1 tablespoon tomato paste
Salt and ground black pepper to taste
Crackers or French bread

1. Heat oven to 400°F. Place eggplant in a baking dish and roast on the middle rack of the oven until very well done, about 1 hour; cool. Cut the eggplant in half and scoop out the soft pulp with a serving spoon. Place on a cutting board and chop thoroughly, until it has the consistency of oatmeal.

2. Heat the olive oil in a large skillet over medium heat for 1 minute. Add onions; cook until they are very soft, but not brown, about 10 minutes; add garlic and cook 1 minute more. Stir in tomato paste; cook 1 minute.

3. Add chopped eggplant and cook until mixture is thickened. An indentation should remain when a spoon is depressed into the mixture. Season with salt and pepper to taste. Serve with crackers or sliced French bread.

Guacamole VN

Serve guacamole with tortilla chips, or as an accompaniment to spicy food.

INGREDIENTS | SERVES 8

2 cloves garlic, chopped

¼ cup chopped red onion

1 small jalapeño pepper, seeded and finely chopped

4 medium ripe Hass avocados, halved, pitted, and scooped from the skin

2 tablespoons lime juice

½ teaspoon salt

Ground black pepper to taste

¼ cup chopped cilantro

1 medium plum tomato, seeded and chopped (optional)

1. In a mortar and pestle, or in a mixing bowl with a fork, mash together the garlic, onion, and jalapeño. Add the avocado and mash until it forms a chunky paste.

2. Add lime juice, salt, pepper, and cilantro and stir to combine. Garnish with chopped tomato if desired.

Hummus VN

Serve hummus with wedges of warm pita bread or crisp vegetables.

INGREDIENTS | MAKES 2 CUPS

2 cloves garlic

1 (16-ounce) can chickpeas, drained and rinsed

3 tablespoons tahini

½ teaspoon kosher salt

2–3 teaspoons toasted cumin powder

Juice of 1 medium lemon, divided

¼ cup extra-virgin olive oil plus a little extra for garnish

Ground black pepper to taste

Paprika and chopped parsley for garnish (optional)

1. In a food processor, chop the garlic until it sticks to the sides of the bowl. Add chickpeas, tahini, salt, cumin, and half of the lemon juice. Process until smooth, gradually drizzling in the olive oil. Add up to ¼ cup cold water to achieve a softer hummus if desired.

2. Season to taste with black pepper and additional salt and lemon to taste.

3. Spread onto plates and garnish with a drizzle of extra-virgin olive oil, a few drops of lemon, a dusting of paprika, and some chopped parsley.

Manchego-Potato Tacos with Pickled Jalapeños

Serve these slightly spicy tacos with your favorite salsa. If you don't have leftover mashed potatoes, make some instant ones with a little less liquid so they're firm.

INGREDIENTS | SERVES 8

1 cup leftover mashed potatoes

8 soft corn tortillas

¼ pound Spanish Manchego cheese or sharp Cheddar, cut into 16 small sticks

16 slices pickled jalapeño pepper

4 tablespoons unsalted butter

1. Spoon 1 tablespoon of mashed potato into the center of each tortilla. Flatten out the potatoes, leaving a 1" border. Lay 2 pieces of cheese and 2 pieces jalapeño onto each tortilla and fold closed into a half-moon shape.

2. In a large skillet over medium heat, melt half of the butter. Gently lay 4 of the tacos into the pan and cook until nicely browned, about 3–4 minutes on each side. Drain on paper towels. Repeat with remaining tacos. Slice tacos in half before serving.

Mini Goat Cheese Pizzas

Fresh cheese made from goats' milk, called chèvre *in France, has a tangy flavor and smooth, creamy texture, even though it's lower in fat than most other cheeses.*

INGREDIENTS | SERVES 8

1 (17-ounce) package frozen puff pastry dough, thawed

3 medium Roma tomatoes, thinly sliced

1 (4-ounce) package fresh goat cheese

2 tablespoons chopped fresh thyme or parsley

1. Heat oven to 400°F.

2. Spread pastry on a lightly floured surface and cut out 8 (4") disks. Place disks on a large ungreased baking sheet. Stack another matching pan atop the disks and bake until golden brown, about 15 minutes. The second pan will keep the disks from rising too high.

3. Top each disk with 2 or 3 slices tomato, ½ ounce goat cheese, and about ½ teaspoon chopped thyme. To serve, warm again in the oven for 1 minute until the goat cheese attains a slight shimmer; serve hot.

Country Corn Cakes

If you have the room, corn is an easy-to-grow garden vegetable best when just picked off the stalk. Good for either breakfast or supper, these corn cakes may be served with melted butter and maple syrup, fruit syrup, or applesauce.

INGREDIENTS | SERVES 4

1 cup buttermilk

1 large egg, lightly beaten

2 tablespoons melted butter

1 cup uncooked grits or coarse cornmeal

1 cup all-purpose flour

1 cup corn kernels, preferably fresh

1 cup cooked black-eyed peas

1 tablespoon baking powder

1 teaspoon baking soda

Salt and ground black pepper to taste

Vegetable oil for pan-frying

1. Combine the buttermilk, egg, and butter in a large mixing bowl. Stir in the grits, flour, corn kernels, black-eyed peas, baking powder, baking soda, salt, and pepper; the batter will be thick.

2. Heat about 2 tablespoons vegetable oil in a large skillet or on a griddle over medium to medium-low heat. When the surface is hot, spoon about ¾ cup of batter per cake onto the surface, and when the bottom has browned, carefully turn the cake over to cook the second side. Be sure the skillet does not overheat or the·cakes will burn. Repeat until all the batter is used up, adding more oil as needed. Serve hot.

About Black-Eyed Peas

If you live in the South, you know the tradition: eat black-eyed peas on New Year's Day to bring good luck for the rest of the year. But these delicious legumes, also known as "cow peas," should be enjoyed often. These "peas" (they are actually beans) are rich sources of calcium, potassium, protein, and vitamin A.

Vegetable Gado-Gado

This appetizer of vegetables with a spicy peanut sauce is Indonesian in origin.

INGREDIENTS | SERVES 8

16 each: 2" carrot sticks, broccoli florets, trimmed green beans, batons of yellow bell pepper and/or yellow summer squash, and assorted other vegetables

½ cup smooth peanut butter

¼ cup honey

¼ teaspoon salt

⅛ teaspoon cayenne pepper

1 tablespoon lime juice

¾ cup (6 ounces) coconut milk

1. Blanch all the vegetables quickly in lightly salted boiling water; plunge immediately into ice-cold water to stop the cooking process. Drain and arrange in an attractive pattern on a serving platter.

2. Combine peanut butter, honey, salt, cayenne, and lime juice in a food processor or mixing bowl; pulse or whisk together until smooth. Gradually work in coconut milk until a saucy consistency is reached. Adjust consistency further if desired with hot water. Serve sauce alongside blanched vegetables.

Sweet Fennel with Lemon and Shaved Parmigiano

This simple but delicious snack typifies the essence of Italian cuisine: Use the best ingredients without overcomplicating them.

INGREDIENTS | SERVES 4

2 bulbs fresh fennel

½ fresh lemon

1 wedge (at least 4" long) Parmigiano-Reggiano cheese or Asiago cheese

1 tablespoon very high quality extra-virgin olive oil

Pinch of salt

1. Trim the stems and fronds from the fennel tops. Break the bulbs apart, layer by layer, using your hands to make long, bite-sized pieces. Discard the core. Arrange the pieces in a pyramid shape onto a small, attractive serving plate.

2. Squeeze the lemon over the fennel. Using a peeler, shave curls of cheese over the fennel, allowing them to fall where they may; make about 10 curls.

3. Drizzle the olive oil over the plate and sprinkle with salt. Serve at room temperature.

Sweet Potato and Rosemary Pizza

Simple four- or five-ingredient pizzas like this one perfume street corners in some parts of Rome.

INGREDIENTS | SERVES 6

1 can store-bought pizza crust or pizza dough of your choice

1½ tablespoons extra-virgin olive oil

1 large sweet potato, peeled

2 sprigs fresh rosemary, or 1 teaspoon dried rosemary leaves

Salt and ground black pepper to taste

What Is a Doubled-Up Sheet Pan?

To buffer baking foods from the direct heat of oven elements, chefs often stack two identical baking sheets (known in the industry as "sheet pans") together, creating an air pocket that protects food from burning on the bottom. Commercially manufactured pans, such as Bakers' Secret pans, incorporate this concept into their insulated bakeware.

1. Preheat oven to 400°F. Spread dough to ¼" thickness onto a doubled-up, lightly greased sheet pan. Brush on a light coating of olive oil.

2. Shred the sweet potato into a ¼"-thick layer over the pizza crust using the large-holed side of a box grater. Distribute rosemary leaves evenly on top of potato. Sprinkle remaining olive oil over the pizza and season it with salt and pepper.

3. Bake 20–25 minutes until potato is cooked through and begins to brown.

Tomato and Black Olive Bruschetta VN

*Avoid buying canned, pitted olives. They have usually been overprocessed
and retain little or no true olive flavor. It is best to select olives from the
delicatessen department, or buy a good, imported olive in a glass jar.*

INGREDIENTS | SERVES 8

4 slices Italian country bread or other crusty rustic bread, about ½" thick

½ cup extra-virgin olive oil

2 cloves garlic, finely chopped

3 medium ripe tomatoes, roughly chopped

½ teaspoon salt

¼ teaspoon freshly ground black pepper

½ cup Gaeta, Kalamata, or black oil-cured black olives (about 24), pitted

¼ cup roughly chopped Italian parsley

Juice of 1 medium lemon

1. Heat a stovetop grill, barbecue grill, or broiler. Cut the bread slices in half.

2. In a small bowl, combine the olive oil and garlic; brush the bread liberally with some of this garlic oil using a pastry brush or your hands. Grill or broil until well toasted on both sides.

3. In a medium bowl, toss chopped tomatoes with 1 tablespoon of garlic oil (make sure to get some pieces of garlic in there), salt, pepper, olives, and parsley. Season to taste with lemon juice.

4. Top each piece of grilled bread with a small mound of tomato-olive mixture. Arrange neatly on a serving platter.

Spicy White Bean–Citrus Dip

Tangy, spicy, unique, and easy to throw together, this stupendous dip is perfect for tortilla chips, fried plantains, raw vegetables, or as a spread in a burrito.

INGREDIENTS | SERVES 12

2 (15-ounce) cans white navy beans, drained and rinsed

¼ cup sour cream

1 tablespoon orange juice concentrate

1 teaspoon hot pepper sauce

1 teaspoon lime juice

Grated zest of 1 medium orange

½ teaspoon salt

½ cup diced white onions

1 tablespoon chopped cilantro

1. Purée the beans, sour cream, orange juice concentrate, hot pepper sauce, lime juice, orange zest, and salt in a food processor until smooth.

2. Add onions and cilantro; mix with a rubber spatula until combined.

Smoky and Spicy

For a smokier taste, replace the hot pepper sauce with puréed chipotle pepper. Chipotle is a smoked jalapeño pepper. They are sold in small six-ounce cans, and are very useful for imparting a smoky flavor and medium heat to dishes. Purée them with the sauce in which they're packed, using a blender or food processor.

Salsa Fresca (Pico de Gallo) VN

Serve Pico de Gallo with chips, with a cheese omelet, or as a sauce with other Mexican foods.

INGREDIENTS | SERVES 8

1½ cups finely diced tomatoes
1 small white onion, finely chopped
1 medium jalapeño pepper, seeded and finely chopped
1 tablespoon puréed chipotle in adobo
½ teaspoon salt
2 teaspoons lime juice
¼ cup chopped cilantro

1. In a blender or food processor, purée one-third of the tomatoes.

2. In a medium bowl, combine tomato purée with remaining tomatoes, onions, jalapeños, chipotle, salt, lime juice, and cilantro. Best if used within 2 days.

Spiced Pecans

It's important to spread these nuts in a single layer when baking. If they are stacked on top of each other, the consistency will not come out right.

INGREDIENTS | MAKES 3 CUPS

1 ounce (2 tablespoons) unsalted butter
1 pound whole, shelled pecans
2 tablespoons light soy sauce
1 tablespoon hoisin sauce
1 or 2 drops of hot pepper sauce

1. Heat oven to 325°F.

2. Melt butter in a large skillet. Add nuts; cook, tossing occasionally, until nuts are well coated. Add soy sauce, hoisin sauce, and hot pepper sauce; cook 1 minute more. Stir to coat thoroughly.

3. Spread nuts into a single layer on a baking sheet. Bake until all liquid is absorbed and nuts begin to brown. Remove from oven. Cool before serving.

CHAPTER 3

Salads and Dressings

Southeast Asian Slaw VN

This crisp, lightly spiced salad is fine enough to roll in Asian-inspired wraps, and combines beautifully with jasmine rice, cooked in coconut milk to make a unique taste.

INGREDIENTS | SERVES 4

¼ head (about ½ pound) napa cabbage

½ medium carrot, grated

1 small red onion, julienned

1 small Thai "bird" chili or jalapeño pepper, seeded and finely chopped

¼ cup chopped cilantro

Juice of 1 medium lime

1 tablespoon rice wine vinegar

1 teaspoon sugar

1 teaspoon vegetable oil

1 or 2 drops sesame oil

½ teaspoon salt

1. Shred the cabbage as fine as you possibly can using a knife, mandolin, or slicing machine. Place in a large bowl and combine with carrot, onion, chili pepper, and cilantro.

2. Dress with lime juice, rice vinegar, sugar, vegetable oil, sesame oil, and salt; toss thoroughly.

3. Refrigerate for at least 30 minutes before serving.

Tomato and Bread Salad (Panzanella) VN

Panzanella (bread salad) is a favorite side dish with sliced cheeses in Italy. Using both yellow and red tomatoes can make this a festive touch on your plate.

INGREDIENTS | SERVES 4

2 cups diced (½") ripe red tomatoes, any variety

¼ cup finely chopped red onion

½ teaspoon salt

1½ tablespoons extra-virgin olive oil

2 teaspoons fresh lemon juice

2 cups day-old country bread, cut into ½" cubes, air-dried overnight or baked 20 minutes at 325°F

¼ cup roughly chopped basil

Ground black pepper, to taste

1. In a medium bowl, combine tomatoes and chopped onion with salt, olive oil, and lemon juice.

2. Toss gently with dried bread cubes and basil.

3. Season with black pepper.

Salad of Celery Root and Pears

The herby, vegetal flavor of celeriac (celery roots) pairs perfectly with pears. Variations on this combination are popular all winter long.

INGREDIENTS | SERVES 6

1 medium celery root (about the size of a baseball), peeled

¼ cup mayonnaise

½ hard-boiled egg, chopped

1 tablespoon finely chopped Italian (flat-leaf) parsley

2 cornichons (little sour gherkins), finely chopped

2 tablespoons Dijon mustard

Juice of 1 medium lemon

Salt and ground black pepper to taste

2 medium ripe Bartlett or Bosc pears

1. Julienne (cut into very thin strips) the celery root.

2. In a medium bowl, combine mayonnaise, chopped egg, parsley, cornichons, mustard, and lemon; toss with celery root. Season with salt and pepper.

3. Peel pears and slice into 6–8 wedges each. Divide dressed celery root into 6 portions and garnish with pear slices.

How to "Chop" Eggs Through a Roasting Rack

Many racks intended for lining roasting pans are made as crosshatch weaves of thin steel rods spaced about a quarter of an inch apart. Not only are these excellent devices for roasting onions, mushrooms, and chili peppers, but they make a great shortcut for chopping eggs. Simply place a peeled hard-boiled egg on the rack, and push it through with the heel of your hand.

Winter Greens Salad with Green Beans and Roquefort Vinaigrette

This salad highlights the fruitiness of blue cheese and the sweetness of the vegetables with the lightness of a vinaigrette dressing.

INGREDIENTS | SERVES 4

½ pound green beans

1 bunch watercress, torn into bite-sized pieces

2 heads Belgium endive, cored and chopped

1 small red onion, sliced

⅓ cup balsamic vinegar

⅓ cup vegetable oil

⅓ cup extra-virgin olive oil

1 tablespoon chopped chives

¼ pound Roquefort or other good quality blue cheese

Coarse (kosher) salt and freshly ground black pepper to taste

1. In 3 quarts of rapidly boiling salted water, cook green beans in 2 separate batches until just tender, about 5 minutes, then plunge them into salted ice water to stop the cooking process. Drain green beans and place in a large bowl.

2. Add watercress, endive, and onion to the bowl with the green beans.

3. In a small bowl, whisk together vinegar, vegetable oil, olive oil, and chives. Roughly break the Roquefort cheese into dressing; stir with a spoon, leaving some large chunks. Season with salt and pepper.

4. Dress salad with ⅓ cup of dressing. Remaining dressing will keep, refrigerated, for 2 weeks.

5. Arrange salad onto 4 plates, with onion rings and green beans displayed prominently on top.

Tatsoi Salad with Orange-Sesame Vinaigrette VN

Light, floral, and zesty, this salad pairs antioxidant-rich Japanese spinach (tatsoi) with springtime-fresh cross-cultural dressing. The salad works equally well with other types of spinach.

INGREDIENTS | SERVES 4

6 cups tatsoi (Japanese "baby" spinach leaves)

¼ cup Orange-Sesame Vinaigrette (see recipe in this chapter)

½ cup thinly sliced red Bermuda onion

1. Wash and dry the tatsoi leaves, then toss gently with half of the dressing. Distribute onto 4 salad plates.

2. Arrange sliced onions atop each salad and finish with a spoonful of dressing.

Orange-Sesame Vinaigrette VN

This dressing works wonderfully with spinach as well as other lettuces and bitter greens.

INGREDIENTS | MAKES 1¼ CUPS

Zest of ½ orange

Zest of ½ lime

1 pickled jalapeño pepper, chopped and 1 tablespoon of the brine it came in

¼ cup Japanese rice wine vinegar

¼ cup orange juice concentrate

1½ teaspoons Dijon mustard

⅛ teaspoon sesame oil

¼ cup peanut oil

¼ cup olive oil

Salt and ground black pepper, to taste

1. Combine zests, pickled jalapeño and brine, rice vinegar, orange concentrate, Dijon, and sesame oil in a blender.

2. Blend on medium speed, slowly drizzling in the peanut and olive oils. Season to taste with salt and pepper.

Madras Curry Dressing

Perfect as a dip for crudités or a spread on sandwiches, this dressing balances the sweetness of dried fruits with the complexity of Indian spices and light chili "heat."

INGREDIENTS | MAKES 1¼ CUPS

1 tablespoon oil
1 small red onion, finely chopped
2 tablespoons chopped red bell pepper
1 teaspoon finely chopped and seeded jalapeño pepper
2 tablespoons Madras curry powder
1 teaspoon ground coriander
1 teaspoon ground turmeric
1 tablespoon raisins, soaked in ½ cup warm water
2 tablespoons lime juice
1 cup mayonnaise
2 tablespoons chopped cilantro
Salt and ground black pepper to taste

1. In a small skillet, heat oil over medium heat for 1 minute. Add onions, bell pepper, and jalapeño. Cook until onions are translucent, about 2 minutes.

2. Add curry powder, coriander, and turmeric to the skillet. Cook 4 minutes more, stirring with a wooden spoon. Some of the spices may stick—this is not a problem. Remove from heat; allow to cool a few minutes.

3. Drain the raisins. In the bowl of a food processor, combine onion mixture and raisins. Pulse until smooth, scraping sides of bowl frequently.

4. Add half of lime juice and the mayonnaise. Pulse to combine, then stir in cilantro. Season with salt, pepper, and remaining lime juice. Can be made up to 1 week in advance.

Classic American Potato Salad

Fourth of July picnics wouldn't be the same without this favorite. For an interesting twist, try making it with specialty potatoes, like slim "fingerlings," from your produce market.

INGREDIENTS | SERVES 8

¾ cup mayonnaise

1 teaspoon sugar

2 teaspoons Dijon-style mustard

2 pounds potatoes (any variety), boiled, skinned, and cut into chunks

Salt and ground white pepper to taste

2 tablespoons chopped chives

1. In a small bowl, whisk together the mayonnaise, sugar, and mustard.

2. Place the potatoes in a large bowl and add the mayonnaise mixture; toss them gently to coat. Season with salt and pepper to taste. Garnish with chives.

Asian Cucumber Salad VN

This refreshing, crisp dish is the perfect counterbalance with grilled tempeh, spicy corn fritters, and other hearty fare. European-style or "English" cucumbers have a thin, edible skin.

INGREDIENTS | SERVES 4

¼ cup rice wine vinegar

1 teaspoon sugar

1 teaspoon chopped jalapeño pepper

1 European-style long cucumber or 1 large regular cucumber

1 or 2 drops sesame oil

1. In a medium bowl, whisk together rice vinegar, sugar, and chopped jalapeño.

2. If using a European cuke, it is not necessary to peel, but if using an American cuke, peel it. Halve the cucumber lengthwise; remove seeds. Slice seeded cucumber very thinly into half-moons. Combine with dressing, drizzle in a few drops of sesame oil, and toss to coat.

3. Marinate for at least 10 minutes before serving.

Succotash Salad VN

In summer, any excuse to use sweet corn is welcome. In New England, fresh cranberry beans are in the market in June and July, and they are delicious in this complete-protein salad.

INGREDIENTS | SERVES 8

8 ears sweet corn, shucked (or 16 ounces frozen corn)

2 (16-ounce) cans pinto or red kidney beans, drained and rinsed

¼ cup champagne vinegar or rice wine vinegar

¼ cup extra-virgin olive oil

¼ cup chopped chives

Salt and ground black pepper to taste

1. Shave corn kernels from cob, shearing them from the stem end to the tip with a knife. Cook in rapidly boiling salted water for 1 minute.

2. Place corn into a large bowl and toss with beans, vinegar, oil, and chives; season to taste with salt and pepper.

Seasonal Tip

During cooler, autumn weather, substitute chopped shallots for the chives, and add 1 teaspoon toasted ground cumin for seasonality. Serve warm or room temperature.

Summer Vegetable Slaw VN

Bursting with summer's bounty, this slaw is a colorful fiesta. The best renditions of this summer harvest celebration utilize whatever vegetables are freshest and best at the market—the more the better!

INGREDIENTS | SERVES 8

1 small head napa cabbage or regular green cabbage (about 1 pound)

1 large carrot or 2 medium carrots

¼ pound snow peas

1 medium red bell pepper, seeded

1 medium green bell pepper, seeded

1 medium yellow bell pepper, seeded

12 green beans

1 small red onion, peeled

2 ears fresh sweet corn, shucked

½ teaspoon sugar

¼ cup cider vinegar

1 tablespoon vegetable oil (preferably peanut oil)

Pinch of celery seeds

Salt and ground black pepper to taste

1. Quarter and core the cabbage; slice as thinly as possible. Using a swivel peeler, shave carrot into as many paper-thin curls as you can. Discard or save remaining carrot for another use. Cut carrot curls, snow peas, bell peppers, green beans, and onion into fine julienne. Cut corn kernels from the cob.

2. Combine all vegetables in a large mixing bowl; dress with sugar, vinegar, oil, celery seeds, and salt and pepper to taste. Allow to sit at least 10 minutes before serving.

Caesar Salad

Vegetarian Worcestershire sauce is now available in health food stores, and may be added for an additional dimension if you wish, but this vegetarian version of America's favorite salad is authentic in taste.

INGREDIENTS | SERVES 8

1 egg yolk

1 tablespoon Dijon mustard

2 tablespoons lemon juice

2 cloves garlic, finely chopped

½ cup peanut oil

¼ cup grated Parmigiano-Reggiano cheese

Pinch of cayenne pepper (optional)

Salt and ground black pepper to taste

1 medium head romaine lettuce, torn into bite-sized pieces

1 cup croutons

1 small wedge Parmigiano-Reggiano cheese (optional)

1. In a mixing bowl or food processor, combine the egg yolk, mustard, lemon juice, and garlic. Vigorously whisk or process in the oil, starting just a drop at a time and gradually drizzling it in a small stream until all is emulsified into a smooth mayonnaise. Stir in the cheese, cayenne, salt and pepper, and a little extra lemon if desired.

2. Place the lettuce and croutons in a large bowl and toss with the dressing. Divide onto 8 plates, arranging croutons on top. If desired, shave curls of Parmigiano over each salad using a vegetable peeler. Dressing may be made up to 1 week in advance.

Three-Bean Salad VN

When taken as part of a lunch buffet with some form of grain salad, bean dishes like this complete the amino acids necessary in our diet, forming complete proteins. And it's simply delicious!

INGREDIENTS | SERVES 6

1 (16-ounce) can green beans
1 (16-ounce) can yellow wax beans
1 (16-ounce) can red kidney beans
1 medium onion
½ cup sugar
⅔ cup vinegar
⅓ cup vegetable oil
½ teaspoon salt
⅛ teaspoon ground black pepper

1. Drain the beans. Slice the onion thinly, then cut the slices into quarters.

2. In a large bowl, whisk together the sugar, vinegar, oil, salt, and pepper.

3. Add the beans and onions to the dressing and mix well. Chill at least 4 hours or overnight, stirring occasionally. If desired, salad can be drained before serving.

Polynesian Banana Salad VN

Excellent with spicy food and rice, this rich, sweet salad can be part of a meal, snack, or dessert.

INGREDIENTS | SERVES 4

4 medium bananas, peeled
1 cup coconut cream
2 tablespoons curry powder
1 cup soft raisins
4 teaspoons shredded coconut

1. Slice the bananas about ½" thick on a slight diagonal bias.

2. In a medium bowl, whisk together the coconut cream and curry powder. Add the bananas and raisins; toss gently to coat.

3. Transfer to a serving dish and sprinkle with shredded coconut.

Insalata Caprese (Tomato-Mozzarella Salad)

Since the essence of this salad is its purity of flavors, only the highest quality of ingredients should be used. If you are unable to find fresh basil or good, fresh-kneaded mozzarella, make something else.

INGREDIENTS | SERVES 4

4 large, ripe red tomatoes

2 loaves fresh mozzarella (or mozzarella di Bufala)

8 top sprigs of fresh basil

2 tablespoons very high quality extra-virgin olive oil

Coarse (kosher) salt and freshly ground black pepper to taste

1. Slice each tomato into 4 thick slices, discarding the polar ends. Cut each mozzarella into 6 even slices. Shingle alternating tomato and mozzarella slices onto 4 plates, starting and ending with tomato slices.

2. Garnish with 2 sprigs basil each and drizzle olive oil over all. Sprinkle with salt and a few grinds of black pepper. Serve immediately.

The Colors of Olive Oil

Younger, early harvest olives produce greener, gutsier, spicy oils preferred by many. But color can be deceptive, and assertive oils are not right for all applications. "Greener is better" is not always true. Later harvests have a more buttery, smoother flavor.

Grilled Vegetable Antipasto VN

Some people prefer to remove the skin of the eggplant, but this is not a necessary step.

INGREDIENTS | SERVES 8

1 medium eggplant, cut into 16 wedges, lightly salted

2 medium yellow squash, quartered lengthwise

2 medium zucchini, quartered lengthwise

4 plum tomatoes, halved lengthwise

2 medium green bell peppers, halved and seeded

2 medium red bell peppers, halved and seeded

8 portobello mushrooms, stems removed

2 heads radicchio, core intact, quartered

2 tablespoons olive oil

½ cup extra-virgin olive oil

1 tablespoon balsamic vinegar

Pinch of sugar

2 shallots, finely chopped

4 sprigs fresh thyme, leaves picked and chopped

Salt and ground black pepper, to taste

Pinch of crushed red pepper (optional)

8 sprigs parsley

1. Heat grill (or a stovetop grill pan) to medium-hot. In a large mixing bowl, toss eggplant, squash, zucchini, and tomatoes, peppers, mushrooms, and radicchio with olive oil, crushed red pepper, salt, and pepper.

2. Cook vegetables on the grill, without turning, until they are slightly more than halfway done. Eggplant and mushrooms will take longest, while the radicchio will take only a few moments. Cook the tomatoes skin-side down only. Turn the other vegetables to finish, then arrange on a serving platter.

3. In a small bowl, whisk together the extra-virgin olive oil, vinegar, sugar, shallots, and chopped thyme. Season to taste with salt and pepper, and drizzle over cooked vegetables while they're still warm.

4. Marinate 20 minutes before serving, garnished with parsley sprigs.

Wild Rice Salad with Mushrooms and Almonds VN

Pair grains like wild rice with beans and legumes for complete proteins, essential to the vegetarian diet and a curiously good culinary combination!

INGREDIENTS | SERVES 8

8 ounces uncooked wild rice

1 cup whole almonds

1 tablespoon extra-virgin olive oil

8 ounces shiitake or other exotic mushrooms, sliced

Salt and ground black pepper to taste

¼ cup yellow raisins, soaked in 1 cup warm water for 30 minutes up to overnight

2 scallions, chopped

Juice of 1 large lemon (about ¼ cup)

1 teaspoon ground cumin, toasted in a dry pan until fragrant

Salt and ground black pepper to taste

1. Boil the wild rice in lightly salted water until tender and most grains have burst open (about 35 minutes); drain.

2. Lightly toast almonds in a dry skillet over medium heat until most have small browned spots and they attain an oily sheen; spread on a plate to cool to room temperature.

3. Heat oil in a medium skillet over high heat for 1 minute, then cook the mushrooms until tender, about 5 minutes; season with salt and pepper.

4. In a large mixing bowl, combine rice, almonds, mushrooms (with their cooking oil), raisins, and scallions. Dress with lemon and cumin and season with salt and pepper. Toss well to coat. Serve chilled or at room temperature.

Tabbouleh VN

Middle Eastern bulgur wheat absorbs water quickly, giving it a pliable and chewy texture unlike anything else in the world. This is an everyday dish in Egypt. It's perfect with stuffed grape leaves.

INGREDIENTS | SERVES 6

1 cup cracked (bulgur) wheat

1 small cucumber, peeled and chopped

3 scallions, finely chopped

2 medium tomatoes, seeded and chopped

2 tablespoons chopped chives

1 cup chopped Italian parsley

½ cup extra-virgin olive oil

Juice of 2 medium lemons (about ½ cup)

Salt and ground black pepper to taste

1. Soak the wheat in 1 quart of water for 15 minutes (or overnight). Drain and squeeze out excess moisture by tying up in a cheesecloth or clean kitchen towel.

2. Combine with cucumber, scallions, tomatoes, chives, and parsley in a large mixing bowl. Dress with olive oil, lemon juice, salt, and pepper.

3. Set aside to marinate for 2–3 hours before serving.

Olive Oil

Spain is the largest exporter of high-quality olive oil, but the United States imports mostly Italian oil. Most (over half) of Italian production comes from the regions of Puglia, Calabria, and Sicily, but in the United States, the only region most people know is Tuscany, which accounts for only a tiny fraction of Italy's extra-virgin exports.

Tofu Salad

Soy foods are a vegetarian's best way to get complete, natural proteins. Keeping delicious, snackable marinated tofu, like the kind here, on hand for sandwiches, salads, and wraps will ensure that you get these nutrients in a satisfying way. Marinated tofu will remain fresh in the fridge for four to five days. One of the best ways to store the cubes is in a ziplock bag with all the air squeezed out of it.

INGREDIENTS | SERVES 6

5 tofu cakes, cut into 1" cubes

Marinade:

2 tablespoons water

Ground black pepper to taste

2 teaspoons sugar

¼ cup dry sherry or Chinese cooking wine

¼ cup soy sauce

¼ cup white wine vinegar

1 clove garlic, chopped

Pinch of anise seed, toasted and ground

1 tablespoon sesame oil

1 tablespoon vegetable oil

Salad:

1 medium carrot, julienned

¼ pound snow peas, julienned

1 cup finely chopped cabbage

5 cremini or white mushrooms, sliced

4 scallions, julienned

Dressing:

½ teaspoon salt

2 teaspoons sesame oil

2 teaspoons tamari soy sauce

Juice of ½ medium lemon

Ground black pepper, to taste

1 tablespoon sugar

1. Spread tofu into a single layer in a baking dish or sheet pan. In a medium bowl, whisk together the ingredients for the marinade and pour it over the tofu. Marinate for 3 hours or overnight in the refrigerator, turning occasionally.

2. Combine salad ingredients in a medium bowl, toss with dressing, and place in the refrigerator to marinate for 1 hour. Add tofu, and toss gently to combine just before serving.

Sweet White Salad with Shaved Asiago

Despite looking like a tan turnip, jicama, a Mexican tuber, is sweet, crisp, and juicy.

INGREDIENTS | SERVES 4

4 ounces (about 2 heads) frisée or fine curly endive

4 heads Belgium endive, cut into 1" pieces

1 cup julienned jicama

1 small sweet onion, peeled and thinly sliced

2 tablespoons lemon juice

1 tablespoon extra-virgin olive oil

1 teaspoon orange juice concentrate

Salt and ground black pepper to taste

Wedge of Asiago, Parmigiano-Reggiano, or other good "grana" cheese

1. Wash and dry the frisée; add to a large bowl with Belgium endive, jicama, and onions and mix to combine.

2. In a small bowl, whisk together the lemon juice, olive oil, orange juice concentrate, salt, and pepper; toss with salad to coat.

3. Arrange salad onto 4 plates, piling it as high as possible. Using a swivel peeler, gently shave 4 or 5 curls of Asiago cheese over each salad and serve immediately.

What Are Grana Cheeses?

Grana cheeses are the hard, aged "grating" cheeses. Grana, literally, means "grainy," and describes these crumbly cheeses very well. They'll sprinkle into flakes or fine powder on a grater. The undeniable king of the grana cheeses is Parmigiano-Reggiano. This Parmesan cheese has a nutty, savory flavor and, sometimes, delicate crystalline specks in it that impart a dynamic texture.

Barley and Corn Salad VN

Whole grains like barley provide many of the B vitamins vegetarians need to fight off diseases, and are higher in protein, vitamin E, zinc, phosphorus, and other phytonutrients than refined grains.

INGREDIENTS | SERVES 8

1 cup barley

1 pound frozen sweet corn kernels

1 medium carrot, peeled and finely chopped

2 ribs celery, finely chopped

1 medium red onion, finely chopped

1 tablespoon cider vinegar

2 tablespoons extra-virgin olive oil

½ cup chopped fresh herbs, such as parsley, chives, basil, oregano, mint and/ or cilantro

Salt and freshly ground black pepper to taste

1. Boil the barley in 2 quarts of lightly salted water until it is very tender, about 30 minutes. Drain and spread on a platter to cool. Heat a dry cast-iron pan or skillet over high heat for 1 minute. Add the corn and cook without stirring until some kernels attain a slight char and the corn has a smoky aroma, about 5 minutes.

2. Combine the barley, corn, carrot, celery, and onion in a mixing bowl. Add all remaining ingredients and toss well to coat.

Mixed Baby Greens with Balsamic Vinaigrette VN

This is a nice, basic house salad. Experiment with different greens, vinegars, and oils to make it your own.

INGREDIENTS | SERVES 6–8

8 ounces baby mixed greens (mesclun)

1 bunch chives, cut into 2" pieces

1 tablespoon good-quality balsamic vinegar

2 tablespoons good-quality extra-virgin olive oil

1 tablespoon finely chopped shallots

Salt and ground black pepper to taste

Wash greens and spin dry; combine with chives in a mixing bowl. In a small bowl, whisk together the vinegar, oil, and shallots; season with salt and pepper to taste. Add dressing to greens and toss well to coat.

Warm Spinach Salad with Potatoes, Red Onions, and Kalamata Olives VN

Use this recipe as a master recipe—a starting point from which to make myriad variations of your own.

INGREDIENTS | SERVES 4

1 pound fresh curly-leaf spinach, washed, stems removed

¼ cup extra-virgin olive oil

1 pound small red potatoes, cut into ½" slices, boiled 10 minutes, and drained

1 medium red onion, halved, and thinly sliced

20 Kalamata or other black olives, pitted

1 tablespoon balsamic vinegar

Salt and ground black pepper to taste

1. Place spinach in a large mixing bowl.

2. Heat olive oil in a large skillet over high heat for 1 minute; add potatoes and onions. Cook over high heat until lightly browned, about 5 minutes. Remove from heat; add olives, vinegar, salt, and pepper.

3. Pour potato mixture over spinach and invert skillet over bowl to hold in heat. Allow to steam 1 minute, then divide onto 4 plates, arranging potatoes, onions, and olives on top. Serve warm.

Lentil Salad VN

Lentils cook more quickly than other beans and never require soaking. Serve this salad with a bed of dressed baby greens.

INGREDIENTS | SERVES 8

1 pound dried lentils

2 medium onions, finely chopped

3 scallions, chopped

1 medium green bell pepper, seeded and finely chopped

1 tablespoon toasted cumin powder

Pinch of cayenne pepper

Juice of 1 medium lemon (about ¼ cup)

2 tablespoons extra-virgin olive oil

Salt and freshly ground black pepper to taste

1. Wash lentils and pick through to take out any stones. Boil in 2 quarts of lightly salted water until tender but not broken up. Spread on a pan to cool.

2. Once cool, place in a large mixing bowl and combine with onions, scallions, and green pepper. Dress with remaining ingredients.

California Garden Salad with Avocado and Sprouts VN

The fruity taste of large, green Florida avocados gives this salad a lighter, more summery flavor, though the Hass is the more authentic California item.

INGREDIENTS | SERVES 4

1 tablespoon fresh-squeezed lemon juice

3 tablespoons extra-virgin olive oil

1 tablespoon finely chopped shallot or chive

½ teaspoon salt

¼ teaspoon freshly ground black pepper

2 heads Boston or Bibb lettuce

2 medium ripe tomatoes, cored, cut into 8 wedges each

1 medium ripe avocado

1 cup alfalfa sprouts

1. Make the dressing: Combine the lemon juice, olive oil, shallot, salt, and pepper in a small bowl, mixing well.

2. Arrange lettuce leaves, stem-end in, onto 4 plates, making a flower petal pattern. Inner leaves will be too small, so reserve them for another use.

3. Toss tomatoes in 1 tablespoon dressing; place 4 onto each salad. Peel avocado, cut into 8 wedges, and toss with 1 tablespoon dressing. Place 2 wedges on each salad. Divide sprouts into 4 bunches and place a bunch in the center of each salad. Drizzle salads with remaining dressing or serve on the side.

Marinated Beet Salad

The natural sweetness and delicate texture of fresh beets seem to have been forgotten by many Americans, who have relegated this noble root vegetable to a curiosity in many places. This simple salad highlights these distinctive characteristics.

INGREDIENTS | SERVES 6

1 pound fresh beets, stem end trimmed

1 tablespoon red wine vinegar

1 tablespoon rice wine vinegar or white wine vinegar

2 tablespoons extra-virgin olive oil

¼ teaspoon dried oregano leaves

¼ teaspoon dried basil leaves

½ teaspoon freshly chopped parsley

1 teaspoon finely chopped shallots

6 large romaine lettuce leaves, washed

Salt and ground black pepper, to taste

1. Boil beets in a small saucepan with red wine vinegar and enough water to cover. Cook until tender, about 30 minutes. Chill, then peel and cut into ¼" slices.

2. In a medium bowl, combine rice wine vinegar, olive oil, oregano, basil, parsley, and shallots. Season with salt and pepper. Add beets, and marinate 10–15 minutes.

3. Place lettuce leaves on 6 plates, trimming stem end to fit inside rim. Arrange beets in an overlapping pattern atop lettuce leaves and drizzle with remaining marinade. Season with salt and pepper to taste.

Basic Egg Salad

For a healthier option, replace the 4 whole eggs with 6 hard-boiled whites and 2 yolks. You can also replace some of the mayonnaise with plain nonfat Greek yogurt.

INGREDIENTS | MAKES ⅔ CUP

1 tablespoon cream cheese, softened

¼ cup mayonnaise

1 tablespoon finely minced onion

4 hard-boiled eggs, peeled and chopped

1 tablespoon sweet pickle relish, slightly drained

Salt and ground black pepper to taste

1. In a medium bowl combine the softened cream cheese with mayonnaise and onion and mix well.

2. Add the chopped egg and relish. Add salt and pepper to taste. Chill before serving.

The Secret to Making Perfect Hard-Boiled Eggs

The perfect hard-boiled egg has a delicate white and a fully cooked yolk, without even a hint of the unattractive gray shadow that affects improperly cooked egg. The perfect hard-boiled egg is also easy to peel. To achieve this, put the eggs in enough cold water to cover them by 1" and boil for 1 minute only. Then remove from heat, cover the pan, and let it sit undisturbed for exactly 15 minutes. Then, transfer the eggs to a bath of ice water for 15–20 minutes. They should then peel easily.

Warm Potato Salad with Balsamic Vinegar and Onions VN

This substantial main-course salad is highly adaptable. Serve it atop fresh spinach leaves in the springtime for a hearty lunch, or beside scrambled eggs for a winter breakfast.

INGREDIENTS | SERVES 8

2 tablespoons extra-virgin olive oil

2 medium onions, thinly sliced

1 tablespoon fresh thyme leaves (about 3 sprigs) or 1 teaspoon dried

½ teaspoon sugar (optional)

1 tablespoon balsamic vinegar

1 pound small white potatoes, peeled, halved, boiled until very tender, and drained

Salt and ground black pepper to taste

Pinch of fresh chopped Italian parsley

1. Heat olive oil over medium heat in a medium skillet for 1 minute; add onions, thyme, and sugar. Cook slowly, stirring regularly with a wooden spoon, until onions are very soft and browned to the color of caramel, about 10 minutes.

2. Stir in balsamic vinegar; remove from heat. Toss gently with warm cooked potatoes and season with salt and pepper. Allow to rest 10 minutes before serving, garnished with chopped parsley.

Curried New Potato Salad

Simple to make, but with a complex taste, this is a delicious and attractive buffet item for a picnic lunch.

INGREDIENTS | SERVES 8

2 pounds red-skinned new potatoes, cut into bite-sized chunks

3 hard-boiled eggs, cut into bite-sized chunks

1 recipe Madras Curry Dressing (see recipe in this chapter)

1 tablespoon chopped cilantro

1. Boil potatoes in lightly salted water until very tender, about 15 minutes; cool.

2. In a large bowl, combine eggs and curry dressing; add the potatoes and toss to coat. Serve chilled, garnished with cilantro leaves.

CHAPTER 4

Soups, Stews, and Chilies

Miso Soup VN

The delicious cloudy broth you've been served in Japanese restaurants, with diced tofu and seaweed, is made with a fermented soybean and grain paste called miso.

INGREDIENTS | SERVES 4

5 cups vegetable or mushroom stock

1 piece kombu (kelp, a dried seaweed), about 5" square

1 teaspoon soy sauce

3 tablespoons light (yellow) miso, such as shiro mugi miso

2 scallions, chopped

2 ounces firm tofu, diced into small cubes

4 teaspoons wakame seaweed (instant)

Green onions (optional)

1. Bring stock and kombu to a boil in a soup pot. Cover; remove from heat and let stand 5 minutes. Strain; stir in soy sauce.

2. In a mixing bowl, mix about ¼ cup of the warm stock into the miso paste with a wire whisk until the miso is dissolved. Pour this mixture back into the remaining stock. Place scallions, diced tofu, and wakame into 4 bowls. Gently ladle soup into the bowls. Garnish with green onions if desired.

English Garden Pea Soup

Pair this soup with a salad and fine artisanal bread for a hearty and satisfying meal.

INGREDIENTS | SERVES 2

1 tablespoon olive oil

2 cloves garlic, thinly sliced

1 medium leek, thinly sliced

2 cups garden peas

1 cup white wine

3 tablespoons plain yogurt

3 tablespoons heavy cream, optional

Salt and ground black pepper to taste

Snipped chives

Garlic croutons

Soy bacon

Tarragon leaves

1. Heat the olive oil in a medium saucepan over medium heat and sauté the garlic and leek for 3–4 minutes.

2. Spoon this mixture into a blender or food processor. Add the peas, white wine, yogurt, and heavy cream if using. Purée until smooth. Season with salt and pepper.

3. Pour into soup bowls and garnish with chives, croutons, bacon, and tarragon leaves.

Tomato Soup VN

*This classic soup is delicious hot or cold. Add some heavy cream
before blending if you like cream of tomato soup.*

INGREDIENTS | SERVES 6

2 tablespoons olive oil

1 medium onion, chopped

2 cloves garlic, finely chopped

4 pounds ripe tomatoes, peeled,
seeded, and roughly chopped

1 teaspoon salt

¼ teaspoon freshly ground black pepper

1. In a large soup pot over medium heat, heat olive oil for 1 minute. Add onion and garlic; cook 5–10 minutes until onions are translucent but not browned.

2. Stir in tomatoes; simmer 25–30 minutes until tomatoes are submerged in their own juices.

3. Purée in a blender or food processor until smooth. Season with salt and black pepper.

Smooth Moves: Blender versus Food Processor

They seem interchangeable sometimes, but they're not. Blenders and food processors are different tools with different strengths. For ultrasmooth purées, a blender is the first choice. For rougher purées, or chopping jobs with drier ingredients, use a processor.

Gazpacho

Nothing could be simpler than buzzing together a refreshing summer soup in minutes in a blender. Serve with a few drops of garlic-infused olive oil drizzled on top and a crust of country bread on the side.

INGREDIENTS | SERVES 6

8 medium tomatoes, seeded

1 large cucumber, peeled

2 medium green bell peppers, seeded

1 slice bread, torn into postage-stamp-sized pieces

1 clove garlic, sliced

2 tablespoons extra-virgin olive oil

1½ teaspoons red wine vinegar

1 teaspoon salt

1–2 cups tomato juice

Hot pepper sauce (optional)

Roughly chop the tomatoes, cucumber, and peppers. Combine with bread, garlic, olive oil, vinegar, and salt in a food processor or blender. Purée at high speed until consistency is soupy but still slightly chunky. Stir in tomato juice to desired consistency and season with hot pepper sauce to taste.

Creamy Carrot Soup

This soup will surprise your guests who won't believe there's no cream in this sweet, delicious soup. For best smoothness, use a blender to purée, not a food processor.

INGREDIENTS | SERVES 6

2 tablespoons oil

1 medium onion, chopped

2 tablespoons white wine

4 cups thinly sliced carrots

2 cups vegetable stock or broth

1 teaspoon salt

Ground white pepper, to taste

Pinch of nutmeg

1¼ cups milk

2 teaspoons freshly chopped parsley or chives

1. Heat oil in large saucepan over medium-high heat. Add onion and sauté for 5 minutes; add wine and carrots. Cook for 1 minute until wine evaporates.

2. Add stock, salt, pepper, and nutmeg. Bring to a boil, then reduce to simmer for 20 minutes.

3. Ladle into a blender, add 1 cup milk, and blend until very smooth. Adjust consistency with more milk if necessary. Be careful when puréeing the hot liquid, starting the blender on the slowest speed and/or doing the job in 2 batches. Serve garnished with a sprinkling of parsley or chives.

Cream of Asparagus Soup

Asparagus presents a challenge to the frugal chef: what to do with the sizable trimmings from the bottom stalks of this expensive vegetable. Here's the answer.

INGREDIENTS | SERVES 6

2 tablespoons olive oil

1 medium onion, chopped

4 cloves garlic, finely chopped

1 bunch fresh asparagus or trimmings from several bunches equal to 1 pound, roughly chopped

1 teaspon salt plus more to taste

¼ cup white wine or sherry (optional)

3 cups vegetable stock or water

1 package (10 ounces) frozen green peas

2 cups cream or half-and-half

¼ teaspoon freshly ground black pepper

1 teaspoon dried basil

Green Peas for Color

Since asparagus, favas, and some other green veggies fade when cooked in a soup, chefs sometimes add a cup of frozen peas to the hot soup just before puréeing it. It revives the soup's color and adds a touch of sweetness.

1. In a large, heavy-bottomed pot over medium heat, heat olive oil for 1 minute. Add onion, garlic, asparagus, and 1 teaspoon salt; cook 15 minutes until onions are translucent but not browned.

2. Add wine or sherry; cook 1 minute until alcohol evaporates; add the stock. Simmer 20 minutes until asparagus is very tender. Remove from heat; stir in frozen peas.

3. Purée in a blender or food processor until smooth; transfer back to pot and heat just to a simmer. Add cream; season with salt to taste, black pepper, and basil. May be served hot or cold.

Smooth Cauliflower Soup with Coriander

Here's another no-cream "cream soup." This soup is equally delicious hot or chilled.

INGREDIENTS | SERVES 4–6

2 tablespoons unsalted butter or olive oil

1 medium onion, chopped

2 tablespoons white wine or dry sherry

1 medium head (about 2 pounds) cauliflower, cut into bite-sized pieces

2 cups vegetable stock

1 teaspoon salt

Ground white pepper, to taste

1 teaspoon ground coriander

¾ cup cold milk

Chopped chives or parsley for garnish

1. In a large saucepan or soup pot over medium-high heat, melt butter. Add onion; cook until it is translucent but not brown, about 5 minutes. Add wine and cauliflower; cook for 1 minute to steam out the alcohol. Add the stock, salt, pepper, and coriander; bring up to a rolling boil.

2. Simmer until cauliflower is very tender, about 15 minutes. Transfer to a blender.

3. Add half of the milk and purée until very smooth, scraping down the sides of the blender vase with a rubber spatula. Be very careful during this step, since hot liquids will splash out of blender if it is not started gradually (you may wish to purée in 2 batches, for safety). Transfer soup back to saucepan and thin with additional milk if necessary. Garnish with chopped herbs just before serving.

Vichyssoise (Potato and Leek Soup)

Elegant, classic French soups like this make the right first course for a formal occasion. Serve chilled or warm, and make sure to use the prettiest leek pieces, cut very precisely, for the garnish.

INGREDIENTS | SERVES 12

1 tablespoon olive oil

1 medium onion, chopped

1 pound (about 3 or 4) potatoes, any variety, peeled and cut into 1" chunks

2 bunches leeks, chopped, thoroughly washed twice; 1 cup of the best parts set aside for garnish

1 teaspoon dried sage leaves

1 bay leaf

¼ cup white wine

2 quarts vegetable stock or water

Salt and ground white pepper to taste

1. In a large soup pot over medium heat, heat olive oil for 1 minute. Add onion, potatoes, and all but 1 cup of the chopped leeks; cook 10 minutes until onions turn translucent. Add sage, bay leaf, and wine. Cook 1 minute more. Add stock. Bring to a full boil; reduce heat to a simmer and cook for 45 minutes until potatoes are very tender and starting to fall apart.

2. Carefully purée the soup in a blender in small batches. Season to taste with salt and white pepper. Steam, boil, or sauté the remaining cup of leeks, and serve the soup garnished with a spoonful of leeks in the center.

Chilled Curry Potato-Fennel Soup

While this soup is delicious hot or cold, it's particularly refreshing in the summer, with enough substance to stand on its own as a main course.

INGREDIENTS | SERVES 10–12

1 large Idaho russet potato, peeled

1 large Spanish onion

1 head sweet fennel, tassel-like fronds removed and set aside

1 medium red bell pepper, seeded

1 tablespoon olive oil

1 (1") piece fresh gingerroot, peeled and finely chopped

2 cloves garlic, finely chopped

2 teaspoons good-quality Madras curry powder

3 cups vegetable stock

1 jalapeño pepper, seeded and finely chopped (optional)

1 quart buttermilk

1 cup half-and-half

Salt and ground white pepper to taste

1 tablespoon chopped Italian parsley, for garnish

1. Chop the potato, onion, fennel, and red bell pepper coarsely. In a large soup pot over medium-high heat, heat the oil for 1 minute. Add the chopped vegetables, ginger, and garlic. Cook until onions are translucent, about 5 minutes; stir in curry powder and cook 5 minutes more.

2. Add vegetable stock; raise heat to high and bring to a full boil. Reduce to a simmer; cook until potatoes are falling-apart tender, about 15 minutes.

3. Chill and purée the soup in a blender or food processor. Add the chopped jalapeño, buttermilk, and half-and-half. Season to taste with salt and white pepper. Serve garnished with chopped parsley and/or sprigs from the reserved fennel fronds.

Corn and Potato Chowder

Corn and dairy form a complete protein, making this a very nourishing dish for vegetarians.

INGREDIENTS | SERVES 12

8 ears sweet corn, shucked

1 tablespoon olive oil

2 large onions, chopped

2 stalks celery, chopped

1 pound red potatoes, cut into 1" chunks

3 sprigs fresh thyme or 1 teaspoon dried thyme leaves

1 bay leaf

3 teaspoons salt

1 smoked chili (optional)

4 ounces (1 stick) unsalted butter

3 quarts vegetable stock or water

4 teaspoons cornstarch, dissolved in ¼ cup water

1 quart cream or milk

Ground white pepper and additional salt to taste

2 tablespoons chopped fresh parsley for garnish

1. Cut corn kernels from the cob using a slicing motion with a kitchen knife. Reserve the cobs and set kernels aside.

2. In a large soup pot over medium-high heat, heat olive oil for 1 minute. Add the corn cobs, onions, celery, potatoes, thyme, bay leaf, salt, and chili if using. Cook until onions are translucent, about 5 minutes. Add the butter and cook gently, allowing the vegetables to stew in the butter for about 5 more minutes.

3. Add the vegetable stock. Raise heat to high and bring to a full boil. Lower to a simmer and cook 10 minutes more. Remove the corn cobs; add cornstarch mixture and simmer 5 minutes more. Stir in the cream and adjust seasoning with white pepper and salt. Serve sprinkled with parsley.

Brothy versus Thick Chowders

While generations of canned soups have conditioned us to believe that chowder is, by definition, a thick, pasty soup, some of the most delicious handmade versions of these chunky soups feature a thin, though rich, broth.

Pumpkin Soup with Caraway Seeds

Butternut squash or acorn squash substitute very well for pumpkin in this soup. Each imparts its own character, making this three recipes in one. Ground chipotle chili and/ or Spanish paprika impart subtle smokiness for an additional dimension.

INGREDIENTS | SERVES 8–10

2 tablespoons unsalted butter or olive oil

1 medium onion, chopped

1 large carrot, peeled and thinly sliced

2 cups peeled, cubed pumpkin

¼ teaspoon whole caraway seeds

1½ cups vegetable stock or broth

3 cups cold milk

Salt and ground black pepper to taste

½ dried chipotle chili or ½ teaspoon smoked Spanish paprika

1. Melt the butter in a heavy-bottomed soup pot over medium heat. Add the onion, carrot, pumpkin, and caraway seeds and sauté, stirring occasionally, 8–10 minutes until pumpkin becomes tender and begins to brown (some may stick to pan).

2. Add stock (or broth) and simmer for 20 minutes. Remove from heat and stir in 2 cups milk.

3. Purée in batches in a blender until smooth, adjusting consistency with remaining milk. Season with salt and pepper to taste. Sprinkle the chipotle chili or Spanish paprika on top.

Pumpkin-Ale Soup VN

Use fresh pumpkin in place of the canned pumpkin purée when the ingredient is in season. You'll need 3¾ cups of cooked, puréed fresh pumpkin.

INGREDIENTS | SERVES 6

2 (15-ounce) cans pumpkin purée

¼ cup diced onion

2 cloves garlic, minced

2 teaspoons salt

1 teaspoon pepper

¼ teaspoon dried thyme

5 cups vegetable broth

1 (12-ounce) bottle pale ale beer

1. In a 4-quart slow cooker, add the pumpkin purée, onion, garlic, salt, pepper, thyme, and vegetable broth. Stir well. Cover and cook over low heat for 4 hours.

2. Allow the soup to cool slightly, then process in a blender or with an immersion blender until smooth.

3. Pour the soup back into the slow cooker, add the beer, and cook for 1 hour over low heat.

Acorn Squash Soup with Anise and Carrots

When the weather turns chilly, fall and winter squashes like acorn squash start showing up in the markets—just in time to make this smooth, soothing velvety soup. Remove the seeds from the squash. Salt and toast them for 20 minutes in a medium-temperature oven for a crunchy soup garnish.

INGREDIENTS | SERVES 6

1 tablespoon olive oil

2 medium onions, chopped

1 teaspoon salt

1 medium acorn squash (about 2 pounds), peeled and cut into 1" chunks

2 large carrots, peeled and cut into 1" chunks

1 teaspoon anise seeds, toasted in a dry pan for 2 minutes until fragrant

¼ cup cognac or brandy

1 pint vegetable stock

1–2 cups skim milk

Fresh parsley, chopped

1. Heat the olive oil in a heavy medium saucepot over medium heat. Add the onions and salt; cook until translucent and slightly browned, about 10 minutes.

2. Lower heat to medium-low. Add the squash, carrots, and anise seeds; cook slowly, stirring the browned bits from the bottom of the pan frequently with a wooden spoon. These browned natural sugars will give the soup its caramelized complexity.

3. When the squash is soft and browned, add the cognac; cook for 2 minutes to steam off the alcohol. Add the stock; simmer 15 minutes.

4. In a blender, purée the soup with as much skim milk as necessary for a thick but soupy consistency. Season to taste. Serve garnished with a sprinkling of chopped parsley.

Mushroom, Barley, and Collard Greens Soup [VN]

This should be called "Health Soup" for its concentration of cancer-fighting antioxidants, folate-rich greens, nourishing whole grains, and complete protein-forming combinations.

INGREDIENTS | SERVES 12

2 tablespoons olive oil

2 pounds mushrooms (any variety)

1 large onion, chopped

1 medium carrot, peeled and chopped

2 stalks celery, chopped

4 cloves garlic, roughly chopped

2 bay leaves

2 tablespoons fresh or 2 teaspoons dried marjoram or oregano leaves

1½ teaspoons fresh or ½ teaspoon dried rosemary leaves

2 teaspoons salt

½ teaspoon freshly ground black pepper

2 cups pearl barley, rinsed

3 quarts vegetable stock or water

2 (10-ounce) packages frozen chopped collard greens

1. Heat the oil in a large soup pot over medium-high heat for 1 minute. Add mushrooms, onions, carrot, celery, garlic, bay leaves, marjoram, rosemary, salt, and pepper. Cook until vegetables have softened significantly and are stewing in their natural broth, about 15 minutes.

2. Stir in barley and stock. Bring the soup up to a full boil, then reduce to a medium simmer and cook until barley is tender, about 40 minutes.

3. Add the collards; cook about 10 minutes more. Season to taste.

Red Bean and Pasta Soup VN

*This is a hearty winter soup to warm up chilly nights. Serve it
with a dollop of sour cream atop each serving.*

INGREDIENTS | SERVES 8

1 medium onion, chopped

3 cloves garlic, sliced

3 tablespoons olive oil

1 teaspoon oregano

2 bay leaves

1 (8-ounce) can tomato sauce

2 teaspoons salt

1 tablespoon soy sauce

1 (16-ounce) package red beans,
soaked overnight in 1 quart cold water
and drained

10 sprigs Italian parsley, including stems

6 cups vegetable stock or water

2 cups cooked pasta (any small shape,
such as orzo or ditalini)

1. In a pot large enough to hold all ingredients, cook onions and garlic with olive oil over medium heat for 5 minutes until onions are translucent. Add oregano, bay leaves, tomato sauce, salt, and soy sauce. Bring to a simmer and add beans, parsley, and stock (or water).

2. Bring to a boil, then reduce to a low simmer and cook for 90 minutes until beans are tender enough to mash between two fingers.

3. In a blender, purée ⅓ of the beans very well; add them back to the soup. Add cooked pasta and bring back to a boil for 1 minute more before serving.

Jamaican Red Bean Stew VN

Make your own jerk seasoning by combining thyme, allspice, black pepper, cinnamon, cayenne, onion powder, and nutmeg.

INGREDIENTS | SERVES 4

2 tablespoons olive oil

½ medium onion, diced

2 garlic cloves, minced

1 (15-ounce) can diced tomatoes

3 cups diced sweet potatoes

2 (15-ounce) cans red kidney beans, drained

1 cup coconut milk

3 cups vegetable broth

2 teaspoons jerk seasoning

2 teaspoons curry powder

Salt and ground black pepper to taste

1. In a sauté pan over medium heat, add the olive oil, then sauté the onion and garlic for about 3 minutes.

2. In a 4-quart slow cooker, add all ingredients. Cover and cook on low heat for 6 hours.

Smoky Black-Eyed Pea Soup with Sweet Potatoes and Mustard Greens VN

Black-eyed peas offer some of the delicious earthiness of green peas, but also a savory touch. Use any dark leafy greens you'd like, fresh or frozen, in place of the mustard greens. Julienned kale or collard greens are excellent choices and are equally antioxidant-rich.

INGREDIENTS | SERVES 10–12

1 tablespoon olive oil

2 ribs celery, chopped

1 medium carrot, chopped

1 medium onion, chopped

2 teaspoons salt plus more to taste

1 teaspoon dried thyme

2 teaspoons dried oregano

1 teaspoon ground cumin

1 dried chipotle chili, halved

2 bay leaves

1 pound dried black-eyed peas or navy beans, washed and picked through for stones

2 quarts vegetable stock or water

1 large sweet potato, peeled and diced into 1" cubes

1 (10-ounce) package frozen mustard greens, chopped

1 (22-ounce) can diced tomatoes

Ground black pepper to taste

Croutons of cornbread or other bread

Chopped cilantro for garnish

1. In a large, heavy-bottomed Dutch oven over medium heat, heat the oil for 1 minute. Add celery, carrot, onion, and 2 teaspoons salt; cook 5 minutes until onions are translucent. Add thyme, oregano, cumin, chipotle chili, and bay leaves; cook 2 minutes more. Add black-eyed peas and vegetable stock. Bring to a boil, then simmer 2 hours until beans are very tender, adding water or stock if necessary.

2. Add the sweet potatoes and cook 20 minutes more. Stir in mustard greens and tomatoes. Cook 10 minutes more until the potatoes and greens are tender. Adjust seasoning with salt and pepper and consistency with additional vegetable stock or water. The soup should be brothy. Serve garnished with cornbread croutons and a sprinkling of chopped cilantro.

White Bean Soup with Chipotle Croutons VN

If you can find it, be sure to use the soy chorizo in this soup. It's tube shaped and packed in plastic; unwrap the "sausage" and sauté the crumbles until golden. Sprinkle them into the soup once it's hot.

INGREDIENTS | SERVES 4

2 (15.5-ounce) cans navy or other white beans, drained and rinsed

1½ cups fresh or canned tomatoes

1 teaspoon dried oregano

1 teaspoon chipotle sauce

Salt and ground black pepper to taste

2 tablespoons olive oil or 4 tablespoons if using soy chorizo

1 (12-ounce) package soy chorizo "sausage" (optional)

1 cup garlic croutons sprinkled with ground chipotle chiles

2 tablespoons diced red onion

Chopped fresh cilantro for garnish

1. Put 1 can of beans into the blender or food processor. Add the tomatoes, oregano, chipotle sauce, salt and pepper, and 2 tablespoons olive oil and process until fairly smooth. Pour into a large saucepan.

2. If using the chorizo, heat 2 more tablespoons olive oil in a medium skillet over medium-low heat and crumble and sauté the sausage.

3. Heat the soup in a saucepan over medium heat, stirring in the remaining beans and the chorizo "sausage" if using. To serve, ladle soup into individual bowls and garnish with the croutons, red onions, and cilantro.

Lentil Soup with Cumin VN

This is the fastest bean soup you can make, ready in about an hour, without any soaking of beans. It gets better as it sits overnight, when the flavors marry, so make enough for two or more meals.

INGREDIENTS | SERVES 8

1 large carrot

1 stalk celery

1 medium onion

1 medium potato, peeled

1 tablespoon olive oil

2 cloves garlic

½ teaspoon whole cumin seeds, toasted in a dry pan for 1 minute until fragrant

2 teaspoons salt plus more to taste

1 cup lentils

8 cups vegetable stock

Ground black pepper to taste

1. Chop carrot, celery, onion, and potato into bite-sized pieces; cut garlic into very small slices.

2. Heat the oil over medium heat in a pot large enough to hold everything and add the cut vegetables, garlic, and cumin, plus 2 teaspoons of salt. Cook for 5 minutes, then add the lentils and vegetable stock. Raise heat to bring to a boil, then reduce heat to medium-low.

3. Simmer 1 hour, season with salt and pepper, and serve warm.

Tuscan White Bean Soup VN

This northern Italian classic is just as hearty, wintry, and delicious as it was in our grandfathers' generation. Tuscans place a hunk of rustic bread at the bottom of the bowl before adding the soup. The crust of bread soaks up soup and becomes a velvety "reward" waiting to be found.

INGREDIENTS | SERVES 8

1 tablespoon olive oil

1 medium onion, chopped

1 large leek, white part only, finely chopped

3 cloves garlic, finely chopped

3 teaspoons fresh rosemary leaves or 1 teaspoon dried

1 bay leaf

3 quarts vegetable stock or water

2 cups large white (Great Northern) beans (soaked overnight if desired)

Salt and ground white pepper to taste

1 tablespoon extra-virgin olive oil

Flavored Oils

To infuse oil with flavor and complexity, stuff herbs, spices, and garlic cloves into a bottle of it and steep for at least three days and up to two weeks or more. Fine olive oil becomes a transcendent condiment when perfumed by rosemary, thyme, savory, garlic, peppercorns, dried mushrooms, or truffles. Or you can buy infused oils at gourmet stores.

1. In a large soup pot over medium heat, heat olive oil for 1 minute. Add onion, leeks, and garlic; cook 10 minutes, until onions turn translucent, stirring frequently. Add rosemary and bay leaf; cook 5 minutes more.

2. Add stock and beans. Bring to a full boil; reduce heat to a simmer and cook 90 minutes until beans are very tender and starting to fall apart (cooking time will vary depending on age of beans and whether or not they were soaked—assume 30 minutes less for soaked beans).

3. Carefully purée ⅔ of the soup in a blender; add back to rest of soup. Season with salt and white pepper. Serve with a few drops of fine extra-virgin olive oil sprinkled on top.

Mediterranean Stew

Serve this stew, redolent with the flavors of the sunny Mediterranean, with warmed pita bread.

INGREDIENTS | SERVES 4

3 tablespoons olive oil

3 cloves garlic, crushed and minced

1 (15.5-ounce) can chickpeas, drained and rinsed

1 (19-ounce) can cannellini beans, drained and rinsed

2 cups roasted tomatoes

1½ cups artichoke hearts, quartered

1 cup vegetable broth

4 tablespoons grated Parmesan cheese

1 teaspoon crushed red pepper, or to taste

1 teaspoon dried oregano

Salt and ground black pepper to taste

Chopped sun-dried tomatoes

Chopped Italian parsley

Garlic-seasoned croutons

Crumbled feta cheese

Fresh oregano leaves

1. Heat the olive oil in a large saucepan over medium heat and sauté the garlic for 2–3 minutes or until golden.

2. Reduce the heat to medium-low. Stir in the chickpeas, cannellini beans, roasted tomatoes, artichoke hearts, broth, Parmesan cheese, crushed red pepper, oregano, salt, and pepper. Cook and stir for about 10 minutes.

3. Serve in individual bowls, garnishing with sun-dried tomatoes, parsley, croutons, feta, and oregano.

White Bean Cassoulet VN

The longer you cook this cassoulet, the creamier it gets.

INGREDIENTS | SERVES 8

1 pound dried cannellini beans
2 cups boiling water
1 ounce dried porcini mushrooms
2 medium leeks
1 teaspoon canola oil
2 medium parsnips, peeled and diced
2 medium carrots, peeled and diced
2 stalks celery, diced
½ teaspoon ground fennel
1 teaspoon crushed rosemary
1 teaspoon dried chervil
⅛ teaspoon cloves
¼ teaspoon salt
¼ teaspoon freshly ground black pepper
2 cups vegetable stock

1. The night before making the soup, place the beans in a 4-quart slow cooker. Fill with water to 1" below the top of the insert. Soak overnight.

2. Drain the beans and return them to the slow cooker.

3. In a heatproof bowl, pour the boiling water over the dried mushrooms and soak for 15 minutes.

4. Slice only the white and light green parts of the leek into ¼" rounds. Cut the rounds in half.

5. In a nonstick skillet, heat the oil; add the parsnip, carrots, celery, and leeks. Sauté for 1 minute just until the color of the vegetables brightens.

6. Add to the slow cooker along with the spices. Add the mushrooms, their soaking liquid, and the stock; stir.

7. Cook on low for 8–10 hours.

Vegan Chili VN

This hearty warm-up goes especially well with cornbread and a tall glass of lemonade.

INGREDIENTS | SERVES 8

¼ cup olive oil

2 cups chopped onions

1 cup chopped carrots

2 cups chopped assorted bell peppers

2 teaspoons salt

1 tablespoon chopped garlic

2 small jalapeño peppers, seeded and chopped

1 tablespoon ground ancho chili pepper or ½ teaspoon crushed red pepper flakes

1 chipotle in adobo, chopped

1 tablespoon toasted cumin seeds, ground or 4 teaspoons ground cumin, toasted briefly in a dry pan

1 (28-ounce) can plum tomatoes, roughly chopped, juice included

1 (16-ounce) can red kidney beans, rinsed and drained

1 (16-ounce) can cannellini beans, rinsed and drained

1 (16-ounce) can black beans, rinsed and drained

1 cup tomato juice

Finely chopped red onions for garnish

Chopped fresh cilantro for garnish

1. Heat the oil in a heavy-bottomed Dutch oven or soup pot. Add the onions, carrots, bell peppers, and salt; cook 15 minutes over medium heat until the onions are soft. Add the garlic, jalapeños, ancho, chipotle, and cumin; cook 5 minutes more.

2. Stir in tomatoes, beans, and tomato juice. Simmer about 45 minutes. Serve garnished with red onions and cilantro.

Golden West Chili

This chili, which is as bright and sunny as a day in California, can be altered to suit your taste. Just keep the proportions about the same. Serve this with fresh flour tortillas.

INGREDIENTS | SERVES 6

3 tablespoons vegetable oil

1 large onion, diced

12 ounces ground soy "meat" crumbles

1 tablespoon chili powder, or more to taste

1 (15-ounce) can golden hominy

1 (15.5-ounce) can canary beans, drained and rinsed

1 (15.5-ounce) can pigeon peas, drained and rinsed

1 cup green salsa

1 cup Mexican beer, or more as needed

Salt and ground black pepper to taste

3 tomatillos, chopped for garnish

Grated Cheddar cheese

Chopped fresh cilantro

Diced avocados

Toasted pumpkin seeds

1. Heat the oil in a large saucepan over medium heat and sauté the onion until partially golden, about 5 minutes. Add the soy "meat" crumbles and continue cooking for 3–4 more minutes. Stir in the chili powder. Add the hominy, beans, pigeon peas, salsa, and beer and stir well.

2. Reduce the heat to medium-low and continue cooking and stirring about 8 minutes more. Season with salt and pepper. Serve in individual bowls, garnishing with tomatillos, cheese, cilantro, avocado, and pumpkin seeds.

What Is Hominy?

If you are not from the South nor have ever eaten that Mexican classic posole, you may not be familiar with the white corn kernel known as hominy. Made from dried corn kernels that have been treated chemically, hominy has a pleasant texture and mild taste. In the Southwest and in Mexico, larger-kernel hominy is available and is known as posole. The smaller hominy is sold canned in most supermarkets; look for the larger variety at a Latino market.

Five-Pepper Chili VN

Sound the alarm! This chili will set mouths aflame.

INGREDIENTS | SERVES 8

1 medium onion, diced

1 small jalapeño pepper, seeded and minced

1 small habanero pepper, seeded and minced

1 medium red bell pepper, seeded and diced

1 medium poblano pepper, seeded and diced

2 cloves garlic, minced

2 (15-ounce) cans crushed tomatoes

2 cups diced fresh tomatoes

2 tablespoons chili powder

1 tablespoon cumin

½ tablespoon cayenne pepper

⅛ cup vegan Worcestershire sauce

2 (15-ounce) cans pinto beans

1 teaspoon salt

¼ teaspoon black pepper

In a 4-quart slow cooker, add all ingredients. Cover and cook on low heat for 5 hours.

Black Bean, Corn, and Fresh Tomato Chili

*Tofutti makes a delicious nondairy sour cream called Sour Supreme,
and it can be found in some national grocery store chains.*

INGREDIENTS | SERVES 4

1 medium red onion, diced

1 medium jalapeño pepper, seeded and minced

3 cloves garlic, minced

1 (15-ounce) can black beans, drained

1 (15-ounce) can corn, drained

3 tablespoons chili powder

1 tablespoon paprika

1 teaspoon dried oregano

1 teaspoon ground cumin

½ teaspoon chipotle powder

2 cups vegetable broth

1 teaspoon salt

¼ teaspoon black pepper

2 cups diced tomato

¼ cup chopped cilantro

4 tablespoons sour cream or vegan sour cream

1. In a 4-quart slow cooker, add all ingredients except tomatoes, cilantro, and sour cream. Cover and cook on low heat for 5 hours.

2. When the chili is done cooking, mix in the tomatoes and garnish with the cilantro. Top with sour cream or vegan sour cream.

CHAPTER 5

Root Vegetables

Roasted Yukon Gold Potatoes VN

Here's a mess-free way of making roasted potatoes, which works as well on the barbecue grill as in the oven. It calls for wrapping the seasoned, cut potatoes in a foil pouch before cooking.

INGREDIENTS | SERVES 4

1 medium onion, roughly chopped

2 tablespoons olive oil

¼ cup chopped parsley

3 or 4 cloves garlic, minced

1½ pounds Yukon gold potatoes, washed, sliced ½" thick

1 teaspoon salt

Ground black pepper to taste

1. Heat oven to 425°F.

2. Put onion, olive oil, parsley, and garlic in blender or food processor and purée until smooth. Toss with potatoes and salt, then wrap in a ready-made foil oven bag or a sheet of foil crimped to seal. Potatoes should be no more than 2 layers deep.

3. Bake on a sheet pan in center rack for 45 minutes until potatoes are tender when poked with a fork. Season with pepper.

Turnip and Potato Gratin

Warm, bubbly, and delicious, this is comfort food at its best. Serve as a side dish or add some crumbled soy sausage to make this a main dish.

INGREDIENTS | SERVES 8

2 tablespoons unsalted butter

2 garlic cloves, finely chopped

2½ pounds all-purpose potatoes, peeled and cut into ½" cubes

2 pounds turnips or rutabagas, peeled and cut into ½" cubes

4 cups heavy cream

2 teaspoons salt

1 teaspoon freshly ground black pepper

Fresh versus Frozen

Did you know that nutritional content is often higher in frozen vegetables than in fresh? Vitamins begin to dissipate in certain vegetables, such as corn and peas, within minutes of picking. By a few hours, they may have lost up to half of their nutrient value. Freezing quickly after harvest is sometimes the best way to lock in flavor and food value. Also, since the frozen vegetable companies have huge buying power, they often get the best part of the crop.

1. Preheat oven to 350°F. Grease the bottom and sides of a 9" square baking dish with the butter and spoon the garlic all over.

2. Mix the potatoes and turnips and arrange them in the pan.

3. Bring the cream to a boil in a medium saucepan on the stove and season with salt and pepper, then pour it over the vegetables and cover the pan with foil.

4. Bake 30 minutes, then uncover and cook another 20–25 minutes. The potatoes and turnips should be very tender and the sauce should be bubbling and browned on top when done.

Parsnip Purée

In New England, farmers leave some parsnips in the ground at the end of the fall harvest season. Through the winter, starches turn to sugars in these parsnips deep below the frozen earth. When the ground thaws in the spring, the farmers dig these supersweet roots and send them to market.

INGREDIENTS | SERVES 6

2 pounds parsnips
½ cup milk
8 tablespoons unsalted butter
Salt, to taste

1. Peel the parsnips and boil in salted water. Cook until very tender, about 10–15 minutes. Drain in a colander.

2. While the parsnips are draining, heat the milk in a small pot over medium-low heat.

3. Combine the parsnips and milk in a food processor or blender. With the motor going, gradually add the butter, making sure it is well mixed and the purée is very smooth. Season lightly with salt.

Yuca con Mojo (Yuca with Garlic and Lime) VN

Earthy-tasting yuca (cassava) has a potato-like texture, but a nutty, somewhat mushroom-like fragrance and taste. Frozen yuca is also available, and is fine for this dish.

INGREDIENTS | SERVES 8

1½ pounds peeled yuca, cut into 1½" chunks
½ teaspoon salt
2½ tablespoons fresh-squeezed lime juice, divided
¼ cup extra-virgin olive oil
3 large cloves garlic, finely chopped
1 tablespoon chopped fresh herb, such as cilantro or parsley (optional)

1. Simmer the yuca about 25 minutes in enough water to cover it, along with the salt and ½ teaspoon of the lime juice, in a covered pot. It should be fork tender but not mushy. Drain; remove woody center core and discard it. Transfer to a plate and cover to keep warm.

2. In a small skillet, heat the oil. Remove pan from heat and add the garlic. Stir in remaining lime juice and herbs. Pour this sauce over the yuca and serve immediately.

Roasted Beets VN

Roasting brings natural juices to the surface of these magenta roots and caramelizes them into a sweet, intensely flavored crust.

INGREDIENTS | SERVES 8

2 pounds beets (about 8, tangerine-sized), peeled, cut into 1" wedges

1 tablespoon olive oil

¼ teaspoon ground cinnamon

¼ teaspoon salt

Chopped Italian parsley (optional)

Cooking Beets—Preserving Nutrition

The flavorful, nutrient-rich juices in beets are water-soluble. To lock in the sweetness, color, and food value of these wonderful vegetables, consider cooking them in their skins. When boiling them, put a few drops of red wine vinegar in the water, which also helps seal in beet juices. Beets can also be baked whole, like potatoes, then peeled and sliced.

1. Heat oven to 350°F.

2. In a large bowl, toss beets with olive oil, cinnamon, and salt. Spread into a single layer on a baking sheet (preferably nonstick).

3. Roast on the middle rack of the oven until tender, about 1 hour, turning once after 30 minutes. If desired, serve sprinkled with chopped parsley.

French Fries VN

The key to crispy, golden French fries is cooking the rinsed, high-starch potatoes twice—once at a moderate temperature to cook them through, then a second time at a higher temperature to crisp them.

INGREDIENTS | SERVES 8

2 pounds (about 5) high-starch potatoes, such as Idaho baking potatoes or Yukon golds, peeled

Peanut oil for frying

Salt to taste

Frying versus Sautéing

Frying means cooking at moderate temperature (usually 340°F–360°F) in a large amount of oil, such as a pan filled two inches deep, or a pot filled with oil for deep-frying. Sauté is a cooking method using small amounts of oil, usually measured in teaspoons or tablespoons, and very high heat—nearly at the oil's smoking point.

1. Cut potatoes into 2½"-long strips, ½" wide and thick; soak in enough cold water to cover them for 30 minutes. Drain and dry with absorbent towels.

2. Heat oil to 350°F. Fry potatoes in small batches until they are soft and tender enough to mash between your fingers, about 2 minutes (make sure to allow time between each batch for the oil to come back up to temperature—a fry thermometer is essential); drain on paper towels. The potatoes may be fried again once cooled (about 5 minutes) or set aside to be refried later.

3. Heat oil to 365°F. Fry again in small batches, stirring lightly with a tool so they don't stick together. When golden brown (about 2–3 minutes), remove from oil, shake off any excess, and drain on paper towels. Sprinkle immediately with salt and serve in a napkin-lined basket.

Honey-Orange Beets

If you are able to find fresh beets with the greens still attached, wash them thoroughly, dress them with lemon and olive oil, and use them as a bed for this dish, creating a warm-salad main course.

INGREDIENTS | SERVES 4

6 medium-sized fresh beets
1 teaspoon grated orange zest
2 tablespoons orange juice
2 teaspoons butter
1 teaspoon honey
¼ teaspoon ground ginger
Salt and freshly ground pepper to taste

1. Boil beets in enough water to cover for 40 minutes or until tender. Drain beets and let cool slightly. Slip off skins and slice.

2. In a saucepan, heat the orange zest, orange juice, butter, honey, and ginger over low heat until the butter melts.

3. Add the beets and toss to coat. Season with salt and pepper.

Rutabaga Oven Fries VN

Though not really fried, these golden batons look and feel like French fries and are great for dipping in ketchup or aïoli (garlic mayonnaise).

INGREDIENTS | SERVES 4

1 large rutabaga, peeled
1 tablespoon olive or vegetable oil
Kosher salt, to taste
1 tablespoon finely chopped thyme, rosemary, or parsley
Ground black pepper to taste

1. Heat oven to 400°F. Slice rutabaga into 2½" × ½" sticks (batons); soak in cold water for 30 minutes. Dry thoroughly with towels.

2. Toss rutabaga gently with oil and a light sprinkling of salt. Spread fries into a single layer on a sheet pan and bake, turning occasionally, until lightly browned and tender, about 30–40 minutes.

3. Remove from oven and toss with thyme and salt and pepper to taste.

Herb-Mixed Turnips

Rutabagas and turnips have a naturally buttery flavor, especially when young and fresh in the autumn. This makes the pairing with herbs and crisp bread crumbs natural.

INGREDIENTS | SERVES 4

1½ pounds turnips and rutabagas, peeled

2 tablespoons butter

1 tablespoon chopped parsley

2 teaspoons chopped chervil or tarragon

2 tablespoons chopped chives

1 clove garlic, finely chopped

Kosher salt and ground black pepper, to taste

½ cup fresh bread crumbs browned in 1 tablespoon olive oil or butter

1. Cook the turnips and rutabagas separately in salted water until they're al dente (tender but firm—approximately 10 minutes for turnips, 20 minutes for rutabagas); drain.

2. In a large skillet over medium heat, melt the butter. Add the turnips and rutabagas and cook over medium-high heat until golden brown. Add herbs, garlic, salt, and pepper and toss to coat. Serve topped with bread crumbs.

Curried Parsnips

The herby sweetness of parsnips lends itself well to curries. Try this one over brown rice with a little lentil dal for a delicious dinner that's a complete protein dish to boot!

INGREDIENTS | SERVES 4

1½ pounds parsnips, peeled, cut into bite-sized pieces

2 tablespoons butter or oil

1 medium red onion, thinly sliced

2 medium Bosc pears or Golden Delicious apples, peeled, cored, and thinly sliced

1 teaspoon Madras curry powder, toasted in a dry pan until fragrant

½ teaspoon ground coriander, toasted in a dry pan until fragrant

Kosher salt and black pepper, to taste

¼ cup yogurt

¼ cup mango chutney (such as Major Grey's)

2 tablespoons chopped cilantro

1. Boil the parsnips until halfway done, about 5 minutes; drain.

2. Melt the butter in a large, heavy-bottomed skillet. Add the onion, pears, curry, and coriander and cook over medium heat, stirring regularly until onions are soft, about 10 minutes.

3. Add the parsnips, season well with salt and pepper, and cook 5 minutes more until the parsnips brown lightly. Remove from heat before stirring in the yogurt, chutney, and cilantro.

Heavy Metal

Burnt onions? It may be the pan you're using. Thin, flimsy stainless steel pans don't conduct heat well, resulting in hot spots where foods burn and cold spots where they don't cook at all. Better pans have a thick core of highly conductive aluminum or even copper bonded to their bottoms. The best are made completely of conductive metal, except for a stainless steel "jacket," which is neutral (nonreactive) and won't give food an "off" flavor.

Celery Root Mash

Celery root is sometimes called "celeriac" or "apio." It has a mild, celery-like flavor and a starchy, potato-like texture.

INGREDIENTS | SERVES 6

2 pounds celery root

1 pound white potatoes

½ cup milk

8 tablespoons unsalted butter

1 tablespoon snipped chives (optional)

Salt to taste

1. Peel and dice the celery root and potatoes roughly into 1" pieces. Boil in lightly salted boiling water until very tender, about 20 minutes. Drain in a colander, then return to the pot and heat for 30 seconds to steam out any residual water.

2. Heat the milk and butter in a small saucepan.

3. Using a stiff wire whisk or potato masher, crush the vegetables until they are a soft mash. Gradually mash in the milk-butter mixture, making sure it is well mixed before adding more; fold in the chives if desired. Season lightly with salt.

Gingered Mashed Sweet Potatoes

This may become a staple on your Thanksgiving table.

INGREDIENTS | SERVES 6

4 medium sweet potatoes or yams (about 1½ pounds)

¼ cup milk

2 tablespoons butter

1 tablespoon mashed candied ginger or 1 tablespoon brown sugar plus ½ teaspoon ground ginger

1. Peel and quarter the sweet potatoes and cook in boiling salted water until tender, about 20 minutes. Drain and return to the pan.

2. In a small saucepan or in the microwave, heat the milk and butter; add to the potatoes, along with the candied ginger; mash by hand or with an electric mixer. Texture will be thicker than mashed white potatoes.

Chipotle and Thyme Sweet Potatoes VN

To substitute fresh thyme for dried thyme, use ½ tablespoon of the fresh herb.

INGREDIENTS | SERVES 6

6 cups cubed sweet potatoes

4 tablespoons vegan margarine

3 cloves garlic, minced

1 teaspoon dried chipotle pepper

½ teaspoon dried thyme

1 teaspoon salt

¼ teaspoon black pepper

Add all ingredients to a 4-quart slow cooker. Cover and cook on medium heat for 4 hours.

Parsnip and Carrot Bake

If you can't find fresh chervil or tarragon, use Italian (flat-leaf) parsley.

INGREDIENTS | SERVES 4

1 pound carrots, peeled and cut roughly into 2½" × ½" batons

8 ounces parsnips, peeled and cut roughly into 2½" × ½" batons

¾ cup vegetable stock

2 tablespoons butter, chopped

½ teaspoon salt

Chopped fresh chervil or tarragon

Ground black pepper to taste

1. Heat oven to 375°F.

2. Place carrots, parsnips, stock, butter, and salt into a shallow baking dish. Cover with aluminum foil and bake until the vegetables are soft, about 45 minutes.

3. Uncover and bake until vegetables brown lightly, 10–15 minutes more. Sprinkle with chervil and black pepper before serving.

Carrot and Mushroom Terrine

Loaded with beta carotene, which is essential for healthy eyes, skin, and cell respiration, carrots are a nutritional superfood that's cheap and available year-round.

INGREDIENTS | SERVES 8

¼ cup plus 1 tablespoon butter, divided

1 pound mushrooms, chopped

2 cloves garlic, chopped

1 cup roughly chopped shallots

4½ cups grated carrots

5 large eggs

1 cup bread crumbs

1 cup grated pecorino Romano or Parmesan cheese

Salt and ground black pepper, to taste

½ teaspoon oregano

½ teaspoon rosemary

1. Heat oven to 350°F.

2. Grease a 2-quart terrine or loaf pan with 1 tablespoon butter. Melt remaining butter in a heavy-bottomed skillet. Add the mushrooms, garlic, and shallots; cook until shallots soften, about 10 minutes.

3. In a mixing bowl, combine the shallot mixture with the carrots, eggs, half of the bread crumbs, the cheese, salt and pepper to taste, oregano, and rosemary. Pour mixture into terrine and sprinkle with remaining bread crumbs and dot with remaining butter; cover with foil.

4. Bake 30 minutes, then uncover and bake 5 minutes more until browned. Let stand 10 minutes before serving.

Crisp Potato Pancakes

These scrumptious, simple latkes make wonderful snacking, and can be made as miniature hors d'oeuvres. It's traditional to serve them with either sour cream or applesauce.

INGREDIENTS | SERVES 4

1 large egg
3 large baking potatoes, peeled
1 medium onion
1 teaspoon salt
1 tablespoon flour
Clarified butter (ghee) or olive oil for frying

Why Butter Is Better for Crisping Potato Cakes

For browning and crispness, clarified butter achieves the best results. This may be because residual proteins in the butter caramelize on foods, or it may simply be the high temperatures that clarified butter can reach without burning. When sautéing, start off with a neutral oil, such as peanut oil, and add a nugget of whole butter to get a better brown.

1. Beat the egg in a large bowl. Using the large-hole side of a box grater, shred the potatoes in long motions, forming the lengthiest shreds possible. Quickly grate in the onion. Add the salt and sprinkle in the flour; toss with your hands to combine well.

2. Heat the clarified butter in a large skillet until it shimmers but does not smoke (a piece of potato should sizzle upon entry). Form 8 pancakes from the batter and pan-fry them in batches of 3 or 4, squeezing out excess water before gently sliding them into the pan. Cook slowly without moving them for the first 5 minutes; then loosen with a spatula. Turn after about 8 minutes, when the top appears ⅓ cooked. Finish cooking on other side, about 4 minutes more. Drain on paper towels.

Fiery Indian Potatoes VN

This unusual potato dish is not for the faint of heart, for the chili component can singe your eyebrows. Yet it is a delicious dish and pairs well with thick plain yogurt or as an accompaniment to other vegetarian dishes. Look for the Indian red chili powder at an Indian market; otherwise, use ground cayenne.

INGREDIENTS | SERVES 6

6 large potatoes, peeled and cubed

3 tablespoons vegetable oil, or more as needed

5 dried red chilies, crushed

1 tablespoon mustard seeds

1 teaspoon ground turmeric

1 teaspoon red chili powder

Salt and ground black pepper to taste

1 tablespoon ground coriander

1 cup chopped fresh cilantro

1. Steam the potato cubes until just tender. Set aside.

2. Heat the oil in a large skillet or wok and sauté the potatoes for 2 minutes. Add the chilies, mustard seeds, turmeric, chili powder, salt, and pepper and continue cooking over medium heat, stirring, until the seasonings are well mixed and the potatoes begin to brown.

3. Stir in the coriander, garnish with the cilantro, and serve.

Rosemary New Potatoes VN

Fresh rosemary perfumes the cooking oil in this Italian classic, imparting its robust herbal flavor to the browning potatoes.

INGREDIENTS | SERVES 4

1 pound golf-ball-sized red-skinned new potatoes

2 tablespoons extra-virgin olive oil

3 sprigs fresh rosemary

Kosher salt and ground black pepper to taste

What Does "Lightly Salted Water" Really Mean?

Lightly salted water tastes like tears. Thoroughly salted water tastes like seawater. For foods that absorb a lot of water as they cook, like beans or pasta, lightly salted is the way to go, since your aim is to draw out the natural flavors of the food, not to make them "salty." For foods that don't absorb water, such as green vegetables, the point is to use salt's properties of sealing in nutrients, color, and flavor. For that reason, you would salt the water more assertively. Excess salt can easily be washed from those vegetables.

1. Heat oven to 375°F.

2. Slice the potatoes into ½"-thick rounds and boil them in lightly salted water until crisp tender, about 7 minutes. Drain well and dry very well with a towel.

3. Heat the olive oil in a large, heavy, ovensafe skillet until it shimmers but does not smoke. Add the rosemary sprigs (they should sizzle) and then slip in the potatoes. Cook without disturbing for 5 minutes. Once potatoes have browned lightly on the first side, turn them over and put the pan in the oven. Cook 10 minutes.

4. Transfer potatoes to a serving platter, season with salt and pepper, and garnish with additional rosemary sprigs.

Slow Cooker Rosemary Fingerling Potatoes VN

Fingerling potatoes are small, long potatoes that look a little like fingers.

INGREDIENTS | SERVES 6

2 tablespoons extra-virgin olive oil

1½ pounds fingerling potatoes

1 teaspoon salt

¼ teaspoon black pepper

2 tablespoons fresh rosemary, chopped

1 tablespoon fresh lemon juice

1. Add the olive oil, potatoes, salt, and pepper to a 4-quart slow cooker. Cover and cook on low heat for 3–4 hours.

2. Remove the cover and mix in the rosemary and lemon juice.

Time Saver

To save on time when cooking potatoes, always cut them into the smallest pieces the recipe will allow and cook at the highest temperature. For this recipe, you can quarter the potatoes and cook on high heat.

Overly Stuffed Baked Sweet Potato

To reduce calories in this robust dish, use reduced-fat cheese. And for even more flavor, you may increase the amount of salsa, or select one of the types that now include fruit and other interesting add-ins.

INGREDIENTS | SERVES 1

1 large sweet potato

½ cup mild or hot salsa

¾ cup grated Cheddar cheese

1 medium jalapeño pepper, seeded and diced

½ cup cubed Monterey jack cheese

1 cup vegetarian chili

Chopped fresh cilantro for garnish

1. Bake the sweet potato in a 350°F oven until tender. Remove from the oven and, when it is cool enough to handle, slit open the top and scoop out the flesh into a medium bowl, leaving a thin layer of flesh around the interior.

2. Mix the sweet potato flesh with the salsa, grated cheese, and jalapeño. Spoon it back into the skin and dot the top with the cubed cheese. Return the sweet potato to the oven to cook until the cheese melts.

3. Meanwhile, heat the chili, and when the cheese has melted, put the sweet potato on a serving plate and spoon the chili over top. Garnish with the cilantro and enjoy.

Roasted Garlic Mashed Potatoes

The amount of garlic in this recipe may seem huge, but the garlic mellows and sweetens as it roasts. All your guests will taste is heavenly, rich, light potatoes.

INGREDIENTS | SERVES 6

3 heads garlic
2 pounds red bliss potatoes, peeled
8 tablespoons butter
½ cup milk or cream
1½ teaspoons salt
Ground white pepper, to taste

1. Heat oven to 350°F. Wrap all three garlic heads into a pouch fashioned from aluminum foil and place in the center of the oven. Roast until garlic is very soft and yields to gentle finger pressure, about 1 hour and 15 minutes. Cut the garlic bulbs in half laterally. Using your hands, squeeze out the roasted garlic and push it through a sieve.

2. Roughly cut potatoes into large chunks and boil in enough lightly salted water to cover until very tender, about 25–30 minutes depending on type and size of potato pieces. Drain the potatoes well, then return them to the pot, put them on the stove, and cook over moderate heat for 30 seconds to 1 minute to steam off any excess moisture.

3. Heat the butter and milk together in a small saucepan over medium-low heat until the butter melts.

4. For smoothest mashed potatoes, force the potatoes through a ricer. Otherwise, mash them with a potato masher or stiff wire whisk. Add the roasted garlic purée, salt, pepper, and the cream mixture to the potatoes and mix just enough to incorporate. Serve immediately or keep warm for later service in a double boiler.

Old-Fashioned Glazed Carrots

For added finesse to this lovely classical dish, cut the carrots on a 45-degree bias, rotating them a quarter turn after each cut to make an angular shape chefs refer to as "oblique."

INGREDIENTS | SERVES 8

1 pound carrots, peeled and cut into 1" chunks

2 tablespoons unsalted butter

½ cup water

1½ teaspoons sugar

¼ teaspoon salt

Combine all ingredients in a heavy-bottomed skillet or pan large enough to accommodate a crowded single layer. Over medium-high heat, simmer about 5 minutes, then toss or flip the carrots. Continue cooking until the liquid is mostly evaporated and what remains is a glaze adhering to the carrots. Be careful not to go too far or the glaze will break and become oily.

CHAPTER 6

Grains, Beans, and Legumes

Mexican Rice VN

This rice combines nicely with refried beans for an excellent lunchtime meal.

INGREDIENTS | SERVES 6

1½ cups long-grain white rice

1 large tomato, peeled, seeded, and chopped

⅓ medium white onion, roughly chopped

1 clove garlic, roughly chopped

⅓ cup peanut or safflower oil

3½ cups vegetable stock

2 teaspoons salt

½ medium carrot, peeled and finely chopped

⅓ cup fresh or frozen green peas

1. Soak rice in hot water for 15 minutes, then rinse and drain. Purée the tomato, onion, and garlic in a blender.

2. In a large saucepan, fry the rice in the oil until it turns light gold in color, about 10 minutes. Pour off excess oil. Stir in the tomato purée and cook until almost dry, about 3 minutes.

3. Add stock, salt, carrots, and peas, cover, and simmer over low heat for 18 minutes; liquid should be absorbed and rice tender. Remove from heat and let stand 5 minutes, then fluff with a fork.

Green Rice Pilaf

Green with fresh herbs, this rice is a great stuffing for vegetables, base for curries, or accompaniment to a hearty vegetable stew.

INGREDIENTS | SERVES 4

3 tablespoons butter

2 cups chopped onion

2 cups long-grain rice

½ cup (packed) mixed chopped herbs, such as chives, chervil, tarragon, parsley, and dill

4 cups vegetable stock

Salt and ground black pepper to taste

1 bay leaf

1. In a medium saucepan, melt the butter over medium heat. Add the onion; cook until translucent, about 5 minutes.

2. Add the rice; cook, stirring often, until the rice is well coated and becomes golden.

3. In a blender, combine the herbs, stock, salt, and pepper; blend until herbs are finely chopped. Add to the rice; bring to a boil, add the bay leaf, and then lower to a very slow simmer. Cover tightly; cook until rice has absorbed all liquid, about 25 minutes. Fluff with a fork, then cover and let stand for 5 minutes before serving.

Fried Rice with Green Peas and Egg

This all-purpose fried rice can be adapted to your taste—try it with sliced mushrooms, snow peas, water chestnuts, or your own favorite garnishes.

INGREDIENTS | SERVES 4

3 large eggs, beaten

2 tablespoons peanut or other oil

2 tablespoons chopped ginger

2 tablespoons chopped garlic

½ cup chopped scallions

4 cups cooked white rice

1 (10-ounce) package frozen green peas

1 small carrot, peeled, diced, and blanched

1 tablespoon soy sauce

Sesame seeds for garnish

1. Heat a 10" nonstick skillet with a few drops of oil over medium heat; add the eggs. Cook without stirring until completely cooked through, about 3 minutes. Slide the cooked egg sheet onto a cutting board; let it cool for 5 minutes. Roll the egg into a cylinder and crosscut to form long julienne.

2. Heat the oil in a large skillet or wok. Add the ginger, garlic, and scallions and cook for 1 minute; they should sizzle. Add the rice. Over high heat, chop and stir the rice to break up any lumps; cook until very hot and some rice forms crunchy bits, about 5 minutes. Add peas and carrots. Cook until peas are hot, then stir in the egg julienne and soy sauce. Serve garnished with additional chopped scallions and sesame seeds.

Easy Saffron Vegetable Risotto

This is about the fastest risotto you can make and still achieve the creamy, saucy, flavorful dish of northern Italy. The key is the gradual addition of hot liquid while stirring, which extracts natural starches in the short-grain rice, thickening the sauce.

INGREDIENTS | SERVES 6

3 pinches saffron

10 cups vegetable stock

2 tablespoons olive oil

1 medium onion, roughly chopped

1 pound short-grain Italian rice for risotto, such as Arborio, carnaroli, or roma

½ cup dry white wine

1½ cups grated Parmesan cheese

1 pound frozen mixed vegetables

Salt and ground black pepper to taste

1 tablespoon unsalted butter

Lemon wedges (optional)

1. Combine the saffron with 1 cup of the stock and let steep for 10 minutes; heat the remaining stock separately until hot but not boiling.

2. Heat the oil in a heavy-bottomed saucepan over medium heat; add the onion and cook until translucent, about 5 minutes. Stir in the rice and mix with a wooden spoon until rice is well coated and begins to change color, about 5 minutes.

3. Add the white wine; cook until all wine is absorbed. Add the saffron mixture; cook, stirring, until the liquid is absorbed.

4. Begin adding the hot stock in 1-cup increments, stirring each time until all the liquid is absorbed before adding the next cup, until rice is soft and creamy and you have only 1 cup of liquid left.

5. Fold in the cheese, vegetables, salt, pepper, and butter. Stir until well combined; remove from heat. Adjust consistency with remaining stock. Rice should have a saucy consistency and be soft, but still have a little bite. Serve with lemon wedges.

Wild Rice with Apples and Almonds VN

*To add extra texture to your Indian curry dinner, serve it in a ring
of this chewy, crunchy mixture of nuts and fruits.*

INGREDIENTS | SERVES 8

½ cup wild rice

½ cup slivered almonds

1 tablespoon vegetable oil

1 large onion, roughly chopped

1 Rome or Golden Delicious apple,
peeled, cored, and diced

¼ cup raisins

Salt and ground black pepper to taste

1 tablespoon olive oil

¼ cup chopped cilantro or parsley

Saving Cooking Liquids as "Stock"

Water and broth from boiled wild rice, simmered beans, blanched vegetables, soaked dry mushrooms, and other cooking processes are free gifts. These no-work byproducts come packed with flavor, nutrients, and body, ready to use in any soup, stew, or dish that calls for "water or stock." Freeze them in portion-sized plastic tubs for use anytime.

1. Boil the rice in 2½ quarts salted water until tender, about 40 minutes; drain, saving cooking liquid.

2. Crisp the almonds by toasting them in a dry skillet until fragrant.

3. Heat vegetable oil in a large skillet or Dutch oven over medium heat for 1 minute. Add onions; cook until softened, about 5 minutes. Add the apples, raisins, and a splash of the rice cooking liquid. Cook 5 minutes more until the apples are translucent.

4. Combine the cooked rice, the apple mixture, the nuts, and salt and pepper. Stir in olive oil and serve garnished with cilantro or parsley.

Quinoa Salad with Tomatoes and Cilantro VN

Quinoa has a very attractive light golden hue and a springy, crunchy texture, and the kernels have an appealing, ringlet-like shape. It cooks quickly.

INGREDIENTS | SERVES 6

1 cup quinoa, boiled for 15 minutes and drained

1 cup Red and Yellow Plum Tomato Chutney (see recipe in Chapter 8)

¼ teaspoon kosher salt

1 tablespoon extra-virgin olive oil

In a mixing bowl, combine the cooked quinoa and tomato chutney. Season to taste with salt. Dress with olive oil, and serve with extra olive oil at the table.

Kasha Varnashkas

While Jewish cooking is pretty meat-centric, there are a few really good vegetarian dishes like this one.

INGREDIENTS | SERVES 8

2 cups coarse or medium granulation kasha (toasted buckwheat)

2 large eggs (or 3 egg whites)

4 cups hot vegetable stock or water

3 tablespoons butter or margarine

1 tablespoon olive oil

1 medium onion, roughly chopped

1 (10-ounce) package sliced mushrooms

1 pound farfalle or egg noodles, cooked medium-soft

1 (10.5-ounce) can condensed cream of mushroom soup

Salt and ground black pepper to taste

1. Heat over to 350°F.

2. Heat a large skillet over high heat. In a medium bowl, combine kasha and eggs and mix with a wooden spoon until well coated. Pour the kasha mixture into the hot pan and cook, stirring and breaking up lumps, until the egg has dried onto the kasha and grains are separate.

3. Add the hot stock and the butter carefully (it may spatter). Reduce heat to low, cover tightly, and cook 7–10 minutes until all liquid is absorbed.

4. In a separate pan, heat the olive oil. Sauté the onions and mushrooms together until soft, about 5 minutes.

5. In a mixing bowl, combine the cooked kasha, onions, mushrooms, cooked pasta, and cream of mushroom soup; mix well. Salt and pepper to taste. Transfer to a casserole and bake 20 minutes until hot and slightly crusty on top.

Indian Chapati Pan Bread VN

The fastest, easiest bread you'll ever make, this recipe takes under an hour for sixteen breads. It's the traditional partner to Indian curries, which are eaten by scooping up morsels into the bread, to be eaten from the hand.

INGREDIENTS | MAKES 16

1 cup chapati flour (Indian whole-wheat flour)

⅓ cup warm water (generous)

1 teaspoon oil

1. In a mixing bowl, make a well in the center of the flour. Pour the warm water and oil into this depression; fold ingredients together with a fork until a dough forms. Knead the dough in the bowl for 10 minutes. It should be smooth and elastic.

2. Divide the dough into 4 pieces. Roll 1 of the pieces against the table with your hands to form a cylinder; cut the cylinder into 4 nuggets. Cover remaining dough with a damp cloth while you work. Form each nugget into a ball the size of a marble and roll it on a floured surface with a rolling pin into thin disks (1/16"—a little thicker than a CD). Repeat with remaining dough. They can be stacked.

3. Heat an iron skillet over medium heat for 5 minutes until hot enough for a drop of water to sizzle on it. Dust off the excess flour from a chapati and place it flat into the dry pan. Leave it until bubbles and air pockets are visible on the top; flip it to cook the other side. Some brown spots are fine. Repeat with remaining dough. Stack the cooked chapatis on a plate and cover with a dry towel to keep warm.

Granola

This crunchy, healthful cereal is a delicious snack that travels well.

INGREDIENTS | SERVES 8

3 cups rolled oats

1½ cups wheat germ

1 cup chopped walnuts, almonds, peanuts, or a combination

1 cup shredded coconut

½ cup sesame seeds

½ cup nonfat dry milk

¼ cup oil

½ cup honey

1 cup brown sugar

1 cup raisins

1. Heat oven to 350°F. Spread the oats onto a baking sheet; bake for 15 minutes. Lower oven to 325°F.

2. In a large mixing bowl, combine the toasted oats with wheat germ, nuts, coconut, sesame seeds, nonfat dry milk, oil, honey, and brown sugar. Mix well with your hands. Transfer to a baking sheet; spread into a single layer. Bake for 10–15 minutes until lightly browned. Toss with raisins. Cool to room temperature before serving.

Polenta with Butter and Cheese

Delicious as a base for stews and ragouts, such as chunky tomato sauce, sautéed wild mushroom ragout, or a vegetable stew, polenta is also excellent when allowed to chill, then grilled or fried.

INGREDIENTS | SERVES 4

4 cups water or stock, boiling

1 teaspoon salt

1 cup coarse yellow cornmeal (polenta)

½ cup grated Parmesan cheese

1 tablespoon butter

1. Add salt to the boiling water. Whisking constantly with a stiff wire whisk, gradually pour cornmeal into water in a steady stream, whisking out any lumps. Continue whisking constantly until mixture thickens noticeably.

2. Lower heat to a very low simmer. You should see only the occasional bubble plopping up through the polenta—beware: The polenta is molten lava at this point, and spattering can be hazardous. Stir regularly with a wooden spoon until full thickening is achieved, about 25 minutes.

3. Stir in cheese and butter; remove from h[...] immediately or allow to cool for grilling [...]

Polenta with Wild Mushrooms

Northern Italian comfort food like this was often placed directly onto the center of a wooden farmhouse table in Italy. Diners would draw portions from the center pile over to their plates. It's the perfect winter dinner.

INGREDIENTS | SERVES 4

1 recipe Polenta with Butter and Cheese (see recipe in this chapter)

1 tablespoon olive oil

1 pound assorted wild or exotic mushrooms, such as hedgehogs, shiitakes, oysters, and chanterelles, sliced into large pieces

8 ounces white button mushrooms, sliced

2 tablespoons butter, divided

1 teaspoon salt

¼ cup chopped fresh herbs such as rosemary, thyme, oregano, and parsley, or 1 tablespoon dried

Juice of 1 medium lemon

Ground black pepper to taste

Grated Parmesan cheese (optional)

1. Keep polenta warm over very heat.

2. Heat the olive oil until very hot, almost smoking, in a large skillet. Add the wild and white mushrooms and 1 tablespoon of butter; do not stir. Cook mushrooms undisturbed over high heat for 5 minutes to give them a nice browning. Season with salt; add the herbs, stir, and cook until the mushrooms are wilted and juicy. Remove from heat and swirl in a little lemon juice and remaining butter.

3. Pour the hot polenta into a deep serving dish or bowl—it should be thick but liquidy. In a minute, make an indentation in the center of the polenta and spoon in the mushrooms. Serve with a few grinds of fresh black pepper and pass grated cheese if desired.

Wheat and Corn Wraps with Tofu

Wraps are neater to eat and easier to hold than sandwiches. Substitute almost any grain, like spelt or faro, for the wheat berries used here.

INGREDIENTS | SERVES 4

½ cup wheat berries boiled until tender, about 30 minutes

1 (10-ounce) package frozen sweet corn, thawed

Juice of 1 medium lemon

1 tablespoon extra-virgin olive oil

½ teaspoon ground cumin

Salt and ground black pepper to taste

2 tablespoons mayonnaise

4 (10"–12") medium flour tortillas

½ recipe marinated tofu from Tofu Salad (see recipe in Chapter 3)

1. In a medium bowl, toss the cooked grain, corn, lemon juice, olive oil, cumin, salt, and pepper until combined.

2. Spread the mayonnaise in a line across the equator of each tortilla. Spoon in the grain salad; arrange the tofu alongside the grain.

3. Roll, jellyroll style, away from yourself. Tuck in ends.

Cuban Black Beans and Rice (*Moros y Cristianos*) VN

This recipe takes a while to cook, but it's mostly hands-off time. Use the black beans in this recipe for many other uses, including Huevos Rancheros in Chapter 12 and Black Bean Burritos in this chapter.

INGREDIENTS | SERVES 8

Beans:

1½ cups black beans, soaked overnight, drained

2 tablespoons vegetable oil

2 cloves garlic, minced

½ medium Spanish onion, finely chopped

¼ teaspoon ground cumin

¼ teaspoon oregano

1 bay leaf

1 teaspoon salt

¼ teaspoon freshly ground black pepper

½ cup chopped fresh cilantro leaves and stems

Rice:

1 clove garlic, peeled and crushed with the side of a knife

4 teaspoons vegetable oil, divided

1½ cups long-grain white rice, rinsed and drained

1½ teaspoons salt

1. Simmer beans in 6 cups water until very tender (about 90 minutes).

2. Meanwhile, heat the oil in a medium saucepan over medium heat. Add the garlic, onion, cumin, oregano, bay leaf, salt, and pepper and sauté until onions are soft. Add this mixture to the beans and simmer 20 minutes more. Stir in cilantro.

3. Make the rice: In a soup pot over medium heat, sauté garlic gently in 3 teaspoons oil until it begins to brown. Add rice and stir to coat.

4. Add 2 cups water and salt; bring to a boil and cover. Lower heat and simmer 20 minutes.

5. Remove from heat; pour in remaining oil and fluff to separate grains. Serve topped with a ladle of black beans.

Black Bean Burritos

It's probably no accident that these burritos (which can be made vegan by substituting soy cheese for the Cheddar and Monterey jack) are a source of complete protein, since their origins are hot Mexican lands, where many local residents considered animal protein a luxury.

INGREDIENTS | SERVES 4

1 tablespoon oil

1 cup chopped onions

4 large (12") flour or whole-wheat tortillas

1 cup shredded Cheddar or Monterey jack cheese

2 cups cooked brown or white rice, hot

1½ cups Cuban Black Beans (see recipe in Chapter 13) or 1 (15-ounce) can black beans, heated with some cumin and garlic

½ cup Salsa Fresca (see recipe in Chapter 2)

1 medium ripe Hass avocado, peeled and sliced

½ cup fresh cilantro sprigs

1. In a medium skillet, brown the onions in the oil until soft.

2. Soften a tortilla over a gas burner or in a hot oven; place on a clean work surface. Spoon a quarter of the hot onions into a line, one-third the way up on the tortilla; sprinkle on a quarter of the shredded cheese. Immediately spoon on ½ cup hot rice; this should be hot enough to melt the cheese. Ladle on a quarter of the beans, including some of its sauce; top with the salsa, avocado slices, and cilantro.

3. Fold edge nearest to you up to cover the fillings. Fold side flaps in, to seal ingredients into a pocket. Roll the burrito away from yourself, keeping even tension and tucking with your fingers as you roll. Repeat with remaining tortillas.

Tuscan White Bean Ragout

Eaten on its own, or over Polenta with Butter and Cheese (see recipe in this chapter), this hearty stew packs flavor and nutrition. This stew can be prepared through step 1 and refrigerated for up to 3 days. The flavors will mingle, and the dish will be even better.

INGREDIENTS | SERVES 8

2 tablespoons olive oil

2 tablespoons chopped garlic (about 5 cloves)

2 medium onions, diced

2 teaspoons chopped fresh rosemary, or 1 teaspoon dried rosemary leaves

1 dried New Mexico chili, or ¼ teaspoon crushed red pepper flakes

1 (28-ounce) can large white beans

2 cups vegetable stock

6 cups torn escarole or spinach leaves

6 medium ripe plum tomatoes, seeded and diced

2 ounces unsalted butter

¼ cup roughly chopped Italian parsley

½ cup grated Parmigiano-Reggiano cheese

Kosher salt and ground black pepper to taste

A few drops top-quality extra-virgin olive oil

1. Heat the olive oil in a large skillet or Dutch oven over medium heat; add the garlic and cook until it turns white and fragrant, only about 30 seconds. Stir in the onions, rosemary, and chili. Cook gently until the onions are very soft, about 10 minutes, stirring occasionally. Add the beans and stock; simmer 5 minutes.

2. Stir in the escarole; simmer until it is all wilted. Add the tomatoes, butter, parsley, and cheese.

3. Remove from the heat and stir until the butter is melted in, adding additional stock as necessary to keep it brothy. Season well with salt and pepper. Serve warm drizzled with extra-virgin olive oil.

Puerto Rican Gandules (Pigeon Peas) VN

Pigeon peas are the beloved bean of Puerto Rico, where they are usually served over long-grain white rice.

INGREDIENTS | SERVES 6

1½ cups pigeon peas, soaked overnight, rinsed, and drained

1 tablespoon olive oil

1 small Spanish onion, chopped

⅓ medium green bell pepper, seeded and chopped

2 cloves garlic, minced

2 bay leaves

1½ teaspoons salt

¼ teaspoon freshly ground black pepper

¼ cup chopped fresh thyme or 1 tablespoon dried

1 medium tomato, seeded, chopped

1. Simmer beans in 4 cups water for 1 hour until tender.

2. Meanwhile, heat the olive oil in a 10" skillet, then add onion, green pepper, garlic, bay leaves, salt, pepper, and thyme and sauté until onion is translucent (about 5 minutes). Add chopped tomato and cook 2 minutes more.

3. Add the vegetables to the beans and cook 45 minutes more until beans are very soft.

Soaking Beans

Dried beans, when submerged for several hours or overnight, absorb much water and swell to as much as 150 percent of their original size. They'll cook much more quickly than starting from dried, and the results may be more even, especially if the beans are old. Never cook them in the soaking water.

Avocado-Beet Wraps with Succotash VN

Be careful when working with beets; their dark red juices can stain your hands and your clothing.

INGREDIENTS | SERVES 4

4 flour tortillas (10" diameter or larger)

2 tablespoons vegan mayonnaise or vegan sour cream

2 cups Succotash Salad (see recipe in Chapter 3)

1 large or 2 small beets (about 8 ounces), boiled until tender and peeled

1 medium ripe avocado, peeled and cut into 1" wedges

Kosher salt to taste

1. Soften and lightly brown the tortillas by placing them directly over the burner of a gas stove and flipping them until the surface blisters slightly (alternately, steam, broil, or toast them for a minute until soft).

2. Spread ½ tablespoon of mayonnaise into a line across the center of each tortilla. Spoon ½ cup of succotash onto each tortilla.

3. Halve the beets and cut the halves into ½" slices. Divide the beets and avocado slices evenly onto the tortillas, placing them on the side of the succotash line closest to you.

4. Place 1 of the tortillas on a work surface directly in front of yourself. Fold the near edge of the tortilla over the fillings and roll it, jellyroll fashion, away from yourself, keeping even pressure to ensure a tight roll. Place seam-side down on a plate; repeat with remaining tortillas.

Connie's Delicious Refried Beans VN

Although canned refried beans are convenient, starting from scratch yields a spectacular flavor absent in the canned version. These also are terrific for breakfast topped with eggs poached in a thick salsa.

INGREDIENTS | SERVES 6

1 (1-pound) bag dried pinto beans, rinsed and picked clean

1 cup chopped onion

1 package dried hot chili seasoning

1 package dried mild chili seasoning

1 tablespoon roasted cumin seeds, pounded with a mortar and pestle

1 small jalapeño pepper, seeded and diced

Salsa, to taste

Salt, to taste

2 tablespoons vegetable oil, or more as needed

1. Soak the rinsed beans overnight in cold water to cover by 2". Drain them well and rinse the beans again.

2. Put the beans and the onion in a large saucepan with about 8 cups water or to cover by 2 inches. Bring the water to a boil and reduce the heat to medium-low; skim off any scum. Stir in the chili seasonings, the cumin seeds, and the jalapeño. Cook, checking on the water level and stirring occasionally, for 3–4 hours or until the beans are tender and the water is almost absorbed. Add the salsa and salt.

3. Heat the vegetable oil in a large skillet over medium heat and, by spoonfuls, put the beans in the skillet and, using a potato masher of the back of a large spoon, mash and fry them until the beans are relatively smooth, repeating until all the beans are mashed and fried.

Raj's Chickpeas in Tomato Sauce VN

This quick, delicious healthful dish can be thrown together in minutes using ingredients from the pantry. Serve it with basmati rice and Indian breads, such as chapati.

INGREDIENTS | SERVES 6

2 tablespoons peanut or safflower oil

1 tablespoon cumin seeds

1 tablespoon chopped fresh ginger

¼ teaspoon crushed red pepper flakes

1 large onion, halved and sliced into half-moons

1 (15–20-ounce) can crushed or diced tomatoes

Salt and ground black pepper to taste

2 (15-ounce) cans chickpeas, drained and rinsed

Chopped cilantro (optional)

1. Heat the oil in a large saucepan over medium heat. Add the cumin seeds and cook until they are fragrant, about 1 minute. Stir in the ginger, crushed red pepper, and onions; cook until the onions are soft, about 5 minutes. Add the tomatoes and cook 5 minutes more until they become saucy.

2. Season the sauce with salt and pepper and add the chickpeas; cook 5 minutes more. Sprinkle with chopped cilantro if desired.

Chickpeas in Potato-Onion Curry VN

Thirty-minute main dishes like this are a lifesaver when you come home hungry and nothing's ready. Put on a pot of basmati rice before you start this dish, and you'll be dining before you know it.

INGREDIENTS | SERVES 4

2 cups chopped (1") onions

3 tablespoons oil, divided

1½ cups cubed (1") potatoes

1 (14-ounce) can coconut milk

1 (15-ounce) can chickpeas, drained and rinsed

5 or 6 cloves garlic, peeled

1 teaspoon kosher salt

1½ teaspoons ground coriander

½ teaspoon ground turmeric

1 teaspoon chili powder

1 teaspoon ground cumin

Juice of ½ medium lemon

1. In a medium skillet over high heat, cook the onions in 1 tablespoon oil until lightly browned, about 5 minutes.

2. Add the potatoes and coconut milk; cover and cook until potatoes are tender, about 20 minutes; add the chickpeas.

3. In a food processor, combine the garlic, salt, coriander, turmeric, chili powder, and cumin; process until it becomes a paste, scraping down sides as needed.

4. Heat remaining oil in a small skillet and fry the garlic mixture for 1 minute, allowing it to become fragrant and slightly browned. Add the garlic mixture to the chickpea pot. Simmer for 2–3 minutes; season to taste with lemon and additional salt.

Fried Chickpeas with Yogurt

A flavorful Indian favorite spiked with chutney, this entrée comes together in minutes and is a perfect accompaniment to cooked basmati rice and hot, fresh naan, the popular Indian bread.

INGREDIENTS | SERVES 2

2 tablespoons vegetable oil

1 medium onion, diced

1 medium tomato, seeded and diced

2 tablespoons minced fresh ginger

1 tablespoon minced garlic

1 teaspoon ground turmeric

1 (15-ounce) can chickpeas, drained and rinsed

1 teaspoon curry powder, or more to taste

1 teaspoon ground cumin

½ bunch fresh cilantro, coarsely chopped

Salt to taste

½ cup plain nonfat or whole milk yogurt

½ cup sweet or hot chutney

1. Heat the oil in a large skillet over medium heat and sauté the onion and tomato until the vegetables soften. Add the ginger, garlic, and turmeric and cook 2–3 minutes more or until the flavors are combined.

2. Add the chickpeas, curry powder, and cumin and cook, stirring often, for about 5 minutes. Add the cilantro and salt, stirring well. Stir in the yogurt and cook 2 minutes more.

3. Serve with a dollop of chutney on each portion.

Hummos bi Tahini with Sprouts and Cherry Tomatoes in a Pita Pocket VN

These beautiful, healthful sandwiches are colorful and attractive to serve when afternoon guests arrive. They're quick to make. Serve with pepperoncini or other spicy pickles.

INGREDIENTS | SERVES 4

1 (15.5-ounce) can chickpeas, drained and rinsed

2 tablespoons tahini (sesame paste)

1 tablespoon ground cumin

Juice of 1 large lemon

⅓ cup plus 1 tablespoon olive oil

Coarse salt and freshly ground black pepper to taste

4 (7") loaves pita bread

1 cello box alfalfa sprouts

12 ripe cherry tomatoes, washed and halved

1. Purée together the chickpeas, tahini, cumin, and half of the lemon juice at high speed in a food processor. While machine is running, gradually add ⅓ cup olive oil. Adjust flavor to taste with salt, pepper, and remaining lemon juice.

2. Make an opening at the top of each pita and slather each generously with hummos. Into each pocket, stuff a tuft of alfalfa sprouts the size of a golf ball and 6 cherry tomato halves. Drizzle remaining olive oil over contents of all sandwiches.

The Great Tahini

That hard-to-define, slightly smoky, slightly nutty dimension to many Middle Eastern foods is a fine-ground sesame seed paste called tahini. It's excellent in dressings, and combines beautifully with anything containing chickpeas for both wonderful flavors and complete proteins.

Fava Bean Hummus with Pistachios VN

If you need extra liquid to help purée the fava beans, you may add olive oil or a splash of vegetable broth, but don't overdo it. The hummus should be thick, not runny. Serve this with toasted pita pieces or bagel chips or with fresh vegetables for dipping.

INGREDIENTS | SERVES 6

1 (15-ounce) can fava beans, drained and rinsed

3 cloves garlic, or to taste

Juice from large 1 lemon, or more to taste

3 tablespoons olive oil, or more as needed to process

1–2 tablespoons tahini paste

Salt and ground black pepper to taste

½ cup minced parsley

¾ cup toasted pistachios

1. Put the beans, garlic, lemon juice, olive oil, tahini, salt, and pepper into a food processor or blender and purée.

2. Spoon the mixture into a bowl and stir in the parsley and pistachios. Chill until serving time.

Minted Sweet Peas VN

Shelling peas is one of the great pleasures of springtime cooking. A trick to opening them is to bend a piece of pod inside out until it snaps, then peel back the tough outer skin like you would the backing of a self-adhesive sticker.

INGREDIENTS | SERVES 4

2 cups shelled fresh peas (about 2 pounds unshelled)

½ teaspoon sugar

2 tablespoons vegan margarine

Salt and ground black pepper to taste

3 tablespoons chopped fresh mint leaves

In a medium saucepan over medium heat, simmer the peas and sugar until bright green and tender, about 5 minutes; drain. Toss peas with butter, salt, pepper, and mint.

Egyptian Lentils and Rice VN

Amino acids in the lentils and rice combine to form complete proteins, making this warming, comforting dish nutritionally powerful. Try adding a dab of Egyptian chili sauce (harissa) or other chili paste.

INGREDIENTS | SERVES 8

1 tablespoon olive oil

¼ teaspoon cumin seeds

1 medium onion, roughly chopped

1 cup rice

½ cup brown or green lentils

2 teaspoons juice plus ½ teaspoon zest from a lemon

1 teaspoon salt

3 cups vegetable stock or water

1. Heat the oil and cumin seeds in a medium saucepan over medium heat until the seeds are fragrant, about 30 seconds. Add the onion; cook until translucent, about 5 minutes.

2. Stir in the rice and lentils, mixing with a wooden spoon until well coated. Add the lemon juice, zest, salt, and stock. Cover tightly and simmer until all water is absorbed, about 20 minutes. Remove from heat and allow to stand for 5 minutes before fluffing with a fork and serving.

CHAPTER 7

Leafy Greens and Cruciferous Vegetables

Spinach and Tomato Sauté

The subtle addition of coriander brings this dish an understated elegance, perfect for a dinner main course. Always wash spinach twice, submerging it in fresh water each time and agitating it well by hand. Growing low to the ground, spinach usually hides plenty of soil in its crevices.

INGREDIENTS | SERVES 4

3 teaspoons butter

6 medium plum tomatoes, roughly chopped

1 teaspoon coriander

2 bunches flat-leaf spinach, washed very thoroughly

½ teaspoon salt

Ground black pepper to taste

1. In a large skillet or heavy-bottomed Dutch oven, melt 2 teaspoons of the butter over medium-high heat. Add the tomatoes and coriander; cook until softened, about 5 minutes.

2. Add the spinach in handfuls, allowing each handful to wilt before adding the next. Season it well with salt and pepper. Finish by swirling in the remaining butter.

Nonreactive Pots

Aluminum and copper, commonly used materials in pots and pans, react with (and alter the flavor and color of) acidic foods. Always use pans with a stainless steel or glass cooking surface to avoid sour tomato sauce, discolored green beans, and "off"-tasting soups. For the lightweight and even heat of aluminum and copper, combined with the nonreactive property of steel, buy aluminum or copper alloy pots clad to a steel "jacket" (inner lining).

Aloo Gobi (Cauliflower and Potato Curry) VN

This classic North Indian curry is a hearty main course. It's also an excellent filling for wraps known as roti. You can make your own garam masala by combining 1 teaspoon each of ground cardamom, cumin seed, cloves, black pepper, and cinnamon.

INGREDIENTS | SERVES 8

1 large head cauliflower

2 pounds potatoes

3 tablespoons oil

2 large onions, finely chopped (about 5 cups)

4 medium jalapeños or other chili peppers, seeded and finely chopped

1 (1") piece fresh ginger, finely chopped

3 medium tomatoes, finely chopped

1¼ teaspoons chili powder

1 teaspoon turmeric

1 teaspoon coriander

2 teaspoons kosher salt

1 teaspoon garam masala

Chopped cilantro for garnish

1. Cut the cauliflower and potatoes into large chunks.

2. Heat the oil in a heavy skillet over medium-high heat and cook the onions, chilies, and ginger until brown, about 10 minutes. Add the tomatoes, chili powder, turmeric, coriander, and salt; cook 5 minutes more until spices are fragrant and evenly disbursed.

3. Mix in the potatoes and cauliflower plus enough water to come halfway up the vegetables. Cover the pan and cook for 20 minutes, stirring occasionally, until the potatoes and cauliflower are very tender.

4. Add the garam masala powder; cook 5 minutes more. Serve garnished with cilantro.

Stir-Fried Asian Greens

Heaping ceramic bowls of jasmine rice with portions of this stir-fry constitute Asian "comfort food" at its best. This may require two large pans, or need to be cooked in two batches.

INGREDIENTS | SERVES 8

1 bunch (about 1 pound) collard greens, thinly sliced

1 small head (about 1 pound) Chinese (napa) cabbage, thinly sliced

1 bunch watercress, stem ends trimmed

2 tablespoons peanut oil

1 (10-ounce) package white or cremini mushrooms

1 large carrot or 2 medium carrots, thinly sliced on the diagonal

¼ pound snow peas, halved diagonally

1 medium red onion, halved, and sliced

2" piece ginger, julienned

3 cloves garlic, finely chopped

Salt and ground white pepper to taste

2 tablespoons soy sauce

1 tablespoon Chinese cooking wine or dry sherry

1 teaspoon Asian sesame oil

Black sesame seeds or toasted white sesame seeds for garnish

1. Mix together the collards, cabbage, and watercress; wash thoroughly and dry.

2. Heat the peanut oil in a large skillet over high heat until it is shimmery but not smoky. Add the mushrooms, carrots, snow peas, onion, ginger, and garlic; sauté 2 minutes, stirring frequently, allowing some parts to brown. Season well with salt and white pepper.

3. Add the greens, soy sauce, wine, and sesame oil. Toss or stir; cook only 1 minute until the greens begin to wilt. Serve immediately with a sprinkling of sesame seeds.

Braised Swiss Chard

Handsome, broad-leafed, and cool, Swiss chard has come back into vogue, thanks in great part to its striking beauty (especially of the red-veined varieties) and cancer-fighting possibilities. The juicy stems and tender leaves are cooked separately.

INGREDIENTS | SERVES 4

1 large bunch red or green Swiss chard (about 1½ pounds)

1 cup strong vegetable stock, mushroom stock, or liquid from cooking beans

Salt and ground black pepper to taste

1 tablespoon olive oil

2 medium shallots, finely chopped (about ¼ cup)

1 tablespoon unsalted butter

Lemon wedges for garnish

1. Wash the chard thoroughly under running water and shake dry. Using your hands, tear the leafy parts away from the stems; set aside. Cut the stems into bite-sized pieces.

2. In a nonreactive skillet, bring the stock to a boil; add the stem pieces. Season with salt and pepper; cook until tender. Transfer them to a bowl or plate, reserving their cooking liquid. Wipe out the skillet.

3. Return the skillet to the heat and add the olive oil and shallots. Cook 1 minute until they sizzle and soften slightly. Add the chard leaves and cook only until they wilt.

4. Add back the stems, plus 2 tablespoons of their cooking liquid. Bring to a simmer and swirl in the butter. Taste for seasoning. Serve with lemon wedges.

Cabbage Stewed in Tomato Sauce VN

Hearty winter food like stewed cabbage goes beautifully with seasoned brown rice.

INGREDIENTS | SERVES 8

2 tablespoons olive oil

1 medium onion, roughly chopped

1 small head green or red cabbage, chopped

1 teaspoon caraway seeds

Salt and ground black pepper to taste

2 cups Basic Fresh Tomato Sauce (see recipe in Chapter 8) or tomato sauce of your choice

2 teaspoons brown sugar

1. Heat the oil in a large Dutch oven. Add the onions and cook until they are translucent, about 5 minutes.

2. Add the cabbage, caraway seeds, and a little salt and pepper; cook over medium heat until soft and saucy, about 5 minutes more.

3. Stir in tomato sauce and brown sugar. Reduce heat to a simmer and cook covered, stirring occasionally, for 1 hour until the cabbage is very tender and has taken on color from the sauce.

Creamy Carrot Soup (Chapter 4)

Mini Goat Cheese Pizzas (Chapter 2)

Banana Nut Bread (Chapter 14)

Chocolate Mousse (Chapter 14)

Ratatouille (Chapter 8)

Miso Soup (Chapter 4)

The Best Pesto (Chapter 11)

Fettuccine Alfredo (Chapter 11)

Pumpkin Bread (Chapter 14)

Indian Chapati Pan Bread (Chapter 6)

Salsa Fresca (Pico de Gallo) (Chapter 2)

Corn and Potato Chowder (Chapter 4)

Okra Gumbo (Chapter 13)

Polenta with Wild Mushrooms (Chapter 6)

Spaghetti Ai Pomodori (Chapter 11)

Tomato and Bread Salad (Panzanella) (Chapter 3)

Basic Buttered Brussels Sprouts (Chapter 7)

Flourless Chocolate Cake (Chapter 14)

Crisp Potato Pancakes (Chapter 5)

Grilled Marinated Portobello Mushrooms
(Chapter 10)

Classic American Potato Salad (Chapter 3)

Baba Ghanouj (Chapter 2)

Challah French Toast (Chapter 12)

Spinach Manicotti (Chapter 11)

Spinach with Pine Nuts and Garlic VN

*Based on a Roman dish, this antioxidant-rich spinach dish picks up nuttiness
not just from the pine nuts but also from the toasted garlic.*

INGREDIENTS | SERVES 4

¼ cup pine nuts

3 tablespoons extra-virgin olive oil

2 cloves garlic, finely chopped

2 pounds washed spinach leaves, stems removed

Salt and ground black pepper to taste

Lemon wedges, for garnish

1. Gently toast the nuts in a dry sauté pan until they start to brown. Set aside.

2. In a very large pan, heat the olive oil and garlic over medium heat until it sizzles and starts to brown.

3. Add ⅓ of the spinach and the pine nuts and sauté until it's wilted and lets off some liquid. Add the rest of the spinach in batches, seasoning with salt and pepper as it cooks. Serve with lemon wedges.

The Incredible Shrinking Spinach!

Leafy green vegetables look huge when they're taking up cubic yards of refrigerator space, but seem to shrivel into mouse-sized portions when you trim the stems and cook them. They shrink to one-sixth their raw volume upon cooking. Figure on a half pound of raw greens per person (slightly less if the stems are eaten, as with Swiss chard).

Basic Buttered Brussels Sprouts

Brussels sprouts are an excellent fall and winter vegetable that hold very well for a long time, making them perfect for busy working people who can keep them on hand in the refrigerator for whenever they're needed.

INGREDIENTS | SERVES 4

1 pint Brussels sprouts
2 ounces (½ stick) unsalted butter
Salt and ground white pepper to taste
Pinch nutmeg (optional)

Where Vegetarians Shop

Seek out your nearest natural foods and/or "gourmet" specialty food shop. That's where you'll find the delectable grains, spices, chilies, and whole foods essential to healthy vegetarian life. Mainstream supermarkets carry most or all of what you'll see in this book, but you'll be surprised at the difference in quality (and sometimes, believe it or not, lower prices) you'll find at these stores.

1. Remove outer leaves from sprouts and trim the stems so that they're flush with the sprout bottoms. Halve the sprouts by cutting through the stem end.

2. Boil in small batches in 4 quarts of well-salted, rapidly boiling water for about 5 minutes each. Drain.

3. In a medium sauté pan over medium heat, melt the butter and add the cooked sprouts, tossing with salt, pepper, and nutmeg to coat.

Southwestern Sprouts

*Don't turn up your nose at Brussels sprouts, especially when these are kicked up
a notch with seasonings and texture. You'll want to serve these often.*

INGREDIENTS | SERVES 4

1 pound Brussels sprouts, trimmed
and halved

1 tablespoon olive oil

1 tablespoon taco seasoning, or to taste

½ cup crushed spicy taco chips

½ cup spicy or mild salsa

½ cup shredded Cheddar cheese

½ cup sunflower seeds

1. Preheat oven to 350°F.

2. Add the sprouts with the oil and taco seasoning to a
   roasting pan and toss to combine. Cook for about 30
   minutes or until the sprouts become tender.

3. Put them in a serving bowl and toss with the taco
   chips, salsa, cheese, and sunflower seeds. Serve hot.

Smoky Spiced Collard Greens with Turnip VN

The smokiness in this dish comes from the chipotle chili, a smoked jalapeño pepper available dried or canned in most supermarkets in the Mexican foods section or at Latino specialty markets. For milder greens, remove the seeds and veins from the chili before use. Collards are high in usable calcium, essential in the vegetarian diet.

INGREDIENTS | SERVES 4

1 bunch collards or turnip greens

1 medium white turnip, peeled and diced into ¼" pieces

1 medium onion, chopped

1 chipotle chili, dried or canned, cut in half

1 tablespoon olive oil

1 teaspoon salt

1 cup vegetable stock or water

1. Wash greens and remove the stems. Cut leaves into long thin strips (julienne).

2. In a heavy-bottomed pot, sauté the turnip, onion, and chili in olive oil until the onion is translucent, about 5–7 minutes. Add the greens and salt and sauté a few minutes more until greens are wilted.

3. Add stock or water, bring to a boil, and reduce heat to simmer for 20 minutes or until greens are very tender and turnips are soft.

Sautéed Mixed Greens with Kielbasa "Sausage"

*Bursting with flavor and nutrients, this greens medley suits a
casual dinner; offer this with a toasted baguette.*

INGREDIENTS | SERVES 4

2 tablespoons olive oil

1 large onion, thinly sliced

1 (12-ounce) package Kielbasa soy "sausage," thinly sliced

1 bunch chard, coarsely chopped

1 bunch collards, julienned

½ cup grated Parmesan cheese

1. Heat the oil in a large stockpot over medium heat and sauté the onion and "sausage" slices until the onion turns golden.

2. Add the greens and a sprinkling of water, cover the stockpot, and steam the greens until they are wilted and tender.

3. Sprinkle the greens with the Parmesan cheese and serve.

Braised Red Cabbage (*Chou Rouge à la Flamande*)

This classic European winter dish pairs marvelously with Crisp Potato Pancakes in Chapter 5 and a helping of Wild Rice with Apples and Almonds (Chapter 6).

INGREDIENTS | SERVES 8

1 small head red cabbage (about 2 pounds)

1 teaspoon salt

Pinch of grated nutmeg

1 tablespoon oil

1 tablespoon red wine vinegar

4 medium Granny Smith apples, peeled, cored, and cut into ¼" slices

1 tablespoon brown sugar

1. Wash cabbage and discard tough outer leaves; quarter, core, and thinly slice it (julienne). Sprinkle shredded cabbage with salt and nutmeg.

2. Heat oil in a large Dutch oven or ovenproof casserole dish with a tight-fitting lid; add cabbage and red vinegar. Cover and cook over low heat for at least 1 hour, either on the stovetop or in a low (325°F) oven.

3. Add the apples and sugar; cook for another 30 minutes until cabbage is very tender and apples are mostly dissolved.

Scented Escarole with Fennel

Greens need a thorough wash and dry before they go into your mouth. Pesticide residue isn't part of a healthy diet, and even organic sandy grit ruins a dish. Proper washing means washing twice.

INGREDIENTS | SERVES 6

2 tablespoons extra-virgin olive oil

2 cloves garlic, finely chopped

1 small onion, finely chopped

12 cups coarsely chopped escarole

1½ teaspoons fennel seeds, lightly toasted in a dry pan

Salt and ground black pepper to taste

1 tablespoon grated Parmesan cheese (Parmigiano-Reggiano)

1. Heat the oil over a medium heat. Add the garlic and cook about 1 minute until it starts to brown. Add onion and cook to translucent, about 5 minutes.

2. Add the escarole and fennel seeds, season with salt and pepper, and cover. Cook until escarole is wilted and simmer in its own juices.

3. Remove cover, raise heat to medium-high, and cook to evaporate most of the liquid, about 5 minutes. Serve garnished with grated cheese.

More Than Milk? Calcium in Leafy Greens

It'd be great if all the good things said about leafy greens were true, but beware: While it's true that beet greens, spinach, chard, and rhubarb provide more calcium than dairy products, it is in a form that your body cannot use. A better source comes from fortified soy beverages, tofu processed with calcium, broccoli, nuts, legumes, and certain leafy greens such as kale, collards, and mustard greens.

Broccoli Florets with Lemon Butter Sauce

White butter sauce, or beurre blanc, is a simple, smooth base that can be tailored to whatever it is served with—whole-grain mustard, herbs, and/or various citrus flavors.

INGREDIENTS | SERVES 4

2 small shallots, finely chopped

¼ cup white cooking wine

Juice of 1 medium lemon

8 ounces cold, unsalted butter, cut into small pieces

Salt and ground white pepper to taste

1 large head broccoli, broken into florets

Antioxidants

Antioxidants are vitamins and other substances that help your body expel "free radicals," harmful byproducts of cellular oxygen use. Antioxidants are believed to have cancer-fighting properties, aid in heart regulation, and strengthen immune systems. Dark leafy greens are high in antioxidants such as beta carotene (which your body turns into vitamin A), selenium, and vitamins C and E. Scientists are still unsure exactly which antioxidants work on which parts of the body, so a balanced diet is still the best diet.

1. Place the shallots, wine, and half of the lemon juice in a small saucepan over medium heat. Simmer until almost dry. Reduce heat to very low and stir in a few small pieces of butter, swirling it in with a wire whisk until it is mostly melted. Gradually add the remaining butter, whisking constantly, until all is used and sauce is smooth. Never boil. Season the sauce with salt, white pepper, and remaining lemon juice to taste. Keep in a warm place, but not over heat.

2. Wash the broccoli and boil in 4 quarts of rapidly boiling, salted water. Drain and serve with lemon butter sauce.

Chilled Broccoli Trio

To parboil the broccolis, plunge each batch into boiling water from 3–5 minutes, depending on the variety. Rinse each batch under cold running water and drain very well.

INGREDIENTS | SERVES 4

2 cups broccoli florets, parboiled

2 cups chopped broccoli raab, parboiled

2 cups chopped Chinese broccoli, parboiled

4 cloves garlic, chopped

1 cup toasted walnuts

½ cup crumbled Gorgonzola cheese

½ cup balsamic salad dressing

Salt and fresh ground black pepper, to taste

Crushed red pepper to taste

1. Combine the three broccolis in a large mixing bowl and toss with the garlic. Chill until ready to serve.

2. Just before serving, add the walnuts, cheese, dressing, salt, pepper, and crushed red pepper. Toss well.

Creamed Spinach

To add richness and silky texture to a meal, add a spoonful of this savory classic vegetable dish to the plate. It works especially well as a counterpoint to crunchy foods like Crisp Potato Pancakes (see recipe in Chapter 5) or toasted crostini.

INGREDIENTS | SERVES 4

2 pounds spinach, stemmed and washed

½ cup heavy cream

½ teaspoon salt

¼ teaspoon grated nutmeg

Ground black pepper to taste

1. Heat a large nonreactive skillet or Dutch oven over medium heat and cook the spinach with a few drops of water until just wilted. Drain, rinse, and squeeze dry in a colander. Chop the spinach finely.

2. In a skillet, bring the cream to a boil; add the salt, nutmeg, and pepper. Stir in the spinach; cook until most of the water has cooked out and the spinach is thick. If desired, purée in a food processor.

Gai Lan (Chinese Broccoli) with Toasted Garlic VN

Darker, leafier, and more slender-stemmed than Western broccoli, gai lan is nonetheless a cousin in the brassica family, which also includes most cabbages, cauliflower, mustard greens, and bok choy. It's worth seeking out in Asian grocery markets, but if you can't find it, this recipe will work just as well with regular broccoli or broccoli raab.

INGREDIENTS | SERVES 4

1 pound gai lan (Chinese broccoli) or other type of broccoli

2 tablespoons peanut oil

5 cloves garlic, finely chopped

Pinch of crushed red pepper flakes (optional)

Kosher salt and freshly ground black pepper to taste

Lemon wedges for garnish

1. Prepare a deep bowl full of salted ice water; set aside. Bring a large pot of salted water to a rapid, rolling boil. Trim any frayed ends from the stems of the gai lan. Cook it by handfuls only until crisp tender; plunge immediately into the ice bath. Drain.

2. In a large skillet or wok, heat the oil over a medium heat until it is hot. Add the garlic and red pepper (if using) and cook without stirring until the garlic begins to turn golden brown. Immediately add the blanched broccoli, and toss gently to stop the garlic from browning further. Cook until the broccoli is thoroughly hot. Season well with salt and pepper. Serve with lemon wedges.

Spinach Pancakes with Cardamom VN

These cakes are popular in cafés in Berlin, where they are served with a cracked wheat pilaf and caramelized onions.

INGREDIENTS | SERVES 4

1 tablespoon olive oil

2 teaspoons finely chopped garlic

2 pounds fresh spinach, washed and stemmed

4 pods cardamom, cracked open, or ½ teaspoon ground

1 teaspoon salt

Ground black pepper to taste

2 ounces egg substitute

1 cup plus 2 tablespoons bread crumbs

Oil for frying

Lemon wedges for garnish

1. Heat the olive oil in a large skillet or Dutch oven over high heat; add the garlic. Cook for 30 seconds until garlic becomes clear and fragrant; add the spinach, cardamom pods, salt, and pepper to taste. Cook just until spinach is wilted; transfer to a colander to cool.

2. Squeeze all excess water from spinach and place in a large bowl. Add egg substitute and 2 tablespoons of bread crumbs to the bowl and mix well. Form into 4 pancakes; dredge in remaining bread crumbs.

3. Heat oil in a heavy-bottomed skillet and fry cakes until browned on both sides and hot in the center. Serve with lemon wedges.

Spinach and Feta Pie

Every June on Manhattan's Ninth Avenue, there's an international food festival. The owners of a Greek bakery features a spinach and feta pie like this one.

INGREDIENTS | SERVES 8

1 bunch fresh spinach (about 4 cups)
3 tablespoons olive oil
1 medium yellow onion, chopped
1 cup grated Swiss cheese
2 large eggs
1¼ cups light cream
½ teaspoon salt
¼ teaspoon freshly ground black pepper
Pinch of nutmeg
¼ cup grated Parmesan cheese
1 (10") deep-dish pie crust, prebaked 5 minutes at 375°F
6 ounces feta cheese, crumbled
2 medium tomatoes, sliced (optional)

1. Heat oven to 350°F.

2. Wash and stem the spinach; steam until wilted. Squeeze out excess water and chop. Heat the olive oil in a small skillet and cook the onion until golden, about 7 minutes; toss with the spinach. Stir in the Swiss cheese.

3. Combine the eggs, cream, salt, pepper, nutmeg, and Parmesan cheese in a blender. Blend 1 minute.

4. Spread the spinach mixture into the crust. Top with feta cheese and decorate with tomatoes if desired. Pour on the egg mixture, pressing through with your fingers to make sure it soaks through to the crust.

5. Bake 45 minutes until a knife inserted in the pie comes out clean. Serve hot or room temperature.

Baked Spinach Tart

Popeye loved his spinach from a can, but you will love it fresh with its bright flavor and color.

INGREDIENTS | SERVES 6

2 large eggs

1 cup plain nonfat or whole-milk yogurt

1 cup feta cheese

1 cup shredded mozzarella cheese

1 bunch fresh spinach, preferably organic, well rinsed, wilted, and chopped

½ cup chopped onion

Salt and ground black pepper to taste

1 (9") unbaked deep-dish pie shell

½ pint grape tomatoes

1. Preheat oven to 350°F.

2. In a medium bowl, beat the eggs until foamy. Stir in the yogurt, feta cheese, mozzarella cheese, spinach, and onions, mixing well until combined. Season with salt and pepper.

3. Spoon the mixture into the pie shell and push the tomatoes into the top of the mixture.

4. Bake for about 40 minutes or until the mixture is firm to the touch. Let it cool slightly before slicing and serving.

Grilled Radicchio VN

Radicchio, a bittersweet, purplish red head lettuce, mellows and becomes juicy when it's lightly dressed and cooked on a grill or in a grill pan. Select tight round heads that are heavy for their size, without wilted leaves or blemishes.

INGREDIENTS | SERVES 4

4 heads radicchio

1 tablespoon extra-virgin olive oil

1 large lemon, halved

Salt and ground black pepper to taste

1. Quarter the radicchio heads through the root end. In a mixing bowl, drizzle the olive oil over the pieces, squeeze on the lemon juice, and season with salt and pepper; toss to coat.

2. Heat a grill or stovetop grill pan to medium heat. Lay the radicchio, cut-side down, across the grill ribs. Cook until wilting is visible from the sides, only about 2 minutes. Turn to the other cut side and cook for 1–2 minutes more, pulling it from the grill before it goes completely limp. Serve with extra lemon wedges on the side.

Kale with Garlic and Thyme

Antioxidant-rich, dark leafy greens like kale are nutritional powerhouses loaded with calcium, beta carotene, and vitamin C. They're also high in fiber and phytochemicals.

INGREDIENTS | SERVES 4

2 pounds kale, stems and ribs removed

1 tablespoon olive oil

1 medium red onion, chopped

1 tablespoon chopped garlic

Pinch of crushed red pepper

2 teaspoons chopped fresh thyme leaves or ½ teaspoon dried

¼ cup dry sherry or white wine

Salt and ground black pepper to taste

1. Bring a large pot of well-salted water to a rolling boil. Add the kale and cook for 10 minutes until it has lost its waxy coating and the leaves are tender. Transfer to a colander to drain, reserving about ½ cup of the cooking liquid. Roughly chop the kale.

2. Heat the oil in a large skillet or Dutch oven. Add the onion, garlic, red pepper, and thyme. Cook over medium heat until the onions are soft and starting to brown around the edges.

3. Splash in the sherry; cook for 5 minutes until all alcohol has evaporated. Add back the kale and reserved liquid; cook 10 minutes more. Season with salt and pepper.

Szechuan Stir-Fried Cabbage with Hot Peppers

You don't have to have a wok to cook this dish. You could also use a large skillet, but the wok's distinctive shape is ideal for the high-heat, fast cooking this dish requires.

INGREDIENTS | SERVES 4–6

¼ cup plus 2 tablespoons peanut or other neutral oil

8 dried red chili peppers, quartered and seeded

1 (1") piece fresh ginger, peeled and finely chopped

1 medium head Chinese cabbage, chopped into 2" pieces

½ teaspoon cornstarch

1 tablespoon soy sauce

1 teaspoon dry sherry or Chinese cooking wine

1 teaspoon sugar

1 teaspoon rice wine vinegar

1 teaspoon Asian sesame oil

1. Heat ¼ cup of the oil in a wok or skillet over high heat. Stir in the peppers and fry, stirring, for 1 minute until the peppers darken in color. Transfer the peppers and oil to a bowl and set aside.

2. Pour remaining 2 tablespoons of oil into the wok; add the ginger and cook for a few seconds until fragrant. Add the cabbage all at once. Fry, stirring, for 1 minute.

3. Combine the cornstarch, soy sauce, and sherry together in a small bowl. Add to the wok. Stir until the cornstarch cooks and forms a thick sauce; add the sugar and vinegar. Sprinkle in the sesame oil and pour in the peppers and their oil. Stir to combine well. Transfer to a serving bowl.

Garlicky Broccoli Raab VN

The key to the toasty flavor of this dish is to brown the garlic to a golden color before adding the blanched raabs. Their moisture stops the garlic from cooking, preserving its browned, but not burned, flavor.

INGREDIENTS | SERVES 4

1 pound broccoli raab, bottoms trimmed

2 tablespoons good-quality olive oil

2 tablespoons finely chopped garlic

Pinch of crushed red pepper flakes (optional)

Salt and ground black pepper to taste

Lemon wedges, for garnish

Spicy Variations

In place of or in addition to pepper flakes, substitute toasted cumin seeds, fennel seeds, anise, or chopped fresh ginger for different character.

1. Blanch the raabs in rapidly boiling salted water; shock in ice water and drain.

2. Heat the olive oil in a large, heavy-bottomed skillet over medium heat for 1 minute. Add the garlic and red pepper flakes, if using, and cook stirring with a wooden spoon until garlic is golden.

3. Add all of the raabs at once; toss to coat. Season well with salt and pepper. When the vegetable is hot, serve with lemon wedges on the side.

Collard Greens with Tomatoes and Cheddar

The assertive vegetal taste of collards benefits from a marriage with equally gutsy tomatoes and Cheddar cheese. Try this with a grain pilaf, such as soaked bulgur wheat, for a chewy textural contrast.

INGREDIENTS | SERVES 4

2 pounds collard greens, stems and ribs removed

2 tablespoons olive oil

1 tablespoon finely chopped garlic (about 2 cloves)

4 medium ripe red or yellow tomatoes (or a combination)

1 teaspoon salt

1 teaspoon oregano

4 ounces Cheddar cheese, shredded

1. Bring a large pot of salted water to a rolling boil. Cook the greens until tender, about 10 minutes; drain and roughly chop.

2. Heat the oil in a large, heavy-bottomed skillet over medium-high heat. Add the garlic; allow it to sizzle for 30 seconds before adding the collards, tomatoes, salt, and oregano. Cook for 4 minutes just until the tomatoes are hot.

3. Serve topped with the shredded cheese.

Cumin-Roasted Butternut Squash VN

Choose butternuts with a large, cylindrical barrel and small, bulbous bottom, so you yield the most squash and fewest seeds. Since the squash is peeled for this dish, the longer barrel means easier preparation.

INGREDIENTS | SERVES 8

1 medium butternut squash (2–3 pounds)

2 tablespoons ground cumin

2 tablespoons olive oil

Salt and coarsely ground black pepper, to taste

1 tablespoon roughly chopped Italian (flat-leaf) parsley

1. Preheat oven to 375°F.

2. Cut the butternut in two, crosswise, just above the bulbous bottom. Place the cut side of the cylindrical barrel down on a cutting board and peel it with a knife or potato peeler, removing all rind. Repeat with the bottom part, then cut bottom in half and remove seeds.

3. Dice squash into 1" chunks. In a large mixing bowl, toss squash with cumin, oil, salt, and pepper.

4. Spread into a single layer on a doubled baking sheet and roast in oven for 40 minutes, turning after 25 minutes, until browned and tender. Serve sprinkled with chopped parsley.

Mushroom-Stuffed Tomatoes

Use any ripe tomato you prefer for this dish. Late in the season, Roma plum tomatoes are usually the best choice, since they keep a long time even when ripe. If using a processor to chop the mushrooms, pulse them in small batches, stopping before they clump.

INGREDIENTS | SERVES 6

4 shallots, finely chopped

2 tablespoons olive oil, divided

1 pound white mushrooms, washed and finely chopped

1 teaspoon salt plus 2 pinches

Splash of white wine (about ¼ cup)

¼ cup finely chopped parsley

Ground black pepper to taste

6 large ripe plum tomatoes, halved crosswise, bottoms trimmed flat

3 tablespoons bread crumbs

1. Preheat oven to 350°F.

2. Sauté chopped shallots with 1 tablespoon olive oil in a large skillet over medium heat. Add chopped mushrooms (if some don't fit, you can add them later, when the rest have wilted down) and 1 teaspoon salt and raise heat to high. Cook, stirring occasionally, until mushrooms have given up their water and most of it has evaporated.

3. Add the white wine and cook until it has mostly evaporated. Stir in chopped parsley, remove from heat, and season with black pepper.

4. Scoop the innards from the tomatoes and season the tomato cups with 2 pinches salt. Fill each tomato with mushroom filling so that it mounds slightly, topping each with a sprinkle of bread crumbs. Line into a baking dish and drizzle with remaining olive oil. Bake 25 minutes or until soft.

Tomato Confit with Fine Herbs VN

The term "confit" refers to items cooked in their own liquid, which these tomatoes do inside their skins. Oven roasting intensifies the sweetness of tomatoes by cooking out some of their water. They'll keep, refrigerated, for 4 days.

INGREDIENTS | SERVES 5

5 large ripe but firm beefsteak tomatoes, cored, halved crosswise, seeded

12 large sprigs assorted fresh herbs like thyme, oregano, rosemary, or parsley

3 tablespoons olive oil

1 teaspoon salt

1. Preheat oven to 275°F. Toss the tomatoes gently with the herbs, olive oil, and salt, then arrange cut-side down in a baking dish, so that the herbs are under and touching them.

2. Bake 2 hours until flesh is very soft to the touch and skin looks wrinkled.

3. Cool until you can touch them, then carefully remove the skins. Serve warm.

Red and Yellow Plum Tomato Chutney VN

This summer salsa accompanies fried tofu very well, and is also a great base for grain salads, such as the Quinoa Salad with Tomatoes and Cilantro (Chapter 6).

INGREDIENTS | MAKES 3 CUPS

⅓ cup sugar

Juice of 1 medium lemon

6 medium red plum tomatoes, seeded and roughly chopped

6 medium yellow plum tomatoes, seeded and roughly chopped

¼ cup finely diced red onion

¼ cup fresh cilantro, roughly chopped

Chopping Tender Herbs

Keep fresh herbs looking neat and clean by cutting them with a slicing action rather than a chopping motion. Even though recipes call for "chopped" leafy herbs, it's best to bunch gentle leaves like basil, oregano, or mint into small piles or stacks, then slice them against the cutting board with the sharpest knife you can find. If your knives are dull, snipping with scissors is a gentler action than chopping. Chopping can result in unattractive black edges, clumps, and rapid spoilage. Heartier herbs, such as fresh thyme, parsley, and rosemary, can stand up to a rough chop.

1. Mix sugar with ½ cup water in a medium saucepan. Cook over high heat until water is evaporated and molten sugar begins to turn golden brown. Pour in lemon juice to stop the sugar from cooking and bring it up from the bottom of the pan.

2. Add the chopped tomatoes and red onion. Simmer for no more than 5 minutes (this is to warm the tomatoes, not cook them). Remove from heat. Allow to cool in a colander, letting the excess water released from the warmed tomatoes drain out. Stir in chopped cilantro.

New Mexico Chili Sauce VN

This tomato-based Southwestern sauce is the ultimate salsa for Black Bean Burritos (Chapter 6), a wonderful accompaniment to scrambled eggs or omelets, and the base for the sauce in Chilaquiles (see recipe in this chapter).

INGREDIENTS | MAKES 3 CUPS

1 teaspoon olive oil

1 medium onion, roughly chopped

5 New Mexico chilies, seeded, soaked, and puréed (see sidebar)

1 (28-ounce) jar roasted-garlic-flavored marinara sauce

½ teaspoon ground cumin

½ teaspoon dried oregano

1. Heat the oil in a saucepan over medium heat. Add onion; cook, stirring occasionally, until translucent, about 5 minutes. Add chili purée; cook 3 minutes more. Add the marinara sauce, cumin, and oregano. Simmer 10 minutes.

2. Purée in a blender until very smooth.

Softening Dried Chilis

Make dried chilies ready for use by toasting them in a 350°F oven for 5 minutes, until they soften, become fragrant, and smoke lightly. Then, soak them in enough water to cover for 1 hour, and purée in a blender with just enough soaking liquid to make a thick purée circulate in the blender vase. For less "heat," remove the seeds before soaking.

Chilaquiles (Tortilla Stew)

Pronounced "chill-uh-KILL-ehs," these softened tortilla chips are a favorite hearty breakfast item in Mexico. They're perfect for brunch, because they only take a few minutes to throw together once the ingredients are assembled.

INGREDIENTS | SERVES 2

4 cups tortilla chips

2 cups vegetable stock

1 cup New Mexico Chili Sauce (see recipe in this chapter) or spicy tomato sauce

2 tablespoons butter

4 large eggs

2 tablespoons sour cream

Chopped cilantro for garnish

1. Place the chips in a large skillet over high heat. Add 1 cup of vegetable stock and the chili sauce. Bring to a boil, then lower to a simmer, adding more stock as needed to keep the mixture soupy. Cook until the tortillas are softened but not mushy.

2. Melt butter in a large skillet over medium heat. Cook eggs over easy in the melted butter.

3. Serve the chilaquiles on 2 plates, topped with fried eggs, a dollop of sour cream, and a sprinkling of chopped cilantro.

Avocado Sashimi with Miso Dressing VN

Avocados provide healthy fats and impart a luxurious richness to foods. There are two types commonly available in American markets: the Florida avocado is large (about the size of a grapefruit or bigger), and the California-grown avocado, known as a Hass avocado, is about the size of an average pear and has a smoother, silkier texture.

INGREDIENTS | SERVES 2

1 large ripe Hass avocado, halved, seeded, and peeled

1 medium lemon

1 teaspoon white or yellow miso

1 teaspoon grated gingerroot

1 teaspoon light soy sauce

1 teaspoon sugar

1 teaspoon sesame oil

Wasabi paste for garnish

Pickled ginger for garnish

1. Place the avocado halves cut-side down on a board; score them at ⅛" intervals, leaving the stem end connected to hold them together. Squeeze the lemon over the scored avocados to prevent browning. Fan the avocados onto 2 small plates.

2. In a small bowl, whisk together the miso, ginger, soy sauce, sugar, and sesame oil until the sugar is dissolved. Spoon some of the dressing over the avocadoes. Serve garnished with wasabi and pickled ginger.

Ratatouille VN

*A classic Provençal dish, this is a perfect way to make the most of summer's harvest.
If you can find it, try using purple basil to garnish this colorful dish.*

INGREDIENTS | SERVES 6

2 tablespoons olive oil

1 large onion, diced

2 medium zucchini, diced

2 medium yellow squash, diced

1 small eggplant, diced

1 medium red bell pepper, seeded
and diced

1 tablespoon flour

3 medium tomatoes, seeded and cut
into 6 pieces

2 teaspoons dried Herbes de Provence
(or a combination of oregano, thyme,
rosemary, marjoram, savory, and/or
lavender)

1 teaspoon salt

Ground black pepper to taste

Fresh basil leaves, chopped

1. Heat the olive oil in a heavy-bottomed Dutch oven until hot but not smoky. Add onion; cook until translucent, about 5 minutes.

2. Combine the zucchini, yellow squash, eggplant, and bell pepper in a large paper bag; dust with flour, fold bag closed, and shake to coat. Add floured vegetables to the pot, along with the tomatoes, herbs, salt, and pepper.

3. Reduce heat to a simmer, cover, and cook gently for 1 hour until all vegetables are tender. Serve hot or at room temperature. Garnish with basil.

Quick Tomato and Oregano Sauté VN

This versatile pan stew accompanies steamed, baked, or sautéed mushrooms as easily as it does grilled tempeh or fried tofu. It also works beautifully as a simple pasta sauce.

INGREDIENTS | SERVES 4

1 tablespoon olive oil

2 cloves garlic, finely minced

2 cups chopped tomatoes

½ teaspoon salt

2 tablespoons chopped fresh oregano or ½ teaspoon dried

Ground black pepper to taste

1. Heat olive oil in a medium skillet over medium heat. Sprinkle in minced garlic and stir with a wooden spoon for only a moment until the garlic whitens and releases its aroma. Do not allow it to brown.

2. Add chopped tomato, salt, and, if you are using dried oregano, add that now. Simmer 10 minutes until most of the water has evaporated, stirring occasionally.

3. Season with freshly ground black pepper, and if you are using fresh oregano, stir it in and simmer 1 minute more.

Basic Fresh Tomato Sauce VN

August and September are tomato harvest season in the East, when thousands of cooks pack summer's bounty into jars of fruity tomato sauce to last them the whole year. This sauce freezes well and can also be canned.

INGREDIENTS | MAKES 1 QUART

4 pounds Roma tomatoes

2 tablespoons olive oil

1 large onion, roughly chopped

5 cloves garlic, chopped (about 2 tablespoons)

1 teaspoon sugar

2 tablespoons tomato paste

Salt and ground black pepper to taste

1 cup washed fresh basil leaves, stems removed

1. Halve the tomatoes and squeeze out as many seeds as you can. Dice the tomatoes.

2. Heat the olive oil in a large nonreactive saucepan or Dutch oven over medium heat until hot enough to sizzle when a piece of onion is added. Add the onions; cook until soft and beginning to brown slightly, about 10 minutes. Stir in the garlic, sugar, and tomato paste; cook 2 minutes more, stirring constantly. Add the tomatoes; cook 10 minutes until mixture becomes brothy.

3. Uncover, lower heat to a slow simmer, and cook 30 minutes more until all tomatoes are fully softened; season with salt and pepper to taste. For smooth sauce, purée and strain, then add the basil leaves at the end.

Quick Tomato Sauce VN

This sauce can be assembled in 20 minutes from ingredients right in the house. It is an excellent all-purpose red sauce for pasta or any recipe calling for tomato sauce.

INGREDIENTS | MAKES 1 QUART

2 tablespoons olive oil

1 medium onion, chopped

2 tablespoons chopped garlic (about 5 cloves)

1 teaspoon dried oregano

1 tablespoon tomato paste

1 teaspoon sugar

1 (28-ounce) can crushed tomatoes

1 (14-ounce) can diced tomatoes in purée

Salt and ground black pepper to taste

1. Heat the oil in a medium saucepan for 1 minute over medium heat. Add onions, garlic, and oregano; cook 5 minutes until onions are translucent.

2. Stir in tomato paste and sugar; cook, stirring, 5 minutes more. Add crushed tomatoes, diced tomatoes, salt, and pepper. Simmer 10 minutes.

Be Creative with Your Tomato Sauce

There are many options available to you when preparing a tomato sauce. Try replacing the oregano with a bay leaf or some basil. Try a finely diced pepper or even cilantro in place of (or in addition to) the onion.

Simple Salsa VN

This simple condiment pairs magnificently with burritos, tacos, empanadas, tortilla chips, and all kinds of other Mexican savories. The salsa keeps in the refrigerator for 2 days, but is best used the day it's made.

INGREDIENTS | MAKES 1 CUP

2 large tomatoes
1 small onion, finely diced
2 small jalapeño peppers, seeded and finely chopped
½ teaspoon fresh-squeezed lime juice
Salt and ground black pepper to taste
½ teaspoon chipotle purée

1. Quarter the tomatoes. Cut out the inside viscera; reserve. Cut the remaining petals into a fine dice. Purée the insides in a food processor until smooth.

2. Toss purée with diced tomatoes, onion, jalapeños, lime juice, salt, pepper, and chipotle.

Stir-Fried Snow Peas with Cilantro VN

This dish should be very quickly cooked. The entire cooking time for the peas should not exceed 5 minutes.

INGREDIENTS | SERVES 4

2 tablespoons peanut oil
1 cup thinly sliced scallions
1 cup snow peas
½ cup strong vegetable stock
2 teaspoons cornstarch
2 tablespoons cold water
½ cup finely chopped cilantro leaves
Dash of soy sauce
Pinch of sugar

1. Heat oil in a large skillet until very hot, almost smoking. Add scallions and snow peas, tossing or stirring quickly to coat them with oil. Add stock, cover the skillet, and cook for 2 minutes.

2. Meanwhile, in a small bowl, mix the cornstarch with 2 tablespoons of cold water and the cilantro.

3. Stir the cornstarch mixture quickly into the peas, stirring constantly until the sauce thickens, about 2 minutes more; season with soy sauce and sugar. Serve immediately.

Eggplant and Tomato Sauté VN

Serve this as a sauce with pasta or chilled as a summer salad
with bulgur wheat pilaf or another grain salad.

INGREDIENTS | SERVES 8

1 medium eggplant (about 1 pound), cut lengthwise into 8 wedges

Kosher salt to taste

3 tablespoons olive oil, divided

2 medium onions, cut into ½" slices

¼ teaspoon crushed red pepper flakes

1 tablespoon chopped garlic (about 3 cloves)

2 cups chopped plum tomatoes

¼ cup chopped fresh oregano or parsley

1. Sprinkle the eggplant wedges liberally with kosher salt; set aside for 10–15 minutes until water visibly pools under the wedges (this extracts some bitter juices, making the eggplant especially mellow for this recipe). Dry the eggplant off with a towel.

2. Heat 2 tablespoons of olive oil in a large, heavy-bottomed skillet until a piece of vegetable sizzles when added. Fry the eggplant wedges until they are lightly browned and bubbling with juice. Transfer to a cutting board and cut into large (2") pieces.

3. Put remaining olive oil in the skillet and heat 1 minute over medium heat. Add onions, crushed pepper, and garlic; cook, stirring occasionally, until onions are very soft, about 10 minutes.

4. Add tomatoes and cook just until they begin to break down into a chunky sauce. Add the eggplant and chopped oregano or parsley. Bring to a simmer; remove from heat.

Asparagus-Shallot Sauté VN

Asparagus is loaded with beneficial insoluble fiber, which aids in digestion, sweeping unwanted potentially harmful items through the system before they can do damage.

INGREDIENTS | SERVES 6

1 bunch asparagus

Kosher salt, to taste

1 tablespoon olive oil

½ cup finely chopped shallots (about 4 shallots)

Pinch of roughly cracked black pepper

1 tablespoon dry white wine or sherry

Lemon wedges for garnish

Roughly Cracked Black Pepper

Release inner tension while liberating black pepper's inner fruitiness, perfume, and fresh taste by cracking against a counter or board with the bottom of a pan. Like many seeds, black pepper's best flavor remains locked inside until it's smashed. Place ten peppercorns at a time on a flat, hard surface. Using a small saucepot or small skillet, apply pressure with the heel of your hand to break the seeds a few at a time. Roll logs of goat cheese in this exceptionally fresh seasoning, or use it as you would ground black pepper.

1. Bring a large pot of water to a rolling boil and blanch the asparagus for about 2–3 minutes, shocking them in salted ice water when they are fully cooked but tender. Transfer to a cutting board and cut on a diagonal angle into 2" pieces.

2. Heat the olive oil in a large skillet; add the shallots and black pepper. Cook until translucent, about 3 minutes; add the wine and asparagus; cook until heated through. Serve with lemon wedges on the side.

Roasted Asparagus with Mixed Summer Squashes and Peppers VN

Don't skip this warm-weather dish if you can't find the mini sweet peppers; simply substitute red, yellow, or green bell peppers.

INGREDIENTS | SERVES 4

¼ cup olive oil

3 tablespoons balsamic vinegar

1 tablespoon minced garlic

1 pound asparagus, stem ends trimmed

1 pound mixed summer squashes, thinly sliced

1 pound mini sweet peppers, stemmed, seeded, and sliced in half lengthwise

2 or 3 hot peppers or to taste, chopped

Seasoning salt to taste

1. Preheat oven to 400°F.

2. In a small bowl, mix the olive oil, balsamic vinegar, and garlic together and set aside.

3. Place the vegetables into a large roasting pan, mixing them together so the flavors will mingle. Pour the olive oil mixture over top, lifting and gently mixing the vegetables so they are all coated with oil. Sprinkle the vegetables with seasoning salt.

4. Roast the vegetables uncovered for about 45 minutes or until they begin to darken; stir occasionally. Serve hot.

Peck of Peppers Tart

For this colorful entrée, mix and match the colors, sizes, and heat quotient of the peppers you select. If you don't want it too piquant, go easy on the hot chiles. Otherwise, live it up!

INGREDIENTS | SERVES 6

2 tablespoons olive oil

1 tablespoon minced garlic

2 cups coarsely chopped peppers of your choice

4 large eggs, beaten

1 cup milk

1 cup shredded Swiss cheese

2 teaspoons smoked paprika

Salt and ground black pepper to taste

1 (9") deep-dish pie crust

1. Preheat oven to 350°F.

2. Heat the oil in a large skillet over medium heat and sauté the garlic. Add the peppers and sauté for 2–3 minutes.

3. Meanwhile, in a mixing bowl, mix the eggs, milk, cheese, paprika, salt, and pepper together until well combined. Stir in the peppers and pour the mixture into the pie crust.

4. Bake the tart for 30 minutes or until the center is firm and the top browns. Serve hot.

Turkish-Style Stuffed Pepper

You can easily double or triple this recipe to serve more people, but it's so easy to prepare, it's fine just for one. For added texture, add a tablespoon or two of toasted pine nuts.

INGREDIENTS | SERVES 1

1 large red bell pepper

Olive oil

½ cup cooked brown rice

¼ cup soy "meat" crumbles

2 tablespoons raisins

2 tablespoons chopped dried apricots

2 tablespoons chopped fresh mint

2 tablespoons chopped parsley

2 tablespoons plain yogurt

1. Preheat oven to 400°F.

2. Cut the top off the pepper and clean out the seeds and membranes. Rub the pepper inside and out with the olive oil.

3. In a medium bowl, combine the rice with the soy "meat," raisins, apricots, mint, parsley, and yogurt. Carefully spoon the mixture into the hollow pepper. Prop the pepper upright in a baking dish.

4. Bake the pepper for 30 minutes or until the pepper is tender. Serve.

Roasted Vegetables VN

As an appetizer, main course, or an ingredient in Basic Pasta Salad (Chapter 11), this mélange of roasted veggies is easy comfort food. Cut everything into 1" cubes. You'll probably need two roasting pans or baking dishes for this recipe.

INGREDIENTS | SERVES 8

1 small eggplant (about 1 pound), cubed

1 small butternut squash (about 1½ pounds), peeled and cubed

1 pound red potatoes, cubed

1 pound carrots, peeled and cut into 1" pieces

12 cloves garlic, peeled

2 large white onions, cut into 1" cubes

1 medium zucchini, cubed

1 yellow squash, cubed

10 ounces mushrooms

3 tablespoons olive oil

1 teaspoon kosher salt

½ teaspoon freshly ground black pepper

½ cup mixed chopped herbs, such as rosemary, thyme, oregano, parsley, chives, or less than ¼ cup of dried mixed herbs

¼ cup good-quality balsamic vinegar

1. Heat oven to 350°F.

2. In a large bowl, combine eggplant, squash, potatoes, carrots, garlic, onions, zucchini, yellow squash, mushrooms, olive oil, salt, pepper, and mixed herbs; toss to coat.

3. Spread into a single layer onto 1 or 2 roasting pans, jellyroll pans, or baking dishes. Cook 1–1½ hours until vegetables are very tender and browned lightly. Sprinkle with balsamic vinegar and set out to cool.

Chinese Wrinkled String Beans VN

Remember to leave time in between your batches when frying to allow the oil to com back to temperature. If you rush and skip this step, you will have soggy, oily beans.

INGREDIENTS | SERVES 4

Oil for deep-frying

1 pound fresh green beans, stem ends snipped off

2 tablespoons peanut oil

½ cup chopped scallions

1 (1") piece fresh ginger, peeled and finely chopped

1 tablespoon chopped garlic

1 teaspoon sugar

1 teaspoon white vinegar

Salt to taste

Asian sesame oil

1. Heat 2" of oil in a wok or deep skillet to 350°F (a piece of vegetable should sizzle vigorously, but the oil should not smoke). Carefully fry the green beans in 4 small batches. They will shrivel as they cook—they take about 5 minutes per batch. Leave time in between batches to let the oil come back up to temperature.

2. In a separate skillet, heat the peanut oil. Add the scallions, ginger, garlic, sugar, and vinegar. Cook 1 minute until the garlic turns white. Add the green beans; toss to coat. Season with salt and Asian sesame oil.

Green Beans and Pine Nut Sauté VN

The key to keeping this attractive dish vibrant is to select only exquisitely fresh, plump, unblemished green beans, and cook them in small batches just until tender, shocking them to lock in color, flavor, and nutrients.

INGREDIENTS | SERVES 6

2 tablespoons extra-virgin olive oil

½ cup finely chopped shallots or red onion

¼ cup pine nuts

1 pound fresh green beans, blanched 1 minute in salted water and shocked in ice water

1 cup diced tomatoes

Salt and ground black pepper to taste

1. Heat the oil in a large skillet over medium heat; add the shallots and pine nuts. Cook until the pine nuts begin to brown lightly, 3–4 minutes.

2. Add the green beans, tomatoes, salt, and pepper. Cook only enough to warm through and soften the tomatoes slightly. Serve hot or at room temperature.

Zucchini Ragout VN

A ragout is either a main-dish stew or a sauce. This one can be served as either.

INGREDIENTS | SERVES 6

5 ounces fresh spinach

3 medium zucchini, diced

½ cup diced red onion

2 stalks celery, diced

2 medium carrots, peeled and diced

1 medium parsnip, peeled and diced

3 tablespoons tomato paste

¼ cup water

1 teaspoon freshly ground black pepper

¼ teaspoon kosher salt

1 tablespoon minced fresh basil

1 tablespoon minced fresh Italian parsley

1 tablespoon minced fresh oregano

Place all ingredients into a 4-quart slow cooker. Stir. Cook on low for 4 hours. Stir before serving.

Saving on Herbs

The cost of herbs can add up quickly, but you can save a little money by shopping at an international farmers' market or buying a blend of spices (an Italian blend would work well in this recipe) instead of buying each individually.

CHAPTER 9

The Onion Family

Braised Leeks VN

Silky, delicate braised leeks are juicy and light, making them an excellent foil for spicy dishes and fried foods. Broth from braising leeks is an excellent vegetable stock, so keep it for use in soups, stews, and risottos.

INGREDIENTS | SERVES 4

5 black peppercorns

5 parsley stems

1 bay leaf

1 medium onion, halved

2 medium carrots, peeled and thinly sliced

1 rib celery, sliced

2 teaspoons salt

4 medium leeks, cleaned, halved lengthwise

1 tablespoon extra-virgin olive oil

Chopped chives or parsley

1. Combine peppercorns, parsley stems, bay leaf, onion, carrots, and celery in a nonreactive pot with 3 quarts of water and 2 teaspoons salt. Bring to a boil; lower to a simmer. Add the leeks; simmer very gently for 15–20 minutes until leeks are very tender.

2. Remove leeks from the broth; arrange them cut-side up on a platter. Drizzle with olive oil and sprinkle with chives.

Cleaning Leeks

Leeks tend to trap a lot of earth, sand, and grit in between their layers. It's important to wash leeks twice before using them. For dishes where the leek will be used unchopped, trim the roots leaving the root core still attached to the leek. Fan through the leek layers with your thumb and middle finger while running the leek under cold, clean water. Repeat several times.

Grilled Leeks with Tarragon and Lemon VN

Some vegetables are best grilled after a light blanching. Leeks achieve a tender, silky texture and mild vegetal sweetness on the grill when they've been steamed or blanched in boiling water before they hit the barbecue. Always leave the root core attached to hold cooking leeks together.

INGREDIENTS | SERVES 4

4 medium leeks, cleaned, split lengthwise

3 tablespoons extra-virgin olive oil, divided

Kosher salt and freshly ground black pepper to taste

1 teaspoon Dijon mustard

2 teaspoons freshly squeezed lemon juice (about ½ of a lemon)

1 tablespoon freshly chopped tarragon, chervil, chives, or Italian parsley

1. Heat a grill or stovetop grill pan. Steam or blanch the leeks in boiling salted water for 5 minutes. Shock them by plunging them into ice-cold water; drain well. Lightly brush them with olive oil, top and bottom; lightly season them with salt and pepper. Grill the leeks on both sides until dark brown grill marks appear. Transfer to a platter.

2. Whisk together the mustard and lemon juice. Gradually whisk in the remaining olive oil; season the dressing with salt and pepper. Drizzle this dressing over the grilled leeks. Sprinkle with chopped herbs and serve hot or at room temperature.

Leek Tart

In keeping with the tradition of pies at Thanksgiving, add this savory tart to your holiday table. Leeks are available year-round.

INGREDIENTS | SERVES 6

2 tablespoons unsalted butter

2 pounds leeks, sliced ¼", washed very thoroughly

½ teaspoon salt plus more to taste

Ground black pepper to taste

2 large eggs

½ cup cream or half-and-half

¼ teaspoon ground nutmeg

1 (9") pie crust

1. Heat oven to 400°F.

2. Melt the butter in a skillet and cook the leeks over medium-low heat until very soft, about 30 minutes, seasoning with ½ teaspoon salt and black pepper to taste. Do not brown.

3. In a medium bowl, whisk together the eggs, cream, and nutmeg; season with salt and pepper. Combine the leeks and the egg mixture and pour into the pie shell. Bake until golden, about 25 minutes. Allow to rest 10 minutes before cutting.

Caramelized Pearl Onions

You can use frozen pearl onions, which are already peeled, for this recipe. But the sweetness and crunch of fresh ones elevate the dish, so use them when you have the time and patience to peel for 20 minutes or so.

INGREDIENTS | SERVES 40

2 cups peeled pearl onions

2 teaspoons sugar or brown sugar

¼ teaspoon salt

1 tablespoon butter or olive oil

1 cup cold water

When Are Onions "Translucent," "Soft," and "Caramelized"?

Cooking onions extracts the natural juices that are trapped in the raw onions' cell walls. By adding heat, these walls break down, releasing sugars and flavors, which add complexity and dimension to food. After a few minutes of sizzling gently in oil or butter, onions wilt as their cell walls collapse, giving up their juices. This gives the once-opaque raw onion a watery, "translucent" appearance. The edges, once rough and sharp, are then "soft." As the water evaporates from the juices, the onions' natural sugars concentrate on the exterior of the pieces and brown in the heat. The first stages of this transformation give onions a golden appearance. Since browned sugar is known as caramel, the browning of onions is often referred to as "caramelizing."

1. In a heavy-bottomed skillet over medium heat, combine onions, sugar, salt, and butter with 1 cup cold water; bring to a simmer. Cook gently until all water is absorbed and onions are coated in a light glaze, about 5 minutes.

2. Lower heat to low; cook slowly until glaze browns and onions attain a golden brown appearance, about 5 minutes more.

Onion Tart

With a lightly dressed salad, this makes an excellent lunch. Experiment with your own herb combinations to make this tart your own.

INGREDIENTS | SERVES 8

1 (9") pie crust

2 tablespoons unsalted butter

3 cups thinly sliced onions

3 teaspoons chopped fresh thyme leaves, or other herb, such as oregano or tarragon

1 tablespoon flour

¾ cup half-and-half

¼ cup sour cream

2 large eggs, beaten

¾ teaspoon salt

½ teaspoon freshly ground black pepper

1. Heat oven to 400°F.

2. Prick the bottom of the pie crust lightly with a fork in several places. Place a sheet of waxed paper on the pie shell; fill with pie beads or dried beans and "blind bake" until lightly browned, about 15 minutes; cool on a rack.

3. Lower oven to 350°F.

4. Melt the butter in a skillet over medium heat. Add the onions and thyme; cook slowly until onions are soft and lightly browned, about 15 minutes. Stir in the flour and cook 1 minute more.

5. Transfer mixture to a mixing bowl; combine with the half-and-half, sour cream, eggs, salt, and pepper. Pour into par-baked pie shell; bake in center of oven until filling is set and lightly browned on top, about 35 minutes.

Roasted Sweet Onions VN

*The easiest recipes are sometimes the best. Choose sweet onions such as
Vidalia or Texas Sweets for the most otherworldly experience.*

INGREDIENTS | SERVES 4

4 large sweet onions, all the same size

1. Heat oven to 350°F.

2. Trim the visible roots from the onions, but leave the skins on and the tops untrimmed. Place the onions root-end down in a baking dish. Roast in center of oven until onions are very soft and give easily to gentle pressure. They take between 60–90 minutes, depending on the size of the onions.

3. Peel the outer skin, but leave on the caramelized outer layers, which add extra flavor.

Roasted Shallots VN

*These sweet jewels pair surprisingly well with both Eastern and Western
foods. The Thais actually use shallots as often as the French!*

INGREDIENTS | SERVES 4

16 medium shallots, peeled, ends trimmed, root core left intact
1 teaspoon sugar
2 tablespoons olive oil

1. Heat oven to 350°F.

2. Toss the shallots with the sugar to coat. Heat the oil in an ovensafe skillet over medium heat; add the shallots. Cook 1 minute, just to start the browning. Turn the shallots and place the pan in the oven.

3. Roast for 30 minutes. Transfer to a plate to cool slightly. If necessary, peel off any leathery outer layers before serving.

Grilled Onions with Balsamic Glaze VN

The key to perfect, sweet grilled onions is slow, even cooking. They're custom-made for the outer edges of the grill, or a grill pan over a whisper of a flame.

INGREDIENTS | SERVES 4

4 large sweet onions (about the size of a baseball)

2 tablespoons extra-virgin olive oil

Kosher salt and freshly ground black pepper to taste

1 cup good-quality balsamic vinegar

Sweet Onions

Vidalia onions from Georgia and other varieties of onion that are naturally high in sugar content and low in "burny" sulfurs have been part of Southern cuisine for generations. Now these onions, sweet enough to eat like apples, are sold in mainstream supermarkets nationwide. Slice them on salads, cook them down into "onion jam," or chop them into spreads and salsas. They should not be substituted in stews and dishes that demand a full, "oniony" flavor, since they will fade into the background in highly seasoned preparations.

1. Leaving the skin on, cut off the polar ends of the onions, about a ½" from the root and sprout ends. Halve the onions laterally; a sharp knife will help keep the onion sections together, which makes flipping them on the grill easier. Brush them with olive oil and sprinkle them with kosher salt and black pepper to taste.

2. In a saucepan over medium heat, simmer the balsamic vinegar until it has cooked down to syrup.

3. Heat a grill or stovetop grill pan to a low heat. Place the onion slices on the grill; cook slowly without moving them until dark grill marks appear, about 15 minutes. Turn once, using both tongs and a spatula to keep the rings together. Grill until the second side is well marked and juices begin to pool on the top, another 10 minutes. Brush with balsamic syrup 5 minutes before removing from the grill. Serve brushed with remaining syrup.

Grilled Scallions VN

Over brown rice, with a few Japanese pickles, this is an unconventionally flavored treat.

INGREDIENTS | SERVES 4

16 scallions

1 tablespoon pure maple syrup

2 teaspoons Asian toasted sesame oil

1 or 2 drops Tamari soy sauce

Assorted Japanese pickles, such as pickled daikon, baby carrots, or cabbage

1. Prepare a grill or stovetop grill pan over medium-high heat. Trim the root ends of the scallions and cut off all but 5" of the green parts.

2. In a small bowl, whisk together the syrup and the oil. Brush the scallions with the maple mixture. Place on the grill and cook, turning regularly, until they are golden brown and tender, about 5 minutes. Transfer to a platter; drizzle with soy sauce. Serve accompanied by Japanese pickles.

Onion Jam VN

The concentrated sweetness and naturally complex flavor of this caramelized onion spread come from slow cooking, which breaks down the cell walls of the onions, releasing 100 percent of their flavor. Serve it with French bread slices or crackers as an hors d'oeuvre, or as a component of a dinner meal.

INGREDIENTS | SERVES 8

6–8 large onions

2 tablespoons olive oil

2 sprigs fresh thyme or ½ teaspoon dried (optional)

½ teaspoon salt

1. Halve the onions through the root end, peel them, and slice them very thinly across the grain.

2. Heat the olive oil in a large, heavy-bottomed Dutch oven over medium heat until it shimmers but does not smoke. Add the thyme and the sliced onions. Sprinkle with salt. Lower heat; cook slowly to wilt the onions completely, stirring gently with a wooden spoon.

3. As the onions begin to caramelize (turn brown), use the wooden spoon to scrape dried-on juices from the bottom of the pot; stir regularly to incorporate as much of these browned juices as possible. Cook this way until onions are dark brown and mostly disintegrated into a thick spread, usually about 40 minutes depending on the water content of your onions. Cool to room temperature or serve warm.

Leek Potato Cakes

With a dollop of crème fraîche, sour cream, or applesauce, these crisp disks are a texturally pleasing and comforting component of a complete meal. These are excellent with a small salad and a wedge of soft, ripened cheese such as Camembert.

INGREDIENTS | SERVES 4

2 cups finely chopped leeks, white part only

2 cups finely grated peeled potatoes

½ teaspoon dried sage

2 large eggs, beaten

2 tablespoons flour

1 teaspoon salt

¼ teaspoon freshly ground black pepper

Olive oil for frying

1. Wash the leeks very thoroughly to remove any grit. Combine the potatoes, leeks, sage, eggs, flour, salt, and pepper in a mixing bowl; mix well. Form into 8 (3") pancakes.

2. Heat ¼" of olive oil in a heavy skillet over medium heat until a piece of leek sizzles when added. Transfer 4 of the pancakes into the pan and cook gently without moving them until a crisp brown crust develops, about 5 minutes. Turn and brown the other side; drain on paper towels and repeat with remaining cakes.

Aïoli (Garlic Mayonnaise)

In Belgium, where frites is a national dish, ketchup is a rarity. Instead, the Belgians dip their fried potatoes in seasoned mayonnaises like aioli, flavored with fresh or roasted garlic. Once you've tried this luxurious flavor combination, you may never reach for ketchup again.

INGREDIENTS | SERVES 8

2 large cloves garlic, finely chopped or pushed through a press

¼ teaspoon salt

2 large egg yolks

1 teaspoon Dijon mustard

Juice of 1 medium lemon (about ¼ cup), divided

1 cup extra-virgin olive oil

Roasted Garlic Variation

For a sweeter, more mature flavor, wrap one whole head of garlic in foil, roast in a 350°F oven for 1 hour, and squeeze the resulting golden brown paste through a strainer. Substitute this roasted garlic purée for the fresh garlic cloves in the Aïoli recipe.

1. Mash together the garlic and salt in a large mixing bowl. Wet a cloth towel, wring it out, fold it in half, and set it onto a work surface (this will hold your bowl steady while you work). Set the mixing bowl on the towel and mix in the yolks, mustard, and 2 teaspoons of the lemon juice.

2. Using a rapid whisking action, very gradually whisk ¼ cup olive oil into the yolk mixture. Add a few drops of room-temperature water in, to help incorporate the oil, then repeat with remaining oil, adding it in a slow, steady stream while whisking vigorously. Season to taste with remaining lemon juice.

Garlic Bread

It is always advisable to crisp loaves of crusty bread in the oven just before serving. This simple step improves the texture and flavor of breads immensely. By spreading some garlic and olive oil or butter on a split loaf, you can make the bread even more scrumptious at the same time.

INGREDIENTS | SERVES 6–8

1 loaf Italian bread or other crusty loaf such as a baguette

3 tablespoons extra-virgin olive oil, softened unsalted butter, or margarine

2 cloves garlic, finely chopped (about 1 tablespoon)

Pinch of crushed red pepper flakes (optional)

1. Heat oven to 375°F. Laterally split the loaf of bread.

2. In a small bowl, whisk together the olive oil (or butter or margarine) with the chopped garlic. Using a brush or a rubber spatula, generously slather both cut sides of the bread with garlic oil or butter. Sprinkle with some pepper flakes if desired.

3. Place garlic bread halves on a sheet pan or baking dish and bake in center of oven until crisp and lightly browned, about 20 minutes.

Baked Peppers and Onions VN

The fruity taste of good dark green olive oil pairs very well with the taste of peppers and onions, so don't skimp on this one—use only extra-virgin oil.

INGREDIENTS | SERVES 4

1½ pounds (4 or 5 medium) green and red bell peppers, seeded and cut into 2" pieces

1 pound small red potatoes, cut into 1" slices or chunks

1 large yellow onion, roughly chopped

¼ cup extra-virgin olive oil

Kosher salt and freshly ground black pepper to taste

1. Heat oven to 425°F.

2. Place bell peppers, potatoes, and onions in a shallow ovenproof dish. Pour the olive oil over the vegetables and toss to coat. Sprinkle with salt and lots of pepper.

3. Bake for about 30 minutes until the potatoes are tender.

Vidalia Onion Salad VN

Sweet onion varieties like Vidalia, Maui, Walla Walla, and Oso Sweet are so low in sulfur that they have more of a fruity taste than an "oniony" one. That makes them perfect for eating raw. Thin shavings have a pleasing crunch without the teary pungency of yellow onions.

INGREDIENTS | SERVES 4

1 large (about 8 ounces) Vidalia or other sweet onion

2 tablespoons extra-virgin olive oil

1 large lemon

¼ teaspoon celery seeds

Kosher salt and freshly ground black pepper to taste

French bread or other crusty bread, warmed in the oven to crisp

1. Slice the onion into very thin rings, almost shavings. Arrange them in an attractive mound at the center of a serving plate.

2. Drizzle them well with olive oil and a squeeze of lemon. Sprinkle with celery seeds and season with salt and pepper.

3. Allow them to rest for 30 minutes to an hour before serving with crusty bread.

Pickled Red Onions

Crunchy and beautifully pink, these pair as perfectly with summer grain salads, such as Succotash Salad (Chapter 3), as they do with polenta and a wild mushroom sauté.

INGREDIENTS | SERVES 8

2 large red onions, thinly sliced
1 quart boiling water
½ cup white wine vinegar
½ cup cold water
½ cup honey
1 teaspoon salt
1 teaspoon black peppercorns
½ teaspoon whole allspice (optional)

1. Place the sliced onions in a bowl; pour the boiling water over them and allow them to steep for 5 minutes; drain.

2. In a medium bowl, whisk together the vinegar, cold water, honey, salt, peppercorns, and allspice. Add the onions and allow them to marinate for 10 minutes.

3. Transfer to a jar, cover tightly, and refrigerate until very cold. These pickled onions will keep for several months and get better with age.

CHAPTER 10

Mushrooms and Truffles

Duxelles

This chopped mushroom spread is a classical French preparation. It can be used as a filling for turnovers, stuffed vegetables, or savory strudels. It makes an excellent spread on crusts of baguette, and is great in sandwiches.

INGREDIENTS | MAKES 1 CUP

1 (10-ounce package) mushrooms

1 tablespoon olive oil

3 shallots, chopped (about ½ cup)

½ teaspoon salt

¼ teaspoon freshly ground black pepper

¼ cup dry white wine

1 tablespoon finely chopped parsley

1. Chop the mushrooms finely (this is best done by hand, but may be done by pulsing them in batches of no more than 5 in a food processor until they're chopped, but not puréed).

2. Heat oil in a medium skillet over medium heat until a piece of shallot sizzles. Add the shallots and salt; cook until translucent, about 3 minutes.

3. Add the mushrooms and black pepper; cook until the mushrooms have given up their liquid and the pan is almost dry, 5–7 minutes.

4. Add the wine and cook until almost dry, about 3 minutes. Remove from heat; stir in chopped parsley.

Fettuccine with Morels and Spring Onions

Long pieces of onion pair nicely with the shape of this pasta.

INGREDIENTS | SERVES 4

1 sprig fresh rosemary

8 ounces fresh morels, halved

2 teaspoons olive oil

6 spring onions or scallions cut into 1" pieces

½ pound imported fettuccine, cooked al dente, drained, and tossed with a few drops of olive oil

1–2 cups strong vegetable stock

1 tablespoon unsalted butter

1 tablespoon chopped Italian (flat-leaf) parsley

1. In a skillet large enough to hold all ingredients, sauté the rosemary and morels in olive oil over medium heat for 5 minutes until soft. Add the spring onions and sauté another 1 minute.

2. Add the cooked fettuccine, 1 cup of vegetable stock, and the butter and simmer until sauce is creamy and adhering well to the pasta. Adjust consistency with remaining stock, season to taste, and serve sprinkled with chopped parsley.

Josh's Mushroom Dip

This is a delicious, creamy dip that's perfect for raw vegetables.

INGREDIENTS | SERVES 8

1 teaspoon olive oil

1 large portobello mushroom cap

1 (10-ounce package) white mushrooms

½ packet dried onion soup mix

1 pint sour cream

8 cups assorted raw vegetables, such as carrots, celery, mixed bell peppers, zucchini, and yellow squash, cut into sticks

1. Heat the olive oil in a small skillet over medium-high heat; cook the portobello until tender, about 5 minutes. Cool it and chop it finely.

2. Chop the white mushrooms finely either by hand or by pulsing in a food processor in batches of 5 at a time.

3. In a medium bowl, stir the onion soup mix into the sour cream. Fold in the chopped mushrooms.

4. Transfer to a bowl and serve surrounded by raw vegetables for dipping.

Portobello Pita with Buckwheat and Beans VN

While buckwheat is actually a seed, not a grain, it has an earthy taste and pilaf-like texture that complete this earthy main-course sandwich.

INGREDIENTS | SERVES 4

4 medium-sized portobello mushrooms, stems removed

Kosher salt and freshly ground black pepper to taste

1 tablespoon olive oil

4 pita pocket breads, medium-sized (about 8")

2 tablespoons soy mayonnaise

1 cup buckwheat groats or medium-granulation kasha, cooked according to directions on package

¼ pound cooked green beans

1. Brush the portobello caps clean (do not wash under water); season with salt and pepper. Heat oil in a large skillet until very hot but not quite smoking. Cook the mushrooms top-side down over high heat until cooked through, about 4 minutes. Small pools of juice should appear where the stem was removed.

2. Cut an opening in a pita; slather the inside with soy mayonnaise. Spoon in a layer of cooked buckwheat groats (or kasha) and add a quarter of the green beans. Stuff in 1 mushroom cap. Repeat with remaining pitas.

Ungrainly Grains

Sometimes things aren't what they seem. Most people think of couscous as a grain, but it isn't; it's pasta. Some consider buckwheat a grain; it isn't. It's the seed of a fruit completely unrelated to any kind of wheat. FYI: Wild rice isn't rice at all, but the seed of a native American grass.

Grilled Marinated Portobello Mushrooms

Main-course mushrooms like these go with anything from summer salads to wintry wild rice dishes. They're one of the best vegetarian dinners to pair with red wine. If you don't have a grill, bake the mushrooms on a sheet pan in a 400°F oven for about 10 minutes.

INGREDIENTS | SERVES 4

4 large portobello mushrooms, stems removed

1 cup extra-virgin olive oil

1 cup red wine vinegar

2 tablespoons soy sauce

1 tablespoon sugar

½ cup chopped fresh herbs (such as parsley, chives, tarragon, oregano) or 1 tablespoon dried herbs

1. Brush any dirt from the mushrooms, but do not wash them under water.

2. In a small bowl, whisk together the olive oil, vinegar, soy sauce, sugar, and herbs. If using dried herbs, allow the mixture to steep for 15 minutes. In a shallow dish, pour the marinade over the mushrooms; marinate 10 minutes, turning occasionally.

3. Grill mushrooms 2–3 minutes on each side. Serve whole or sliced. Sauce with leftover marinade or save the marinade for another batch.

Mushroom-Spelt Sauté

Spelt, wheat berries (sold in Hispanic markets as trigo), or barley make great whole-grain alternatives to rice.

INGREDIENTS | SERVES 4

2 tablespoons extra-virgin olive oil

1 large onion, diced

2 cloves garlic, chopped

Kosher salt and freshly ground black pepper to taste

1 (10-ounce package) mushrooms, sliced

¼ cup dry sherry or white wine (optional)

2 cups cooked spelt (available at health food stores) or barley

1. Heat the olive oil in a skillet over high heat until it shimmers and a piece of onion sizzles in it. Add the onion and garlic; sprinkle with a little salt and cook for 5 minutes until translucent.

2. Add the mushrooms and cook, stirring occasionally, until some browning occurs, about 5 minutes; add the sherry and cook until it has almost all evaporated, 2–3 minutes.

3. Add the spelt and cook until heated through; season with salt and pepper to taste.

Chinese Three Slivers VN

The silky texture of slender, white enoki mushrooms contrasts here with crunchy bamboo and "meaty" bean curd. Here, the dish is served "taco style," wrapped in a crisp lettuce leaf.

INGREDIENTS | SERVES 4

2 tablespoons vegetable oil

1 (4-ounce) can sliced bamboo shoots, drained and rinsed

3 cakes (about 8 ounces) firm tofu, sliced into ¼" strips, patted dry with paper towel

1 package enoki mushrooms, trimmed and broken into individual strands

¼ cup Asian dumpling sauce

½ teaspoon sambal or other Asian chili paste (optional)

1 tablespoon cornstarch dissolved in 2 tablespoons cold water

1 head iceberg lettuce

1. Heat the oil in a skillet or wok until very hot but not smoky. Add the bamboo shoots and cook for 1 minute. Slide the tofu into the pan and cook over high heat without stirring until lightly browned. Add the enoki mushrooms, dumpling sauce, chili paste, and cornstarch solution. Cook until thick, about 2 minutes. Transfer to a serving bowl.

2. Select 4 unbroken leaves from the lettuce head; wash thoroughly and tear them in half. Place the bowl of cooked Chinese vegetables in the center of a large serving platter and arrange the lettuce pieces around it. Guests spoon filling into the leaves and eat the lettuce wraps with their hands.

Taiwanese Mushroom Egg

This dish uses only the egg whites and a sweet "mayonnaise," also made with whites only.

INGREDIENTS | SERVES 4

6 large hard-boiled eggs

2 teaspoons vegetable oil

12 shiitake mushrooms, stems removed, diced ¼"

1 egg white

1 teaspoon sugar

¼ teaspoon salt

½ teaspoon rice vinegar or white vinegar

⅓ cup peanut oil

1 tablespoon chopped fresh chives

1. Carefully halve the eggs lengthwise and discard the yolks; rinse out the whites. Heat the vegetable oil in a skillet and cook the mushrooms until well wilted, about 5 minutes; transfer to a plate to cool.

2. In a food processor on high speed, combine the egg white, sugar, salt, and rice vinegar. With the motor running, gradually incorporate the oil until a thick white mayonnaise is formed. Mix 2 tablespoons of this white mayonnaise with the cooked mushrooms. Spoon this mixture into the egg halves, allowing the filling to mound generously. Sprinkle the tops with chopped chives.

Mushroom Bruschetta

In many restaurants in Italy, the waiter will bring you a small plate of bruschetta to nibble on while perusing the menu.

INGREDIENTS | SERVES 4

1 baguette or crusty country bread

4 teaspoons Aïoli (see recipe in Chapter 9) or mayonnaise mixed with chopped garlic

12 ounces mixed mushrooms, such as button, oyster, shiitake, enoki, or portobello

2 tablespoons olive oil

1 teaspoon mixed dried herbs, such as thyme, oregano, rosemary, and basil

Juice of ½ medium lemon

Kosher salt and freshly ground black pepper to taste

Fresh chopped parsley or chives (optional)

1. Heat a stovetop grill (or an oven to 400°F). Slice the bread on a diagonal into 8 (1"-thick) oblong slices; spread the aïoli onto both sides of each slice. Grill or bake the bread slices until dark brown marks decorate their faces, top and bottom. Transfer to a serving plate.

2. Cut the mushrooms into large, uneven chunks and slices and mix all the varieties together. Warm a large, heavy skillet over high heat. Add the mushrooms to the dry pan all at once, then add the olive oil; sprinkle the herbs on top. Cook without stirring for the first 4–5 minutes, allowing the mushrooms to get a brown crust. After 5 minutes, stir to mix in the herbs and cook until the accumulating liquid is mostly evaporated. Season well with lemon, salt, and pepper.

3. Spoon onto the grilled bread and garnish with chopped parsley or chives if desired.

Oven-Roasted Mushrooms VN

Roasting intensifies the flavor of these savory herbed mushrooms, making them an excellent topping for whole grains like brown rice, barley, or wheat berries.

INGREDIENTS | SERVES 4

1 pound white, cremini, or shiitake mushrooms

1 tablespoon extra-virgin olive oil

1 tablespoon chopped fresh thyme or 1 teaspoon dried

½ teaspoon salt

Pinch of crushed red pepper flakes

Chopped Italian parsley

1 teaspoon balsamic vinegar or lemon juice

1. Heat oven to 400°F. If using shiitakes, remove stems.

2. In a bowl, combine mushrooms, olive oil, thyme, salt, and red pepper flakes; toss to coat. Spread in a single layer into a roasting pan. Roast in center of oven for 30 minutes until nicely browned.

3. Toss with parsley and vinegar or lemon juice. Serve hot or room temperature.

Mushroom-Tofu Stir-Fry VN

Dried Chinese black mushrooms make their own delicious stock when you soak them. If you choose to use fresh mushrooms, substitute the soaking liquid with your favorite vegetable stock. Serve this stir-fry with brown rice.

INGREDIENTS | SERVES 4

10 Chinese dried black mushrooms or ½ pound fresh shiitakes

1 medium onion, halved and sliced lengthwise

2 tablespoons vegetable oil

1 tablespoon chopped fresh ginger

1 bunch scallions, chopped

1 tablespoon chopped garlic

½ teaspoon salt

3 tablespoons hoisin sauce mixed with ½ teaspoon Asian sesame oil

½ teaspoon rice vinegar or white wine vinegar

1½ teaspoon cornstarch dissolved in 1 tablespoon of mushroom soaking liquid or water

20 ounces silken tofu, cut into cubes

1. Soak the mushrooms in 4 cups of hot water for at least 20 minutes or overnight. Pour off and reserve the liquid. Remove the stems and slice the mushrooms thickly (¼").

2. Heat the oil in a large skillet; add the ginger, scallions, and garlic. Cook until the onions are translucent, about 5 minutes; add 1 cup of mushroom soaking liquid. Season with salt, hoisin, and vinegar; stir and simmer 5 minutes. Stir in the cornstarch mixture.

3. Spoon the tofu cubes onto the top of the cooking vegetables. Cover and cook slowly until the tofu is hot, about 5 minutes.

Pickled Mushrooms VN

As a snack or as part of a dinner buffet, pickled mushrooms bring an attractive piquancy to the table. They keep refrigerated for weeks.

INGREDIENTS | SERVES 8

1½ pounds small white mushrooms, halved

3 medium carrots, peeled and julienned

1 tablespoon olive oil

½ cup canned pimento peppers, cut into 1" × ½" strips

½ teaspoon oregano

½ teaspoon garlic powder

¼ cup cider vinegar

½ teaspoon salt

¼ teaspoon freshly ground black pepper

1. Boil the mushrooms and the carrots separately; drain.

2. Heat the oil in a medium skillet. Cook the carrots in the oil for 3 minutes; add the mushrooms. Cook 3 minutes more; add the pimento, oregano, garlic powder, cider vinegar, salt, and pepper. Cook until everything is heated through.

3. Refrigerate for 24 hours before serving.

Warm Oyster Mushroom Salad VN

This variation on a popular salad from New York's Orso restaurant can be served warm or room temperature. If you can't grill or broil the mushrooms and onions, sauté them in very hot olive oil instead.

INGREDIENTS | SERVES 4

3 tablespoons extra-virgin olive oil, divided

1 tablespoon good-quality balsamic vinegar

1 tablespoon finely chopped shallots

Kosher salt and freshly ground black pepper, taste

½ pound oyster mushrooms ("pleurots"), root ends trimmed, in small bunches

2 medium red onions, peeled and cut into 12 (1") rings

6 ounces frisée, chicory, or other resilient salad green

1. In a small bowl, whisk together 2 tablespoons olive oil, balsamic vinegar, and shallots; season with salt and pepper.

2. Heat a grill, stovetop grill pan, or broiler. Toss the oyster mushrooms and onions, separately, with the remaining 1 tablespoon olive oil. Season them with salt and pepper and grill or broil separately. The mushrooms will cook quickly—in about 2 minutes. The onions will take longer—about 5 minutes.

3. Spoon some of the dressing onto the hot mushrooms and onions and use the rest to dress the greens. Arrange the hot vegetables atop the greens and serve.

Mushroom-Leek Tart

Savory pies are common in Italy and France, but with the exception of quiche, not too well known here. It's a shame, because they make beautiful presentations, and with the right ingredients they're unforgettable. This one is French in origin.

INGREDIENTS | SERVES 6

1 package refrigerated pie dough

1 large egg

1 teaspoon milk

6 medium leeks, white parts only, chopped and washed twice

1 teaspoon sage

1 cup heavy cream

Kosher salt and freshly ground black pepper to taste

10 ounces white mushrooms, sliced

1. Roll out half the pie dough thinly and press it into a 10" pie pan, leaving excess hanging over the rim of the pan. Roll out the remaining dough into an 11" round and place onto a floured sheet pan. Refrigerate both parts until needed.

2. Whisk together the eggs and milk in a small bowl and set aside. Heat oven to 400°F.

3. In a heavy skillet over medium heat, cook the leeks in a few drops of water until they're bright green, about 3 minutes; transfer to a plate to cool. In a bowl, combine the leeks with the sage, cream, salt, pepper, and mushrooms; mix well.

4. Fill the pie bottom with the vegetable mixture. Brush the rim with egg wash and carefully place the top onto the pie (it's easiest if you fold it into quarters, then unfold it onto the pie). Brush the top well with egg mixture and cut a few vents with scissors or a knife. Bake in center of oven until golden and bubbly, about 35 minutes.

5. Cool for 10–15 minutes before cutting into wedges.

Mushroom Barley

There is no actual barley in "mushroom barley," a popular traditional Jewish dish found at bar mitzvahs, weddings, and funerals. The recipe uses barley-shaped egg noodles. Both Goodman's and Manischewitz make this pasta, usually sold in the "Jewish Ingredients" section of the supermarket.

INGREDIENTS | SERVES 8

1 mushroom-vegetable bouillon cube

2 teaspoons kosher salt, divided

1 (12-ounce) package barley-shaped egg noodle

2 tablespoons olive oil

1 large onion, diced

1 teaspoon garlic powder

10 ounces white mushrooms, sliced

1. Bring 8 cups water to a boil; add the bouillon cube, 1 teaspoon salt, and the pasta. Cook until tender, about 10–15 minutes. Drain.

2. Heat the olive oil in a large, heavy skillet for 1 minute over high heat; add the onion. Cook 5 minutes until translucent. Add 1 teaspoon salt and the garlic powder; cook 1 minute more. Add the mushrooms. Cook over high heat for 5–7 minutes more until mushrooms have given up their liquid and most has evaporated.

3. Toss the mushroom mixture with the cooked pasta.

Mushroom and Olive Blend

Try serving on top of toasted baguette slices, on pasta, or as a savory side dish.

INGREDIENTS | SERVES 6

2 tablespoons butter or vegan margarine

1 clove garlic, minced

½ cup sliced shiitake mushrooms

½ cup sliced oyster mushrooms

½ cup chopped hen of the woods mushrooms

¼ cup pitted and sliced Kalamata olives

½ teaspoon salt

¼ teaspoon pepper

Add all ingredients to a 2-quart slow cooker; cover and cook on low heat for 2 hours. Stir occasionally to make sure the butter or margarine is coating the mushrooms.

CHAPTER 11

Pasta Dishes

Gemelli with Asparagus Tips, Lemon, and Butter

Butter thickens this sauce and helps it adhere to these short, twisted pairs of macaroni.

INGREDIENTS | SERVES 4

2 bunches medium asparagus, cut on bias into 1½" pieces

½ pound gemelli pasta

4 tablespoons unsalted butter, divided

Zest and juice of 2 medium lemons

½ cup vegetable stock or water

Salt and ground black pepper to taste

Grated Parmesan

Garlic Oil

This stuff is indispensable if you make Italian pasta dishes frequently. Combine 1 cup extra-virgin olive oil with ¼ cup finely chopped garlic and stir. The oil keeps refrigerated for up to two weeks. When you sauté in it, just take from the top, which is pure flavored oil; stir it up to get little bits of garlic if you're adding it to already-cooking dishes.

1. Par-cook the asparagus pieces in 3 batches in 6 quarts rapidly boiling salted water, plunging them immediately into salted ice water as they are removed from cooking water (shock), then drain. Boil gemelli in the asparagus cooking water "al dente" (soft, but still slightly chewy in the center). Drain and rinse.

2. Melt 1 tablespoon butter in a skillet large enough to hold all ingredients (12" diameter) and add the lemon zest and asparagus pieces. Sauté on medium heat until asparagus are hot, then add the stock, toss in the pasta, and raise heat to high.

3. When pasta is steaming hot, swirl in the remaining butter, the lemon juice, and salt and pepper to taste. Serve in bowls sprinkled with Parmesan.

Ziti with Peppers and Marinated Mozzarella

Multicolored peppers give this dish a festive look.

INGREDIENTS | SERVES 4

1 pound fresh mozzarella cheese or smoked fresh mozzarella, cut into ½" cubes

3 tablespoons olive oil, divided

½ cup mixed chopped fresh herbs, such as parsley, chives, oregano, mint, etc.

Pinch of crushed red pepper flakes

1 teaspoon red or white wine vinegar

Kosher salt and freshly ground black pepper to taste

1 tablespoon chopped garlic (about 3 cloves)

2 cups sliced onions

3 cups sliced mixed bell peppers

2 cups tomato sauce

8 ounces ziti, cooked al dente

1 tablespoon unsalted butter

¼ cup grated Parmesan cheese

1. In a medium bowl, combine the mozzarella, 1 tablespoon of olive oil, the herbs, pepper flakes, vinegar, salt, and pepper. Marinate at room temperature for 30 minutes.

2. In a small bowl, combine remaining oil with chopped garlic. Heat a large skillet over high heat and bring a pot of water to a boil to reheat the pasta. Add the garlic oil to the pan, sizzle 10 seconds until the garlic turns white, and add the onions and peppers. Cook, stirring occasionally, until the onions are translucent. Add the tomato sauce and lower heat to a simmer.

3. Dip the pasta in boiling water to reheat; transfer hot pasta to the sauce, allowing some of the pasta water to drip into the sauce and thin it. Season to taste with salt and pepper. Remove from heat.

4. Toss with marinated mozzarella, butter, and Parmesan.

Fusilli with Grilled Eggplant, Garlic, and Spicy Tomato Sauce

Smoky, fruity flavors of grilled or roasted eggplant marry beautifully with tomatoes and garlic. Fusilli's deep crannies scoop up every drop of this complex-tasting sauce.

INGREDIENTS | SERVES 4

1 small eggplant (about ½ pound), cut lengthwise into 8 wedges

3 tablespoons olive oil, divided

Kosher salt and freshly ground black pepper to taste

3 cloves garlic, finely chopped (about 1 tablespoon)

¼ teaspoon crushed red pepper flakes

½ cup roughly chopped Italian parsley

4 cups tomato sauce

8 ounces fusilli or other pasta shape, cooked "al dente"

1 tablespoon butter

¼ cup grated Parmesan cheese

Stir Pasta Early

To prevent pasta from clumping and cooking unevenly, wait until water is boiling rapidly before adding dried pasta, and stir the pasta immediately to separate the pieces or strands. Pasta should boil vigorously in a large amount of water, uncovered.

1. Heat grill, grill pan, or broiler. In a medium bowl, toss the eggplant wedges with 1 tablespoon olive oil; season liberally with salt and pepper. Grill or broil it on the largest cut side for 4 minutes until black marks show. Using tongs or a fork, turn to another side and cook 3 minutes more until it is bubbling with juices. Transfer to a cutting board to cool; cut into 1" pieces.

2. In a small bowl, mix remaining olive oil with garlic and red pepper flakes. Heat a large skillet over medium-high heat. Add the garlic mixture; allow to sizzle just 15 seconds, stirring with a wooden spoon, before adding the parsley. Cook 30 seconds; add the eggplant and tomato sauce. Bring to a simmer, add the cooked pasta, and cook until heated through; remove from heat.

3. Finish by adding butter and cheese, adjusting for seasoning, and tossing well to combine. Serve in bowls sprinkled with additional chopped parsley. Pass additional cheese on the side if desired.

Farfalle (Bow-Ties) Fra Diavolo ⓋⓃ

This is a very quick, easy pasta.

INGREDIENTS | SERVES 8

2 tablespoons olive oil

1 tablespoon finely chopped garlic (about 3 cloves)

½ teaspoon crushed red pepper flakes

1 cup roughly chopped Italian parsley

1 (28-ounce) jar marinara sauce

1 pound farfalle, cooked "al dente"

Kosher salt and freshly ground black pepper to taste

1. Bring a pot of water to a boil for reheating the pasta.

2. Heat a large skillet or heavy-bottomed pot large enough to hold all the ingredients over high heat. Add the oil, garlic, pepper flakes, and parsley; allow these ingredients to sizzle for 30 seconds. Add the tomato sauce; bring to a simmer.

3. Using a colander or strainer, dip the cooked pasta into the boiling water for 1 minute to reheat. Transfer the reheated pasta into the sauce, letting the water that adheres to the pasta drip into the sauce and thin it a little.

4. Toss to coat; adjust consistency with additional pasta water and season with salt and pepper to taste. Serve sprinkled with additional chopped parsley.

Quick Pasta Pesto

This dinner comes together in no time. Boil the water while you slice the onions, cook the vegetables and pasta at the same time, and toss everything together in the skillet. What could be easier?

INGREDIENTS | SERVES 4

8 ounces ziti pasta

2 tablespoons olive oil

1 medium onion, thinly sliced

2 cups frozen peas

Salt and ground black pepper, to taste

⅓ cup pesto sauce

1 cup chopped tomatoes

Butter and grated Parmesan cheese (optional)

1. Bring a large pot of water to boil over high heat and stir in the ziti. Cook according to package directions.

2. In the meantime, heat the olive oil in a large skillet over very high heat; add the onions and peas. When onions are translucent (3 minutes), use a slotted spoon or strainer to scoop the cooked pasta from the boiling water into the pan with the vegetables, allowing some of the pasta water to fall into the skillet along with it. Season well with salt and pepper.

3. Remove pan from the heat; add the pesto, chopped tomatoes, and butter and cheese if using. Toss to coat. Serve immediately.

Fettuccine Alfredo

Rich enough to sate the hungriest guest, this creamy pasta was named for the famous Alfredo's restaurant in Rome.

INGREDIENTS | SERVES 4

8 ounces fettuccine

½ cup butter

2 cloves garlic, minced

1 tablespoon flour

1½ cups whole milk

2 tablespoons cream cheese

1 cup grated Parmesan cheese, plus extra for garnish

Salt and ground black pepper to taste

Precooking Pasta

Restaurant chefs have developed a trick for making pasta ready-to-serve in a minute, but still pleasingly al dente. The key is to just par-cook it: Boiling it for less than four minutes, drain it, rinse it well in cold water, and toss it with a few drops of olive oil. It will not seem cooked when you drain it, but it will soften to the chewy consistency of fresh pasta as it sits. This can be done any-where from an hour to a day before ser-vice. When you're ready to serve it, dip it for one minute in boiling water and toss with sauce of your choice. This works best with small dried pasta shapes like penne, ziti, rigatoni, shells, or farfalle (bow-ties).

1. Prepare the pasta according to package directions. Drain and keep warm.

2. In a large saucepan over medium heat, melt the butter; add garlic and cook 2 minutes. Stir in the flour, then add the milk all at once, cooking and stirring over medium heat until thick and bubbly.

3. Add the cream cheese; stir until blended. Add the Parmesan cheese; continue cooking until all cheese has melted.

4. Toss with fettuccine; season with salt and pepper. Serve with extra Parmesan passed on the side.

Linguine with Asparagus, Parmesan, and Cream

In the winter, asparagus are fatter and imported from the other side of the world. They're perfect for pastas like this, which rely on plump stems.

INGREDIENTS | SERVES 6

1 bunch asparagus (preferably chubby-stemmed)

2 teaspoons olive oil

2 medium shallots, thinly sliced

¼ cup white wine

¼ cup vegetable stock or water

2 cups heavy cream

8 ounces linguine, cooked al dente, drained, tossed with a drop of olive oil

¼ cup Parmigiano-Reggiano cheese or other top-quality Parmesan

Juice of 1 medium lemon, plus 6 lemon wedges

Kosher salt and freshly ground black pepper to taste

1. Trim the bottoms of the asparagus and use a vegetable peeler to peel off the skin from the bottom half of the stalks. Cut the asparagus into bite-sized (about 1") pieces. Heat the oil in a large skillet over medium heat; add the shallots and cook 3 minutes to soften them. Add the asparagus and wine; cook until the wine is mostly evaporated, then add the stock (or water).

2. When the asparagus are mostly cooked and the stock is mostly steamed out, stir in the cream and bring to a boil; add the linguine. Cook until the linguine is hot, and the sauce is slightly thick; add the Parmigiano and remove from the heat.

3. Season with lemon juice, salt, and pepper. If necessary, adjust consistency with additional stock or water. Serve with lemon wedges on the side.

Orecchiette with Roasted Peppers, Green Beans, and Pesto

Orecchiette are "little ears" of pasta—dime-sized concave disks that catch sauce very well and have a substantial, hearty bite. If you can't find them, look for conchiglie (small shells), which are similar.

INGREDIENTS | SERVES 6

8 ounces orecchiette or other pasta shape

1 tablespoon olive oil

2 teaspoons chopped garlic

1 cup sliced roasted peppers

¼ pound green beans, blanched

¼ cup dry white wine (optional)

¾ cup homemade pesto or fresh store-bought pesto, divided

¼ cup roughly chopped Italian parsley

Salt and ground black pepper to taste

1 tablespoon unsalted butter

Parmesan cheese for garnish

Lemon wedges for garnish

1. Bring a pot of salted water to boil; cook the pasta until al dente (still a little chewy), drain it, but save a cup of the cooking water for later. Toss the pasta with a drop of olive oil; set aside.

2. Combine the olive oil and chopped garlic in a cup. Heat a large skillet for 1 minute over medium heat. Add the garlic oil; sizzle for 15 seconds, then add the roasted peppers and green beans. Sauté for 3 minutes; add the wine. Cook 1 minute until alcohol has evaporated. Add ½ cup pesto; stir.

3. Add the cooked pasta, parsley, salt and pepper, and butter; simmer until heated through, adding a few drops of the reserved pasta water to make it saucy.

4. Remove from heat; toss with Parmesan cheese. Serve with lemon wedges and a little extra pesto on the side.

The Best Pesto

This is an exquisite sauce for pasta, vegetables, or grilled foods. It also makes a great soup garnish.

INGREDIENTS | SERVES 8

5 cloves garlic, peeled

½ cup pine nuts, toasted to very light brown

1 large bunch basil, stems and veins removed, washed and dried thoroughly

2 cups extra-virgin olive oil, divided

½ cup grated Parmigiano-Reggiano cheese

Coarse salt and freshly ground black pepper to taste

Practical Pasta Picking

Certain shapes work best with certain sauces and garnishes. For thin, brothy sauces, concave shapes like conchiglie (small shells) and orecchiette ("little ears") scoop up flavorful sauce with every bite. They also work best for dishes with small garnishes like peas or chopped vegetables. Longer pastas, which have plenty of surface area to adhere to, are right for thicker sauces, which will stick to long strands of spaghetti or linguine.

1. Pulse garlic in food processor until finely chopped. Add nuts and pulse a few times just to break them into pieces. Scrape the bowl to loosen anything stuck to the sides.

2. Pile in all of the basil. Pour half of the oil over the leaves and pulse until basil is medium chopped (pieces about the size of cooked rice). Transfer to a mixing bowl.

3. Using a plastic spatula or a wooden spoon, fold in the Parmigiano cheese; season with salt and pepper and thin to sauce consistency with the remaining olive oil. It will keep in the refrigerator for 1 week, in the freezer for up to 2 months. When using frozen pesto, do not thaw, but break off what you need from a frozen block.

Spaghetti with Olives, Capers, and Tomatoes VN

Remember to use a boxed variety of pasta when making a vegan pasta dish. Most fresh and many frozen pastas are made with eggs. You should also check the ingredients of any dry pasta you buy, just to be sure.

INGREDIENTS | SERVES 8

2 tablespoons olive oil

1 tablespoon chopped garlic

½ cup assorted olives, such as Picholine, Ligurian, Kalamata, or niçoise, pitted

1 tablespoon small (nonpareil) capers

Pinch of crushed red pepper flakes

½ cup roughly chopped Italian parsley

2 cups chopped tomatoes

2 cups Basic Fresh Tomato Sauce (see recipe in Chapter 8) or other tomato sauce

Salt and ground black pepper to taste

1 pound spaghetti, cooked al dente, drained, rinsed, and tossed with olive oil

1. Heat the olive oil and garlic in a large, heavy-bottomed skillet or Dutch oven until it sizzles; add the olives, capers, red pepper flakes, and parsley. Cook 2 minutes; add the tomatoes. Cook until the tomatoes soften into a chunky sauce; add the tomato sauce, season with salt and pepper to taste, and bring back to a simmer.

2. Add the cooked spaghetti; cook until heated through. Remove from heat and serve immediately.

Skip the Oil in the Boil

Adding oil to the pasta cooking water doesn't do anything but make cleanup harder. Pasta added to oiled water still sticks together. The best way to prevent sticking is to stir the pasta immediately after adding it to a sufficient amount of rapidly boiling water. Stir again after a minute or two to catch any remaining clumps.

Fettuccine with Shiitake Mushrooms and Brown Butter

This is an easy, elegant pasta served at one of New York's legendary theater district dining spots.

INGREDIENTS | SERVES 4

4 ounces (1 stick) unsalted butter, divided

½ teaspoon kosher salt

3 leaves fresh sage or a pinch of dried

1 pound shiitake mushrooms, stems removed, thinly sliced

¼ cup dry white wine

¼ cup vegetable stock or water

8 ounces fettuccine, cooked

¼ cup roughly chopped Italian parsley

Juice of 1 medium lemon plus 6 wedges

1. Place all but 1 tablespoon of the butter in a large skillet with the salt. Cook over medium heat until the butter turns brown and has a smoky, nutty aroma—it should not turn black or smell burnt.

2. Add the sage and then the mushrooms. Cook without stirring for 5 minutes to brown the mushrooms. Stir and cook until the mushrooms are wilted and juicy; add the wine. Cook 1 minute to steam out the alcohol. Add the stock, cooked fettuccine, parsley, and lemon juice.

3. Remove from heat, add remaining 1 tablespoon butter, and toss to coat. Serve with extra lemon wedges.

Angel Hair with Broccoli Raab, Toasted Garlic, Fava Beans, and Pecorino Cheese

Highlight one of spring's most delicious flavors by using fresh fava beans in this dish. If fresh favas are unavailable, use fresh or frozen green peas instead.

INGREDIENTS | SERVES 6

1 cup fresh shelled fava beans or 1 cup fresh or frozen green peas

1 tablespoon olive oil

2 cloves garlic, finely chopped

Pinch of crushed red pepper flakes (optional)

¼ cup black olives, such as niçoise or Kalamata, pitted

1 bunch broccoli raab, cut into bite-sized pieces, blanched

1 pound angel hair pasta

1 tablespoon butter

¼ cup grated Parmesan cheese

¼ pound block pecorino, feta, or other semihard cheese

Lemon wedges for garnish

1. Bring a large pot of salted water to a rolling boil. Drop the fava beans in for 2 minutes, then skim them out with a slotted spoon and shock them by plunging them into ice-cold water. Peel off the outer leathery skin. Set them aside. Keep the water at a rolling boil.

2. Heat the oil in a large skillet over medium heat. Add the garlic, pepper flakes, and olives and cook, stirring, until the garlic begins to brown. Add the broccoli raab; cook until heated through, about 2 minutes. Turn off heat.

3. Put the angel hair pasta into the boiling water, stir well to separate, and cook until tender, about 5 minutes—it cooks very quickly; drain and add to the skillet, allowing some of the water from the pasta to drip into the pan.

4. Toss with butter and Parmesan; season to taste. Divide onto serving plates. Using a swivel vegetable peeler, shave pecorino cheese liberally over pasta. Serve with lemon wedges.

Spaghetti with Sweet Corn, Tomatoes, and Goat Cheese

Late summer is the perfect time to scoop up sweet seasonal vegetables like scallions, corn, and tomatoes. When vegetables are ripe, they do all the work for you in a dish like this.

INGREDIENTS | SERVES 4

8 ounces spaghetti

2 tablespoons butter or oil

4 scallions, chopped

2 cups fresh corn kernels (about 3 ears)

1 cup diced red bell pepper

1 medium jalapeño pepper, seeded and finely chopped

3 medium tomatoes, diced

¼ cup chopped cilantro

¼ cup water or stock

Salt and ground black pepper to taste

2 ounces goat cheese, crumbled

1 large lemon

1. Cook the pasta according to the package directions.

2. Heat the butter (or oil) in a large skillet over medium heat. Add the scallions, corn, red bell pepper, and jalapeño. Cook 3 minutes; add the tomatoes, cilantro, and ¼ cup water (or stock). Season with salt and pepper.

3. Add the pasta. Sprinkle in the crumbled cheese and toss to distribute. Divide into 4 portions and garnish with additional chopped cilantro and lemon wedges.

Baked Ziti

Italian Americans have a cuisine that is distinctly their own, based on an adaptation of ingredients available to their immigrant forefathers when they arrived in the United States. This is a staple of the Italian American table.

INGREDIENTS | SERVES 10

1 pound ziti

Olive oil

1 quart tomato sauce

1 pound whole-milk or part-skim ricotta cheese

1 pound whole-milk or part-skim mozzarella, shredded

Chopped Italian parsley for garnish

1. Prepare ziti al dente according to package directions; drain, rinse, and toss with a few drops of olive oil.

2. Heat oven to 350°F.

3. Line the bottom of a 9" × 13" baking pan with half of the tomato sauce. Distribute half of the cooked ziti into the pan. Distribute the ricotta by the tablespoonful onto the ziti and then sprinkle on half of the shredded cheese. Layer on the remaining ziti. Cover the top with most of the remaining sauce, saving about ½ cup for later—the top layer does not need to be even—or use all the remaining sauce to cover the pasta completely. Sprinkle on remaining shredded cheese.

4. Bake 25 minutes until cheese is bubbly and starting to brown. Serve with additional tomato sauce on the side and garnish with chopped parsley.

Spinach Manicotti

Everybody loves stuffed pasta, and this is one of the easiest stuffed pasta dishes you can make. You can use the same filling for jumbo stuffed shells, cannelloni, or other large, stuff-able pasta.

INGREDIENTS | SERVES 4 OR 5

8–10 manicotti shells

5–6 ounces fresh spinach leaves, washed

1 pound ricotta cheese

½ cup grated Parmesan cheese

1 large egg, beaten

½ teaspoon salt

¼ teaspoon ground black pepper

2 cups tomato sauce

½ cup shredded mozzarella cheese

1. Cook the manicotti shells according to the package directions. Pick the stems from the spinach leaves. Steam or sauté spinach until just wilted.

2. In a large bowl, combine the ricotta, Parmesan, egg, salt, and pepper; stir in the spinach.

3. Heat the oven to 350°F.

4. Stuff the shells lightly (easy with a pastry bag or spoon); line them into a lightly greased 8" × 11" baking dish. Pour the sauce over all; sprinkle with mozzarella cheese. Bake uncovered 30–40 minutes until bubbly in the middle.

Raw Veggie Pasta Toss

While cooking unlocks nutrients in some vegetables, such as the vitamin A in carrots, many vegetables are at their peak of healthful elements before cooking. So eating raw vegetables in dishes like this isn't just refreshing—it's smart.

INGREDIENTS | SERVES 4

1 small yellow squash, diced

1 small zucchini, diced

¼ cup extra-virgin olive oil

3 medium plum tomatoes, seeded and chopped

1 cup shredded broccoli ("broccoli slaw")

3 scallions, sliced

1 clove garlic, finely chopped

¼ cup chopped fresh basil

Salt and ground black pepper to taste

8 ounces ziti or penne pasta

½ cup shredded mozzarella or provolone cheese

¼ cup shredded Parmigiano-Reggiano or other top-quality Parmesan

1. In a large bowl, combine the yellow squash, zucchini, olive oil, tomatoes, broccoli, scallions, garlic, basil, salt, and pepper. Allow to stand while you prepare the pasta.

2. Cook the pasta according to the package directions. Immediately after draining, toss with the cheese until it melts, then toss with the vegetable mixture. Serve warm.

Basic Pasta Salad

The vegetables in this salad are raw, but you could also cook them briefly. Just toss them into the water with the pasta for a minute before draining.

INGREDIENTS | SERVES 6

8 ounces tricolor corkscrew (fusilli or spirali) pasta

1 cup Italian salad dressing, divided

¼ cup sliced scallions

1 cup chopped broccoli (raw or parboiled)

1 cup chopped cauliflower (raw or parboiled)

1 cup shredded or chopped carrots

¼ cup sliced black olives

⅓ cup shredded Gouda or other cheese

⅓ cup cubed Cheddar cheese

⅓ cup shredded Parmigiano-Reggiano or other top-quality Parmesan

Salt and ground black pepper to taste

1. Cook the pasta according to package directions. While it's still warm, toss in a deep bowl with ¼ cup salad dressing; allow to cool to room temperature 30 minutes, stirring occasionally.

2. Meanwhile, combine all the other vegetables in a deep, narrow bowl or container. Add about ½ cup of dressing and stir to coat; add up to ¼ cup more if necessary. Marinate 30 minutes at room temperature, stirring occasionally. Chill and marinate both bowls for at least 6 hours or overnight.

3. When ready to serve, combine the pasta and vegetables. Toss with cheeses and season with salt and pepper.

Roasted Vegetable Pasta VN

*This pasta is perfect for a summer barbecue. For this recipe, it's
best to cook the pasta about 1 minute past al dente.*

INGREDIENTS | SERVES 12

1 recipe Roasted Vegetables (see recipe in Chapter 8), cut into 1" pieces

1 pound good quality fusilli, penne, or other small pasta shape, cooked about 1 minute longer than the package directions

2 tablespoons top-quality extra-virgin olive oil

2 teaspoons balsamic vinegar

Pinch of sugar

1 teaspoon kosher salt

¼ teaspoon freshly ground black pepper

½ cup roughly chopped Italian parsley

Place roasted vegetables in a large bowl and allow them to come to room temperature. Add the cooked pasta, olive oil, vinegar, and sugar. Toss to coat. Marinate 30 minutes. Season with salt and pepper; toss with parsley.

Freezing Baked Pastas

Baked pastas, such as cannelloni and lasagna, freeze very well. Portion them into airtight zipper plastic bags for convenience. Pastas with a lot of watery vegetables in them, such as carrots or zucchini, may lose some of their original texture, but will be fine to eat. Generally, the more rich items there are in the dish, such as cheese or cream, the better they will hold up in the freezer.

Mexi Mac 'n' Cheese

This grown-up version of mac 'n' cheese rouses people with its fiery bite. You can kick this up a notch or two by adding both jalapeño and habanero chilies as a garnish. But you may need a fire extinguisher.

INGREDIENTS | SERVES 6

3 cups crushed taco chips, divided

8 ounces elbow macaroni

3 tablespoons butter

3 tablespoons flour

2 cups milk

1 cup hot or mild salsa

2 cups shredded Cheddar cheese

Salt and freshly ground black pepper to taste

4 ounces habanero cheese, cubed

Jalapeño slices

Flour tortillas for serving

1. Preheat oven to 350°F. Layer 2 cups taco chips on the bottom of a 2-quart heatproof dish.

2. Cook the macaroni in lightly salted water until al dente. Drain and set aside.

3. Meanwhile, in a medium saucepan, melt the butter and whisk in the flour and milk, stirring for a few minutes until the mixture begins to thicken and is lump-free. Stir in the salsa, Cheddar cheese, salt, and pepper. Combine the pasta with the cheese sauce and spoon into the prepared dish. Top with the remaining chips, the habanero cheese, and jalapeño slices.

4. Bake for about 30 minutes or until the cheese is melted throughout. Serve with softened flour tortillas.

Gnocchi and Purple Potatoes with Broccolini VN

By garnishing this dish with a dusting of grated Parmesan cheese or a portion of shredded mozzarella or fontina cheese, you can achieve a different flavor profile. And for a kick of heat, add sparingly some crushed red pepper.

INGREDIENTS | SERVES 4

1 (17.6-ounce) package fresh gnocchi

1 bunch broccolini, chopped and cooked

10 baby purple potatoes, cooked and cubed

1 (13¾-ounce) can artichoke hearts, drained and quartered

3 tablespoons capers

½ cup olive oil

3 tablespoons red wine vinegar

2 tablespoons vegan pesto

Salt and ground black pepper to taste

1. Cook the gnocchi according to package directions, drain, and put into a serving bowl. Add the broccolini, potatoes, artichoke hearts, and capers.

2. In a small bowl, whisk together the oil, vinegar, pesto, salt, and pepper. Pour over the vegetables and toss to combine. Serve.

What Are Gnocchi?

A knot-shaped pasta most commonly made with mashed potatoes and flour, gnocchi, when freshly made and right from the boiling water, are so delicate they seem to whisper. Another less common version is made with semolina flour, milk, and cheese. You can make potato gnocchi yourself, but fresh ones are sold at Italian markets and some supermarkets.

Small Shells with Grilled Vegetables, Olives, Oregano, and Tomatoes VN

Make extra grilled vegetables next time you have the grill or the broiler on. You'll be ready to make this simple pasta quickly later in the week.

INGREDIENTS | SERVES 8

1 pound shell-shaped pasta

1 tablespoon olive oil

¼ cup pitted black olives, such as Kalamata, Gaeta, or niçoise

4 cups Roasted Vegetables (see recipe in Chapter 8) or store-bought grilled vegetables from a salad bar or deli counter

¼ cup chopped fresh oregano leaves or 2 teaspoons dried

1 cup roughly chopped tomatoes

2 cups tomato sauce

¼ cup roughly chopped Italian parsley

Salt and ground black pepper to taste

Vegetable stock or water

1. Cook pasta according to package directions; drain, rinse, and toss with a few drops of oil.

2. Heat olive oil in a large skillet or Dutch oven for 1 minute over high heat; add olives and roasted vegetables. Cook 5 minutes until hot; add oregano leaves. Cook 2 minutes more until oregano is fragrant; stir in the tomatoes and the tomato sauce. Cook 1 minute more, then toss in the pasta, parsley, salt, pepper, and a splash of stock (or water) to keep it saucy. Cook until the pasta is hot.

Linguine with Gorgonzola, Asparagus, and Cream

Gorgonzola is a highly fragrant Italian blue cheese. You may prefer to make this dish using milder French Roquefort, English Stilton, or American Maytag blue cheese.

INGREDIENTS | SERVES 4

½ pound linguine, broken in half

1 tablespoon olive oil

1 teaspoon chopped garlic

1 pound cooked asparagus, cut into 1" pieces

1 cup heavy cream

1 cup crumbled Gorgonzola or other crumbly cheese

1 tablespoon finely chopped chives

Lemon wedges for garnish

1. Cook linguine in a large pot of rapidly boiling, lightly salted water until it's soft but still slightly chewy; drain, retaining some of the cooking water, rinse under cold water, and toss with a few drops of olive oil. Set into a colander for later use. Put another pot of water on to boil for reheating the pasta.

2. In a large skillet, heat the oil for 1 minute over medium heat; add the garlic and let it sizzle for 15 seconds until it turns white. Add cooked asparagus. Sauté for 1 minute until heated through; add cream. Bring to a boil, then lower to a simmer and cook until cream is thick enough to coat the back of a spoon, about 3 minutes; stir in the cheese. Cook, stirring, until cheese is mostly melted but a few lumps remain, about 2 minutes.

3. Using a colander or strainer, dip the pasta into boiling water to reheat it, then add the hot pasta to the cream; toss to coat. If sauce is too thick, add a splash of the pasta cooking water. Serve with a sprinkling of freshly snipped chives and lemon wedges.

Spaghetti Ai Pomodori VN

The simplest pasta requires almost no cooking. Just toss the ingredients in a bowl with the cooked spaghetti.

INGREDIENTS | SERVES 4

½ pound spaghetti

2 cups diced plum tomatoes

2 tablespoons chopped fresh oregano leaves or Italian parsley

1 tablespoon extra-virgin olive oil

1 teaspoon finely chopped garlic

½ teaspoon salt

¼ teaspoon freshly ground black pepper

Cook the spaghetti according to the directions on the package; drain. Transfer the hot spaghetti to a large mixing bowl; add all other ingredients. Toss thoroughly.

"Fresh" Pasta

Pasta that has not been dried is called "fresh" pasta. Fresh and dried pastas are equally good, but have different textures. Most fresh pasta is used for stuffed varieties, like ravioli and tortellini, or for long pastas, like spaghetti or fettuccine. Small shapes, such as ziti, small shells, and elbows, are almost always sold dried.

Tagliatelle Aglio e Olio VN

The name means "cuttings with garlic and oil." Tagliatelle is similar to spaghetti, but is cut rather than extruded (terms describe the method of manufacture), and is usually sold fresh, not dried.

INGREDIENTS | SERVES 4

1 pound fresh tagliatelle, or 8 ounces dried linguine

2 tablespoons extra-virgin olive oil

2 teaspoons finely chopped garlic

Salt and ground black pepper to taste

Italian parsley, chopped

Buying Garlic

When buying fresh garlic, look for heads that are plump, firm, and heavy for their size. Any green shoots or spouts indicate that the garlic is old and will have an off flavor. Store whole bulbs in an open plastic bag in the vegetable drawer of your refrigerator. Markets now carry a variety of processed garlic options, from peeled cloves to fully chopped pastes. They are a great convenience, but buy these in the smallest containers possible, since they lose their fresh taste and become stale very quickly.

1. Cook the pasta al dente; drain in a colander, reserving ½ cup of the hot cooking water.

2. Combine the olive oil and garlic in a large skillet over high heat until the garlic sizzles and becomes fragrant but does not brown.

3. Add all the cooked pasta at once. Season with salt and pepper, add a few drops of cooking water, and toss to coat. Toss with chopped parsley.

Garlicky Pasta Tossed with Sun-Dried Tomatoes

Select the most intriguing pasta shape and use it as a basis for this dish.
Already roasted garlic cloves are sold at some markets.

INGREDIENTS | SERVES 2

4 ounces dried shaped pasta

¼ cup oil-packed sun-dried
tomatoes, slivered

1 whole head garlic, roasted and cooled

1 cup shredded fontina cheese

⅓ cup grated Parmesan cheese

3 tablespoons toasted pine nuts

1 tablespoon olive oil

Salt and ground black pepper to taste

1. Bring a large pot of lightly salted water to a boil and cook the pasta until al dente, 6–8 minutes. Drain and put into a large bowl.

2. Squeeze the cloves out of the roasted garlic and add to the bowl. Toss with the remaining ingredients and adjust seasonings.

Roasting Garlic

You'll find many suggestions for roasting garlic, but the simplest one is this: Preheat the oven to 400°F, slice off about ¼" from the top, remove the outer papery skin, set the head or heads in a small heatproof bowl, and drizzle the garlic with olive oil. Wrap the bowl in aluminum foil and roast for about 1 hour.

Cannellini and Tortellini

For a splash of color, add some chopped-up oil-packed sundried tomatoes to taste. Additionally, you can boost flavors with a garnish of capers and pitted niçoise olives.

INGREDIENTS | SERVES 4

1 (12-ounce) package fresh tortellini

3 tablespoons olive oil

5 cloves garlic, minced

1 (9-ounce) package soy "meatballs"

1 (19-ounce) can cannellini, drained and rinsed

1 (14½-ounce) can roasted tomatoes

Salt and ground black pepper to taste

1. Cook the tortellini according to package directions, drain, and set aside.

2. Meanwhile, heat the oil in a large skillet over medium heat and sauté the garlic and the "meatballs" for 4–5 minutes. Add the cannellini and tomatoes and continue cooking until the mixture is heated through. Season with salt and pepper.

3. Add the tortellini, stirring to combine, and serve.

Summer Salad with Shells

Although shells make an attractive pasta base, feel free to substitute another small pasta of your choice. You may also use a fruit-flavored yogurt for additional flavor interest.

INGREDIENTS | SERVES 4

3 cups mixed young salad greens

2 cups cooked small shells, cooled

1 cup thinly sliced fresh strawberries

1 cup halved grapes

3 tablespoons plain yogurt

2 tablespoons balsamic vinegar

2 tablespoons honey, or to taste

Mint leaves, for garnish

1. In a large bowl, toss the greens with the shells, strawberries, and grapes and set aside.

2. In a small bowl, whisk together the yogurt, vinegar, and honey and toss with the salad ingredients. Before serving, garnish the salad with the mint leaves.

Couscous Fruit and Nut Salad

Don't be alarmed by the long list of ingredients. This salad comes together in minutes, and it bursts with so much flavor and texture you will want to serve it often.

INGREDIENTS | SERVES 6

1 (10-ounce) box quick-cooking couscous

1 cup chopped flat-leaf parsley

1 cup cashews

½ cup raisins

½ cup cubed dried papaya

½ cup chopped dates

½ cup diced dried figs

½ cup chopped dried apricots

3 kiwifruit, peeled and sliced

½ red onion, diced

1 (6-ounce) container nonfat lime yogurt

2 tablespoons balsamic vinegar

1 tablespoon olive oil

Creole seasoning salt to taste

Mint leaves for garnish

1. Cook the couscous according to package directions and when it is cool add to the salad bowl.

2. Meanwhile, add the parsley, cashews, raisins, papaya, dates, figs, apricots, kiwifruit, and red onion to the bowl and stir to combine.

3. In a small bowl, whisk together the yogurt, vinegar, and olive oil. Toss dressing with the salad ingredients. Season with the Creole seasoning salt, garnish with mint leaves, and serve.

Cellophane Noodle Salad VN

In the traditional Thai version of this salad, cooks use fish sauce instead of soy sauce and use ground pork, shrimp, and/ or chicken for the meat.

INGREDIENTS | SERVES 4

4 ounces cellophane, or bean thread, noodles, softened in hot water for 20 minutes

1 (6-ounce) package soy "chicken" strips, optional

½ cup thinly sliced scallions

½ cup fresh cilantro leaves

1–2 tablespoons crushed red peppers

2 tablespoons lime juice

2 tablespoons soy sauce

1 tablespoon pickled garlic, chopped

Sugar to taste

1. Drain the soaked and softened noodles and cut them into serving pieces. Put the noodles, "chicken" strips if using, scallions, cilantro leaves, and crushed red peppers into a serving bowl.

2. In a small bowl, mix together the lime juice, soy sauce, and pickled garlic and toss with the salad ingredients.

What Are Cellophane Noodles?

Called "glass," "cellophane," or "bean thread" noodles, this Asian pasta is made from the starch of mung beans, and when dried, the noodles are so brittle and tough that when you cut them—and the cleanest way is using scissors—they may fly around, so hold them over the sink. They are easier to cut when wet, although when they are wet they are also somewhat gelatinous. Unless you plan to use the softened noodles in a soup, drain them before using them in other dishes. These are readily available at most well-stocked supermarkets and at Asian markets.

CHAPTER 12

Egg and Dairy Dishes

Artichoke and Cheese Squares

*These rich vegetable cakes are easy-to-serve, attractive savories
that can be made ahead, up to three days.*

INGREDIENTS | SERVES 8

1 (12-ounce) jar marinated artichoke
hearts, drained, liquid reserved

1 small onion, finely chopped

2 cloves garlic, finely minced

4 large eggs, beaten

2 tablespoons flour

½ teaspoon salt

¼ teaspoon ground black pepper

¼ teaspoon oregano

¼ teaspoon hot pepper sauce

8 ounces shredded Monterey
jack cheese

2 tablespoons chopped parsley

1. Preheat oven to 325°F. Chop artichokes and set aside.

2. Heat the marinade liquid in a medium skillet and sauté
   the onion and garlic in it until translucent, about
   5 minutes.

3. In a medium mixing bowl, combine eggs, flour, salt,
   pepper, oregano, and hot pepper sauce. Thoroughly
   mix in cheese, parsley, artichokes, and onion mixture.

4. Turn into a 7" × 11" baking dish. Bake for 30 minutes
   until set. Cool to room temp. Cut into squares and
   serve room temperature, or reheat at 325°F for
   10 minutes.

Huevos Rancheros

Rich and delicious, this Mexican ranch breakfast will fuel your whole morning. While this recipe calls for scrambled eggs, it works equally well with any style of eggs.

INGREDIENTS | SERVES 4

1 can Mexican-style black beans in sauce or Cuban Black Beans (see recipe in Chapter 13)

2 cups Rancheros Salsa (see recipe in this chapter) or store-bought Mexican salsa

8 large eggs

½ cup half-and-half

½ teaspoon salt

Unsalted butter, for greasing pan

8 (8″ diameter) soft corn tortillas

1 cup shredded Monterey jack or mild Cheddar cheese

½ cup sour cream

Chopped cilantro

1. Heat the beans and Rancheros Salsa in separate saucepans over low heat.

2. In a medium bowl, scramble together the eggs, half-and-half, and salt. Melt the butter in a nonstick pan; add the egg mixture and cook over low heat until soft and creamy, with small curds.

3. Soften the tortillas either by steaming or flash cooking over an open gas burner. Place 2 tortillas onto each plate. Divide the hot black beans evenly onto these tortillas. Spoon the eggs onto the beans, then sauce with a ladleful of Rancheros Salsa. Garnish with cheese, sour cream, and cilantro. Serve immediately.

Rancheros Salsa VN

This salsa, the best part of Huevos Rancheros, freezes exceptionally well.
Consider making a double batch and storing half for later.

INGREDIENTS | MAKES 4 CUPS

2 tablespoons olive oil

1 medium white onion, peeled and roughly chopped

1 medium red bell pepper, seeded and roughly chopped

1 medium green bell pepper, seeded and roughly chopped

4 large plum tomatoes, seeded and roughly chopped

1 tablespoon chopped garlic (about 4 cloves)

1 (14-ounce) can diced tomatoes in tomato purée

1 (7-ounce) can tomatillos, drained

1 (7-ounce) can green chilies, rinsed, drained, and roughly chopped

1 teaspoon chipotle purée (optional)

1 small jalapeño pepper, seeded and finely chopped

¼ cup chopped cilantro

1 tablespoon frozen orange juice concentrate

1 teaspoon ground cumin, toasted in a dry pan until fragrant

1 teaspoon dried oregano

¼ teaspoon ground cinnamon

Salt and ground black pepper to taste

1. In a large, heavy-bottomed pot, heat the oil over medium-high heat until hot but not smoky. Add onion, peppers, and plum tomatoes; cook 5 minutes until onion is translucent.

2. In a food processor, purée garlic, diced tomato, and tomatillos; add to onion mixture. Cook 5 minutes more.

3. Add chilies, chipotle, jalapeño, and cilantro; stir in orange juice concentrate, cumin, oregano, cinnamon, salt, and pepper. Cook 5 minutes more.

Roasted Vegetable Frittata

This perfect brunch main course can be made ahead and served at slightly above room temperature. It's a perfect way to utilize leftover vegetables of all sorts—any vegetables will work.

INGREDIENTS | SERVES 8

1 medium zucchini, quartered lengthwise

1 medium yellow squash, quartered lengthwise

1 cup small white mushrooms

1 small (Italian) eggplant, or ¼ of a regular eggplant, cut into large chunks

2 tablespoons olive oil

9 large eggs, beaten

¾ cup half-and-half

½ teaspoon salt

2 tablespoons unsalted butter

1 large baked potato, diced

1 medium onion, chopped

2 tablespoons chopped Italian parsley or cilantro

1 cup shredded cheese (Monterey jack, cheddar, or Havarti, for example)

½ cup diced tomatoes (about 1 large)

Ground black pepper to taste

1. Heat oven to 400°F.

2. Toss zucchini, yellow squash, mushrooms, and eggplant in a large bowl with olive oil. Spread into a baking sheet or roasting pan. Roast until tender, about 20 minutes. (Note: This step can be done up to 2 days in advance.)

3. Raise oven temperature to 450°F.

4. In a large bowl, whisk together the eggs, half-and-half, and salt.

5. In an ovensafe, 10" nonstick skillet, melt the butter over medium heat. Add the potatoes, onions, and parsley (or cilantro); cook until the onions are softened and the potatoes are slightly browned.

6. Add the roasted vegetables and the egg mixture to the skillet. Cook, stirring with a wooden spoon, until the mixture begins to thicken but is still mostly liquid. Stir in the cheese and tomatoes. Season with pepper.

7. Place pan on center rack of oven and bake until frittata puffs slightly and begins to brown on top, about 15 minutes. Remove from oven and transfer frittata to a serving plate. Allow it to rest 5 minutes before cutting into 8 wedges and serving, garnished with additional parsley or cilantro.

Spinach Quiche

*There's no yummier way to get the iron, calcium, and other goodness
from spinach than this elegant, simple, savory pie.*

INGREDIENTS | SERVES 6

1 unbaked (9") pie shell

¼ cup scallions, chopped

2 tablespoons unsalted butter

1 pound (1 package) fresh
spinach, washed, stems removed,
roughly chopped

Pinch of nutmeg

½ teaspoon salt

¼ teaspoon freshly ground black pepper

3 large eggs

6 ounces half-and-half or milk

¼ cup shredded Gruyère or
Swiss cheese

1. Heat oven to 350°F.

2. Gently place wax paper over the unbaked pie shell and fill the cavity with dried beans or pie beads. Bake until golden brown, 15–20 minutes (this is known as "blind baking" the crust). Cool on a rack; remove beans.

3. Increase oven temperature to 375°F.

4. Heat the scallions and butter in a skillet until they sizzle. Add spinach, nutmeg, salt, and pepper; cook until spinach is wilted.

5. Whisk together eggs and half-and-half in a medium bowl. Add the spinach mixture.

6. Sprinkle half of the cheese into the prebaked pie crust; add the spinach-egg mixture. Top with remaining cheese; bake for 35 minutes until the top is domed and beginning to brown.

Creamed Carrots

With their appealing color and gentle bite, these carrots have a beautiful color, texture, and flavor. Also, since the vitamin A in carrots is lipid-soluble, the combination of butter and cream aids in the release of this important nutrient.

INGREDIENTS | SERVES 4

1 pound carrots, peeled, quartered lengthwise, and cut into 2" sticks

½ cup water

2 tablespoons unsalted butter

½ teaspoon salt

1½ teaspoons sugar

½ cup light cream

Pinch of grated nutmeg

Ground white pepper to taste

1. Combine the carrots, water, butter, salt, and sugar in a large skillet. Simmer over medium heat until most of the water has evaporated and the carrots are tender.

2. Add the cream; simmer until it lightly coats the carrots and has a saucy consistency. Season carrots with nutmeg and white pepper.

Creamed Corn

Now that sweet corn of good quality is available for much of the year, celebrate with a rich, comforting dish of creamed corn accompanied by a refreshing salad.

INGREDIENTS | SERVES 4

6 ears sweet corn, shucked

1 tablespoon butter

¼ cup finely chopped shallots or onions

½ cup heavy cream

Salt and ground black pepper to taste

Freshly chopped chives (optional)

1. Using a knife, cut the kernels from the cob with a tip-to-stem slicing motion. You should have about 3 cups.

2. Melt the butter in a skillet; add the shallots and cook until soft, about 3 minutes.

3. Add the corn and cream and cook until thickened, about 2 minutes; season with salt and pepper. Garnish with chives if desired.

Corn and Pepper Pudding

This luscious bread and corn pudding with a Southwestern touch is great as an appetizer or a side dish.

INGREDIENTS | SERVES 6

2 tablespoons unsalted butter, melted

3 cups cubed bread, about ½" dice

3 medium roasted poblano or red bell peppers, peeled and diced

6 ears sweet corn, shucked, kernels cut off with a knife (about 3 cups)

¼ cup chopped chives

1 teaspoon salt

½ teaspoon freshly ground black pepper

4 large eggs

2 cups milk

¾ cup shredded jalapeño pepper jack cheese

1. Heat oven to 350°F.

2. Combine the melted butter and bread cubes in a baking dish and bake in a single layer until lightly browned, about 10 minutes.

3. In a mixing bowl, combine the roasted peppers, corn, chives, bread cubes, salt, and pepper. Transfer to a buttered 8" × 11" baking dish.

4. In a medium bowl, whisk together the eggs and milk; pour over bread mixture. Allow to sit for 10 minutes to let the bread absorb the custard; top with the shredded cheese. Bake until set in the center and lightly browned on top, about 1 hour.

Stuffed Eggs

These filled eggs are a variation on deviled eggs, and are a great first course or garnish for a main-course salad. Their tops are attractively browned under the broiler.

INGREDIENTS | SERVES 8

8 large hard-boiled eggs

¼ cup Dijon mustard

3 tablespoons heavy cream

2 tablespoons finely chopped shallot

1 tablespoon rice wine vinegar

1 tablespoon chopped chives

1 tablespoon chopped tarragon

Salt and ground white pepper to taste

Unsalted butter

1. Heat the broiler. Peel and halve the eggs. Take out the yolks and combine them in a medium bowl with the mustard, cream, shallot, vinegar, chives, and tarragon. Season with salt and white pepper. Transfer mixture to a piping bag and pipe it into the egg whites (you could also use a spoon).

2. Place the filled eggs in a baking dish or broiler pan. Dot the tops with a tiny nugget of butter and broil them until lightly browned, about 5 minutes. Serve warm.

Scrambled Egg Burritos

This innovative "wrap" makes a flavorful breakfast.

INGREDIENTS | SERVES 4

1 tablespoon unsalted butter

1 cup finely chopped onion

½ cup sliced roasted peppers

9 extra-large eggs, beaten

½ cup half-and-half

1 or 2 dashes of hot pepper sauce

2 cups shredded jalapeño jack cheese

Salt and ground black pepper to taste

4 (12") flour tortillas

Salsa Fresca (see recipe in Chapter 2) or store-bought salsa

1. In a large skillet over medium heat, melt the butter; add the onions and sliced roasted peppers. Cook until the onions are soft and translucent, about 5 minutes.

2. In a medium bowl, combine the eggs and the cream and add them to the pan. Cook, stirring constantly with a wooden spoon, until the eggs are about half cooked—still very runny; add the hot pepper sauce, cheese, salt, and pepper. Remove from heat. Eggs should be soft, creamy, and have small curds.

3. Soften the tortillas by placing them directly atop the stove burner on medium heat; a few black spots are okay. Spoon a quarter of the egg mixture slightly off center on a tortilla. Fold the sides in upon the egg and roll the tortilla away from yourself, folding the filling in and tucking with your fingers to keep even pressure. Repeat with remaining tortillas. Serve with salsa.

Miso Eggs Benedict

Miso has a salty flavor that replaces the Canadian bacon used in traditional eggs Benedict. Have all of the ingredients ready to go, and set the English muffins to toast at the same time as you put the eggs in to poach, so you can place freshly poached eggs onto freshly toasted muffins.

INGREDIENTS | SERVES 4

3 tablespoons white vinegar

1 teaspoon salt

4 extra-large eggs

2 English muffins, split

½ teaspoon butter

½ teaspoon miso paste

½ cup store-bought hollandaise sauce

Chives for garnish

Hot pepper sauce to taste

Note

Eggs can be poached up to a day in advance and stored submerged in cold water. To reheat, gently place in fresh boiling water for a minute before using.

1. Combine the vinegar and salt in a deep skillet with 2" of water. Crack each egg into its own cup. When water boils, lower heat as low as you can. Gently lower the eggs into the hot water, one by one, and pour them from the cups into the pan. Set the muffins to toast.

2. Poach the eggs for no more than 3 minutes, then remove them with a slotted spoon, allowing excess water to drain back into the skillet. Transfer poached eggs to a waiting plate. Mash together the butter and miso; spread this mixture onto the toasted muffins. Place 1 poached egg onto each.

3. Spoon generous helpings of hollandaise sauce onto each and serve immediately with a sprinkling of chives and hot pepper sauce on the side.

Fricos (Cheese Crisps)

Lacy, cooked wafers of cheese make exquisite garnishes for salads, accompaniments to soups or sandwiches, and handy snack foods. Usually these are made with Parmigiano-Reggiano, but they're equally good made with Asiago, Cheddar, or provolone.

INGREDIENTS | SERVES 4

1 cup finely shredded Parmigiano-Reggiano or other cheese

Heat a nonstick skillet over medium heat. Sprinkle 1 tablespoon of cheese into a small mound on the pan. Cook until the bottom is nicely browned, then transfer to drain on paper towels. They are soft and oozy, and require a little practice to handle them properly, so have a little extra cheese ready in case the first few are less than perfect.

Tomato and Cheese Tart

Store-bought puff pastry makes this an easy, attractive brunch item. Always look for puff made with real butter rather than shortening.

INGREDIENTS | SERVES 4–6

8 ounces frozen puff pastry, thawed

1 tablespoon olive oil

4 leeks, sliced and thoroughly washed

3 sprigs fresh thyme leaves, picked (about 2 teaspoons), or a scant teaspoon dried

Kosher salt and freshly ground black pepper to taste

6 ounces raclette or other semisoft cheese, such as Havarti or Gouda, sliced

2 or 3 medium tomatoes, thinly sliced

Pinch of sugar

1. Heat oven to 375°F. Roll the pastry out to fit a 14" × 4" oblong rectangular tart pan (you can also use a 10" circular tart pan—adjust dough dimensions accordingly); prick the rolled dough with the tines of a fork in several places. Arrange the dough in the pan and refrigerate until ready to use.

2. Heat the olive oil in a medium skillet over moderate heat; sauté the leeks and thyme until the leeks are soft and translucent, about 5 minutes. Season with salt and pepper, remove from heat, and cool to room temperature. Spoon the leeks into the tart shell; cover with the cheese. Arrange the tomatoes in rows or concentric circles (depending on what type of pan you're using) and sprinkle them with a little sugar.

3. Bake for 40–45 minutes until cheese begins to brown and the crust is golden.

Scrambled Eggs Masala

These unique scrambled eggs have a fragrant allure. Serve them with Indian breads for a special brunch.

INGREDIENTS | SERVES 2

2 tablespoons butter

¼ cup chopped onion

¼ teaspoon cumin seed, toasted in a dry pan and crushed (or very fresh cumin powder, toasted a minute in a dry pan)

¼ cup diced tomato

4 large eggs, beaten

Salt and ground white pepper to taste

4 teaspoons chopped fresh mint leaves

1. Melt the butter in a medium nonstick skillet over moderate heat. Add the onions; cook 5–8 minutes until soft. Add cumin and tomatoes; cook 1 minute more.

2. Stir in the eggs, salt, and pepper. Using a wooden spoon, constantly stir the eggs until they form soft, creamy curds; transfer to plates and serve immediately. Garnish with the mint.

Greek Salad Tacos

This fusion of Mediterranean and Central American fare is a wholly North American phenomenon.

INGREDIENTS | SERVES 4

8 (6") corn tortillas

8 ounces feta cheese, cut into 8 slices

2 cups shredded romaine or iceberg lettuce

8 thin slices ripe tomato

24 pitted Kalamata olives

¼ cup extra-virgin olive oil

1 teaspoon dried oregano leaves, preferably Mexican

Salt and ground black pepper to taste

1. Soften the tortillas over a stove burner or in the oven.

2. Place a slice of feta in the center of a tortilla, along with a pinch of lettuce, a slice of tomato, and 3 olives. Repeat with remaining tortillas.

3. In a bowl, whisk together the olive oil, oregano, salt, and pepper. Drizzle the tacos with spoonfuls of dressing and serve with remaining dressing on the side.

Noodle Pudding

Baked side-dish puddings that can do double duty as dessert, such as rice pudding, bread pudding, and noodle pudding, are some of the old-fashioned comfort foods that are making a comeback.

INGREDIENTS | SERVES 6

2 large eggs

¼ cup sugar

1 cup cottage cheese

½ cup sour cream

¼ teaspoon salt

¼ cup raisins, soaked for 15 minutes in a cup of hot tap water

2 cups dried wide egg noodles

3 tablespoons butter, at room temperature

Ground cinnamon

1. Heat oven to 350°F.

2. In a large bowl, combine eggs, sugar, cottage cheese, sour cream, salt, and raisins; stir well.

3. Cook noodles according to package directions, drain, and toss with butter. Add noodles to cottage cheese mixture; toss to coat. Transfer to a buttered 9" square baking dish. Cover with foil.

4. Bake until fully set in the middle, about 45 minutes, uncovering halfway through. Dust with cinnamon and allow to rest 10 minutes before cutting into portions.

Challah French Toast

Challah's richness and golden color make for the most luxurious and attractive French toast. The key here is to let the egg mixture soak all the way to the center of thick bread slices, and then cook slowly, so it gets cooked in the middle without overbrowning the outside.

INGREDIENTS | SERVES 4

½ teaspoon ground cinnamon

3 cups milk

6 extra-large eggs, beaten

1 teaspoon vanilla extract

3 tablespoons sugar

1 teaspoon salt

8 (1") slices challah or other bread

2 tablespoons unsalted butter

Blueberry or raspberry preserves or pure maple syrup

1. In a mixing bowl, make a paste with the cinnamon and a drop of the milk. Whisk in the rest of the milk, the eggs, vanilla, sugar, and salt. Transfer to a wide, deep dish and submerge the bread slices in the egg mixture. Allow to soak for at least 10 minutes, pressing the slices gently under with your fingertips to keep them submerged and turning them halfway through.

2. Heat a large, heavy-bottomed skillet over medium-low heat. A piece of butter should sizzle but not smoke when it is added. Melt ½ tablespoon butter and fry the soaked bread 2 pieces at a time (it's important not to crowd the pan) on both sides until they bounce back when poked with a finger, about 4 minutes per side. Serve them as they come out of the pan or keep them warm in the oven. Do not reuse butter—wipe the pan after each batch. Serve with blueberry or raspberry preserves or pure maple syrup.

Chinese Soy Sauce Eggs

These strikingly dark, double-cooked spiced eggs are an excellent first course with a salad of baby Asian greens dressed with a few drops of rice vinegar and sesame oil.

INGREDIENTS | SERVES 4

8 large eggs

½ cup soy sauce

2 tablespoons sugar

2 tablespoons Chinese five-spice powder

1 tablespoon chopped garlic

1. Hard-boil the eggs, about 10 minutes; run them under cold water and peel them.

2. Bring 4 cups water to a boil in a medium saucepan. Add the soy sauce and sugar. Simmer 5 minutes; add the five-spice, garlic, and peeled eggs. Cover; simmer slowly for at least 1 hour until the soy sauce's color has penetrated well into the eggs, all the way to the yolk. Cool in the cooking liquid and serve warm or room temperature.

Hawaiian Turnovers

You can eat these turnovers right away, but if you let them cool, then wrap and chill them for later use, these become tidy portable breakfast treats.

INGREDIENTS | SERVES 8

1 (8-ounce) package cream cheese, at room temperature

½ cup confectioners' sugar

½ cup crushed pineapple, very well drained

½ cup shredded coconut

½ cup sliced almonds

1 teaspoon vanilla extract

½ teaspoon salt

1 (16.3-ounce) package jumbo buttermilk refrigerator biscuits

Milk for brushing

1. Preheat oven to 350°F. Spray a nonstick baking sheet with nonstick cooking spray.

2. In a large mixing bowl, beat the cream cheese and sugar together until smooth and slightly fluffy. Fold in the pineapple, coconut, almonds, vanilla extract, and salt.

3. Unfold the biscuit circles, one at a time. Roll them out on a lightly floured surface to about 5½" round. Put about 2 tablespoons of the filling mixture into the center of the circle and fold one side over the filling to the other side. Crimp the edges shut and brush the top with milk. Place on the baking sheet. Repeat with the remaining ingredients.

4. Bake for about 15 minutes or until the turnovers turn golden. Remove from the oven and eat hot or set aside for later use.

Fruit-and-Cheese Quesadillas

Bland mozzarella is a perfect backdrop for fruit, and you can vary the fruit and jam according to what's seasonally available. These are knife-and-fork quesadillas, too gooey for finger food.

INGREDIENTS | SERVES 4

4 tablespoons strawberry jam

4 (6"–8") whole-wheat flour tortillas

2 cups shredded mozzarella cheese

1 cup diced fresh strawberries plus extra for sprinkling

4 tablespoons strawberry yogurt for garnish

Confectioners' sugar for dusting

1. Spread 1 tablespoon jam on a tortilla and sprinkle it with ¼ cup mozzarella cheese and ¼ cup diced strawberries. Fold over the tortilla to enclose the filling. Repeat with the remaining tortillas, mozzarella, jam, and strawberries.

2. Spray the skillet with nonstick cooking spray and heat it over medium heat. Cook the quesadillas, one or two at a time, until golden on the bottom, about 3 minutes. Flip over and cook the second side until golden and the cheese has melted.

3. Top each quesadilla with a dollop of yogurt, a sprinkling of strawberries, and a dusting of confectioners' sugar. Serve hot.

Baked Pasta Custard

As a wholesome counterpoint to this rich brunch dish, offer your family a bowl of freshly sliced oranges or grapefruit segments, or whatever slightly tart fruit is in season.

INGREDIENTS | SERVES 4–6

4 large eggs

1 cup part-skim or whole-milk ricotta cheese

1 cup confectioners' sugar

2 cups cooked orzo

½ cup slivered almonds

½ cup heavy cream

1 tablespoon lemon zest

2 teaspoons vanilla extract

1 teaspoon lemon extract

1. Preheat oven to 350°F. Lightly butter a 2-quart baking dish and set aside.

2. In a large bowl, beat the eggs until light and foamy. Beat in the ricotta cheese and sugar. Fold in the orzo, almonds, cream, lemon zest, vanilla extract, and lemon extract and stir until well combined.

3. Pour into prepared baking dish and bake for about 1 hour or until the custard browns and the center is firm. Serve hot or at room temperature.

"Sausage" Bread Pudding

Vary the berry topping to suit your taste by using raspberries, blueberries, blackberries, or strawberries. If these are not available, substitute 2 cups of your favorite seasonal fruits cut into small cubes. This dish is ideal for a leisurely family brunch.

INGREDIENTS | SERVES 4

1 tablespoon olive oil

1 teaspoon minced garlic

1 cup soy "sausage" meat

1 teaspoon Cajun or Creole seasoning or hot sauce to taste

2 cups whole milk

3 tablespoons melted butter

4 large eggs

2 cups shredded Cheddar or Monterey jack cheese

3 cups cubed sourdough bread

2 cups fresh blackberries or blueberries

Soy Sausages

Made from soy proteins, soy "sausages" are available as links or as a compact product packed in a tube. In the tube, the soy meat is easy to crumble and sauté like its pork sausage counterpart; alternatively, it slices easily and pan-fries like a patty. Look for soy sausage products in a refrigerated case displayed with other vegetarian and vegan ingredients.

1. Preheat oven to 375°F. Lightly butter a 2-quart baking dish.

2. Heat the oil in a large skillet over medium heat and sauté the garlic for about 30 seconds. Add and crumble the "sausage" meat, stirring as you crumble, and season with the Cajun seasoning. Reduce the heat to low.

3. Meanwhile, in a medium bowl, beat together the milk, butter, and eggs until foamy. Stir in the cheese and the sausage mixture. Put the bread into the baking dish and pour the milk mixture over the bread.

4. Bake the custard for about 45 minutes or until puffy and golden. Serve hot with the fruit topping.

CHAPTER 13

Slow Cooker Meals

Breakfast Quinoa with Fruit VN

Take a break from oatmeal and try this fruity quinoa instead!

INGREDIENTS | SERVES 4

1 cup quinoa

2 cups water

½ cup dried mixed berries

1 pear, thinly sliced

1 teaspoon dark brown sugar

½ teaspoon ground ginger

¼ teaspoon cinnamon

⅛ teaspoon cloves

⅛ teaspoon nutmeg

Place all ingredients into a 4-quart slow cooker. Cover and cook on low heat for 2–3 hours or until the quinoa is fully cooked.

Quinoa

Quinoa, pronounced "keen-wah," is actually a seed, not a grain, closely related to spinach. It was originally cultivated by the Incas. It contains more high-quality protein than any other grain or cereal and is also high in iron, magnesium, phosphorous, and zinc, and a source of calcium, B vitamins, and fiber.

Pear Oatmeal VN

Cooking rolled oats overnight makes them so creamy they could be served as dessert. Cooking them with fruit is just the icing on the cake.

INGREDIENTS | SERVES 4

2 Bosc pears, cored and thinly sliced

2¼ cups pear cider

1½ cups old-fashioned rolled oats

1 tablespoon dark brown sugar

½ teaspoon cinnamon

Place all ingredients in a 4-quart slow cooker. Cook on low overnight, approximately 8–9 hours. Stir and serve.

A Quick Guide to Oatmeal

Oat groats are oats that still have the bran, but the outer husk has been removed. Rolled oats are groats that have been rolled into flat flakes for quick cooking, a process that removes the bran. Scottish oats are oat groats that have been chopped to include the bran. Quick-cooking or instant oats are more processed rolled oats.

Tofu Ranchero

Bring Mexican cuisine to the breakfast table with this easy Tofu Ranchero.

INGREDIENTS | SERVES 4

3 tablespoons olive oil

1 (16-ounce) package firm tofu, drained and crumbled

½ medium onion, diced

2 cloves garlic, minced

1 large lemon, juiced

½ teaspoon turmeric

1 teaspoon salt

¼ teaspoon black pepper

1 cup pinto beans, drained

8 corn tortillas

½ cup shredded Cheddar cheese or vegan Cheddar cheese

½ cup chipotle salsa

Choosing Salsa

Salsa comes in many delicious and unique varieties. Most are clearly labeled mild, medium, and hot, but one's interpretation of those words can vary greatly. Chipotle salsa has a deep, earthy spice, but you can also use plain tomato salsa or tomatillo salsa in this recipe.

1. Add the olive oil, tofu, onion, garlic, lemon juice, turmeric, salt, black pepper, and pinto beans to a 4-quart slow cooker. Cover and cook on medium heat for 4 hours.

2. When the ranchero filling is nearly done, brown the tortillas on both sides using a small sauté pan.

3. Preheat oven to 350°F.

4. Place the tortillas on a baking sheet and add the filling. Sprinkle the cheese over the rancheros and bake until the cheese has melted, about 5 minutes. Top with the chipotle salsa.

Black Bean Soup VN

You can use the leftover green bell pepper, red bell pepper, and red onion from this recipe to make chili.

INGREDIENTS | SERVES 6

2 tablespoons olive oil

½ medium green bell pepper, diced

½ medium red bell pepper, diced

½ medium red onion, sliced

2 cloves garlic, minced

2 (15-ounce) cans black beans, drained and rinsed

2 teaspoons cumin, minced

1 teaspoon chipotle powder

1 teaspoon salt

4 cups vegetable broth

¼ cup cilantro, chopped

1. In a medium sauté pan, heat the olive oil over medium heat, then sauté the bell peppers, onion, and garlic for 2–3 minutes.

2. In a 4-quart slow cooker, add the sautéed vegetables, black beans, cumin, chipotle powder, salt, and broth. Cover and cook on low for 6 hours.

3. Let the soup cool slightly, then pour half into a blender. Process until smooth, then pour back into the pot. Add the chopped cilantro and stir.

French Onion Soup

Vidalia onions are a sweet variety of onion that work particularly well in French Onion Soup.

INGREDIENTS | SERVES 4

¼ cup olive oil

4 Vidalia onions, sliced

4 cloves garlic, minced

1 tablespoon dried thyme

1 cup red wine

4 cups vegetable broth

1 teaspoon salt

1 teaspoon pepper

4 slices French bread

4 ounces Swiss cheese or vegan cheese such as Daiya Mozzarella Style Shreds

1. In a medium sauté pan, heat the olive oil over medium high heat and cook the onions until golden brown, about 3 minutes. Add the garlic and sauté for 1 minute.

2. In a 4-quart slow cooker, pour the sautéed vegetables, thyme, red wine, vegetable broth, salt, and pepper. Cover and cook on low heat for 4 hours.

3. While the soup is cooking, preheat the oven to the broiler setting. Lightly toast the slices of French bread.

4. To serve, ladle the soup into a broiler-safe bowl, place a slice of the toasted French bread on top of the soup, put a slice of the Swiss cheese on top of the bread, and place the soup under the broiler until the cheese has melted.

Brunswick Stew VN

Try adding barbecue sauce to this stew to spice things up.

INGREDIENTS | SERVES 4

4 cups vegetable broth

1 (15-ounce) can diced tomatoes

1 (6-ounce) can tomato paste

1 cup okra, sliced

1 cup corn

1 cup frozen lima beans

2 cups seitan, diced

¼ teaspoon dried rosemary

¼ teaspoon dried oregano

2 teaspoons vegan Worcestershire sauce

Salt and ground black pepper to taste

In a 4-quart slow cooker, add all ingredients. Cover and cook on low heat for 5–6 hours.

Debate on Origin

Some claim that Brunswick stew was first served in Brunswick, Georgia, in 1898, while others say it was created in Brunswick County, Virginia, in 1828. Today, Brunswick Stew recipe ingredients vary by region.

Okra Gumbo VN

The roux—a combination of oil or butter and flour—is the base for many classic New Orleans dishes.

INGREDIENTS | SERVES 6

½ cup vegetable oil

½ cup flour

1 medium white onion, diced

1 medium bell pepper, diced

4 cloves garlic, minced

4 cups water

2 cups vegetable broth

1 tablespoon vegan Worcestershire sauce

1 (16-ounce) package frozen chopped okra

1 tablespoon Cajun seasoning

1 bay leaf

2 teaspoons salt

2 teaspoons pepper

1 (7-ounce) package Gardein Chick'n Strips, chopped

½ cup flat-leaf parsley, chopped

½ cup scallions, sliced

½ teaspoon filé powder

6 cups cooked white rice

1. In a small sauté pan, bring the oil and flour to medium heat, stirring continuously until the roux achieves a rich brown color, at least 10 minutes.

2. In a 4-quart slow cooker, add the roux and all remaining ingredients except the rice. Cover and cook on low heat for 6 hours.

3. Once done, remove the bay leaf. Pour each serving over 1 cup of cooked rice.

Filé Powder

Filé (pronounced fee-LAY) powder is made from ground sassafras leaves. It is an essential ingredient for authentic Cajun or Creole gumbo. Used to both thicken and flavor, filé powder is thought to have been first used by the Choctaw Indians from the Louisiana bayou region. It can be found in most well-stocked grocery stores.

Seitan Bourguinon

Better Than Bouillon's No Beef Base is a good vegetarian alternative to beef stock.

INGREDIENTS | SERVES 6

2 tablespoons olive oil

1 pound cooked seitan, cut into 2" cubes

2 medium carrots, sliced

1 medium onion, sliced

1 teaspoon salt

2 tablespoons flour

2 cups red wine

2 cups No Beef Base

1 tablespoon tomato paste

2 cloves garlic, minced

½ teaspoon dried thyme

1 bay leaf

¼ teaspoon pepper

1 tablespoon butter or vegan margarine

18 whole pearl onions, peeled

2 cups button mushrooms, sliced

1. Heat the olive oil in a large sauté pan over medium heat. Sauté the seitan, carrots, and onion until soft, about 7 minutes. Stir in the salt and flour.

2. In a 4-quart slow cooker, add the vegetables and roux. Whisk in the red wine and No Beef Base, then add all remaining ingredients.

3. Cover and cook over low heat for 6–8 hours.

Seitan

Seitan is made from wheat gluten and is often used as a vegetarian substitute for all types of meat. It's one of the easiest meat substitutes to cook with at home.

Vegan Alfredo VN

Top cooked fettuccine with this updated version of a classic sauce.

INGREDIENTS | SERVES 8

1 cup raw cashews

1 cup water

½ cup unsweetened soymilk

3 cups vegetable broth

Juice of ½ lemon

½ cup nutritional yeast

1 teaspoon mustard

2 cloves garlic, minced

2 teaspoons salt

1 teaspoon pepper

1. In a blender, place the cashews, water, and soymilk. Process until very smooth.

2. In a 4-quart slow cooker, pour the blended cashew sauce and all remaining ingredients and stir well. Cover and cook over low heat for 1 hour.

Cooking with Cashews

Cashews are an excellent ingredient to use when you want to create a creamy vegan dish, but be sure to use raw cashews, not roasted or cooked in any other way. Also, remember that nuts are high in calories and fat, so they should be consumed in small quantities.

Puttanesca Sauce VN

You can easily omit the anchovies found in the recipes for many puttanesca sauces and replace it with olive brine, the liquid that olives are packed in.

INGREDIENTS | SERVES 6

1 tablespoon olive oil

4 cloves garlic, minced

1 medium onion, diced

1 cup sliced black olives

1 tablespoon olive brine

1 (28 ounce) can crushed tomatoes

1 (15-ounce) can diced tomatoes

1 tablespoon crushed red pepper

2 tablespoons drained nonpareil-sized capers

2 tablespoons fresh basil, chopped

1. In a large sauté pan, heat the olive oil over medium heat. Add the garlic and onion and sauté until soft, about 3–4 minutes.

2. In a 4-quart slow cooker, place the onions and garlic; add the remaining ingredients. Stir to distribute the ingredients evenly.

3. Cook on low for 4–6 hours. If the sauce looks very wet at the end of the cooking time, remove the lid and cook on high for 15–30 minutes before serving.

What Is Sautéing?

Sautéing is a method of cooking that uses a small amount of fat to cook food in a shallow pan over medium-high heat. The goal is to brown the food while preserving its color, moisture, and flavor.

Eggplant Caponata

Serve this on small slices of Italian bread as an appetizer or use as a filling in sandwiches or wraps.

INGREDIENTS | SERVES 8

2 (1-pound) eggplants
1 teaspoon olive oil
1 medium red onion, diced
4 cloves garlic, minced
1 stalk celery, diced
2 large tomatoes, diced
2 tablespoons nonpareil capers
2 tablespoons toasted pine nuts
1 teaspoon red pepper flakes
¼ cup red wine vinegar

1. Pierce the eggplants with a fork. Cook on high in a 4- or 6-quart slow cooker for 2 hours.

2. Allow to cool. Peel off the skin. Slice each in half and remove the seeds. Discard the skin and seeds.

3. Place the pulp in a food processor. Pulse until smooth. Set aside.

4. Heat the oil in a nonstick skillet. Sauté the onion, garlic, and celery until the onion is soft.

5. Add the eggplant and tomatoes. Sauté 3 minutes.

6. Return to the slow cooker and add the capers, pine nuts, red pepper flakes, and vinegar. Stir. Cook on low 30 minutes. Stir prior to serving.

Portobello Barley

This method of cooking barley makes it as creamy as risotto, but with the bonus of being high in fiber.

INGREDIENTS | SERVES 8

1 teaspoon olive oil

2 shallots, minced

2 cloves garlic, minced

3 portobello mushroom caps, sliced

1 cup pearl barley

3¼ cups water

¼ teaspoon salt

½ teaspoon freshly ground black pepper

1 teaspoon crushed rosemary

1 teaspoon dried chervil

¼ cup grated Parmesan or vegan Parmesan

1. Heat the oil in a nonstick skillet. Sauté the shallots, garlic, and mushrooms until softened, about 3–4 minutes.

2. Place the mushroom mixture into a 4-quart slow cooker. Add the barley, water, salt, pepper, rosemary, and chervil. Stir.

3. Cover and cook on low for 8–9 hours or on high for 4 hours.

4. Turn off the slow cooker and stir in the Parmesan. Serve immediately.

Chervil

Chervil is an herb of the parsley family. It has delicate, curly leaves almost like carrot tops. Its mild flavor, which includes hints of anise, is easily overwhelmed by stronger flavors. Fresh parsley, tarragon, or a combination of both can easily substitute for chervil.

Cuban Black Beans VN

Traditionally served with rice, Cuban-style black beans are also great served with tortillas and fresh avocado slices.

INGREDIENTS | SERVES 4

½ teaspoon apple cider vinegar

¼ cup diced onion

1 (15-ounce) can black beans, drained

2 cloves garlic, minced

1 jalapeño pepper, minced

½ teaspoon oregano

¼ teaspoon cumin

1. Place all ingredients into a 2-quart slow cooker. Stir to distribute all the ingredients evenly.

2. Cover and cook on low for 6–8 hours. Stir before serving.

Cuban Cuisine

Cuban cuisine is influenced by French, African, Arab, Chinese, Portuguese, and Spanish cultures. Traditionally primarily a peasant food, it is rarely fried but rather sautéed or slow cooked, and is unconcerned with exact measurements. Many dishes have a sofrito for their base, a mixture of onion, green pepper, garlic, oregano, and ground pepper quick-fried in olive oil, used to cook black beans as well as other dishes.

Hoppin' John VN

Hoppin' John is traditionally eaten on New Year's Day. Eating it as the first meal of the day is supposed to ensure health and prosperity for the coming year.

INGREDIENTS | SERVES 8

1 cup dried black-eyed peas, rehydrated
¾ cup water
1 teaspoon liquid smoke
1 teaspoon red pepper flakes
3 cups diced mustard or collard greens
1 (14.5-ounce) can tomatoes
½ teaspoon freshly ground black pepper
¼ teaspoon salt
1 teaspoon dried oregano

1. Place all ingredients into a 4-quart slow cooker. Stir.

2. Cover and cook on high for 5 hours.

Quick Prep for Black-Eyed Peas

Here's a method to quickly and easily prepare black-eyed peas. Place the peas in a large stockpot. Cover completely with water and bring to a boil. Boil 2 minutes, reduce heat, and simmer for 1 hour.

Ginger-Lime Tofu VN

The slow cooker does all the work in this recipe, creating a healthy yet impressive dish that requires virtually no hands-on time.

INGREDIENTS | SERVES 8

2 (14-ounce) packages extra-firm tofu, pressed and sliced into fourths

¼ cup minced fresh ginger

¼ cup lime juice

1 medium lime, thinly sliced

1 medium onion, thinly sliced

1. Place the tofu fillets in a 6- to 7-quart slow cooker. Pour the ginger and lime juice over the tofu, then arrange the lime and then the onion in a single layer over the top.

2. Cook on low for 3–4 hours.

Cracked!

Before each use, check your slow cooker for cracks. Even small cracks in the glaze can allow bacteria to grow in the ceramic insert. If there are cracks, replace the insert or the whole slow cooker.

Sweet-and-Sour Tofu VN

This recipe is not only kid friendly but vegan and gluten-free. Serve it over rice and garnish with diced green onions.

INGREDIENTS | SERVES 6

1 (12-ounce) package extra-firm tofu, cubed

¼ cup rice vinegar

3 tablespoons water

1 tablespoon sesame seeds

1 tablespoon brown sugar

1 tablespoon tamari

1 tablespoon pineapple juice

1 teaspoon ground ginger

¾ cup pineapple chunks

1 cup snow peas

½ cup sliced onion

1. Spray a nonstick skillet with cooking spray. Sauté the tofu until it is lightly browned on each side. Add to a 4-quart slow cooker.

2. In a small bowl, whisk together the vinegar, water, sesame seeds, brown sugar, tamari, pineapple juice, and ginger until the sugar fully dissolves. Pour over the tofu.

3. Add the remaining ingredients.

4. Cover and cook on low for 4 hours. Remove the lid and cook on low for 30 minutes.

Recipe Variation

For added texture, try breading the tofu with flour or panko bread crumbs and then pan-frying it in 2 tablespoons of oil. You can then proceed with the remainder of the recipe.

General Tso's Tofu

*The combination of sweet and spicy is what makes this dish a
hit at Chinese restaurants across the country.*

INGREDIENTS | SERVES 2

1 (14-ounce) package extra-firm tofu, pressed and cubed

1 cup water

2 tablespoons cornstarch

2 cloves garlic, minced

1 teaspoon ginger, minced

⅛ cup sugar

¼ cup soy sauce

⅛ cup white wine vinegar

⅛ cup sherry

2 teaspoons cayenne pepper

2 tablespoons vegetable oil

2 cups broccoli, chopped

Add all ingredients to a 4-quart slow cooker. Cover and
cook on medium heat for 4 hours.

Coconut Rice Pudding

Rice pudding, also referred to as porridge, is eaten around the world in many different forms.

INGREDIENTS | SERVES 8

1 cup white rice

1 quart soymilk

½ cup butter or vegan margarine

⅛ cup shredded coconut

1 cup sugar

1 teaspoon cinnamon

¼ teaspoon salt

Add all ingredients to a 4-quart slow cooker. Cover and
cook on low heat for 6 hours.

Easy Applesauce VN

Homemade applesauce is easy to make and tastes much better than what you can get in the store. It freezes well, too, so you can make extra when apples are in season.

INGREDIENTS | MAKES ABOUT 4 CUPS

10 medium apples, peeled, cored, and sliced

2 tablespoons fresh lemon juice

2 tablespoons water

6" cinnamon stick (optional)

Sugar to taste (optional)

1. In a 4-quart slow cooker, add the apples, lemon juice, water, and cinnamon stick, if using. Stir to mix.

2. Cover and cook on low for 5 hours or until the apples are soft and tender.

3. For chunky applesauce, mash the apples with a potato masher. For smooth applesauce, purée in a food processor or blender, use an immersion blender, or press through a food mill or large-meshed strainer.

4. While applesauce is still warm, add sugar to taste, if desired. Store covered in the refrigerator for up to 2 weeks or freeze.

Ginger Poached Pears VN

Fresh ginger best compliments pear flavor, but if you only have ground, start by adding a smaller amount and then increasing after tasting.

INGREDIENTS | SERVES 8

5 pears, peeled, cored, and cut into wedges

3 cups water

1 cup white sugar

2 tablespoons ginger, minced

1 teaspoon cinnamon

Add all ingredients to a 4-quart slow cooker. Cover and cook on low heat for 4 hours.

CHAPTER 14

Desserts and Baked Goods

Pumpkin Bread

Don't you dare use canned pumpkin for this bread! If you can't find sugar pumpkins, use butternut squash instead.

INGREDIENTS | SERVES 10

2 cups boiled and mashed pumpkin
1 cup sugar
1 cup brown sugar
½ cup oil
1 large egg
2½ cups flour
½ teaspoon salt
½ teaspoon cinnamon
½ teaspoon cloves
¼ teaspoon nutmeg
2 teaspoons baking soda
1 cup chopped pecans

1. Preheat oven to 350°F.

2. In a large bowl, combine pumpkin, sugar, brown sugar, oil, and egg. Mix well.

3. In a medium bowl, combine the remaining ingredients, except nuts, and mix well. Add to pumpkin mixture. Stir in nuts.

4. Bake in greased loaf pan for 1 hour. Test periodically by inserting a toothpick into the center of the loaf; when the toothpick comes out clean, the bread is done.

Simple Cloverleaf Dinner Rolls

Nothing brings a more comforting aroma to the house than baking rolls. The dough can be made and rolled in advance, then frozen. Just thaw and rise before baking.

INGREDIENTS | SERVES 12

1 envelope active dry yeast
1 cup milk, lukewarm (about 110°F)
6 tablespoons butter, divided
3 tablespoons sugar
1 large egg
1 teaspoon salt
3½–4 cups all-purpose flour

1. In a large mixing bowl, combine yeast with 3 tablespoons of lukewarm water. Let stand 5 minutes.

2. Add milk, 4 tablespoons butter, sugar, egg, and salt; mix well with a wooden spoon.

3. Gradually add 2 cups of flour and mix for 1 minute. Gradually mix in 1½–2 cups more flour until dough is moist but not sticky.

4. Knead dough for 10 minutes until it's smooth and elastic. Form into a ball and place in a mixing bowl with a few drops of oil; toss to coat. Cover bowl with plastic wrap; allow to rise in a warm place until double in size, about 1–1½ hours. Knead dough 1 minute; cover and refrigerate 30 minutes.

5. Form into 36 tight, round balls, rolling them against an unfloured surface. In a buttered muffin tin, place 3 balls in each muffin cup; cover loosely with greased plastic wrap. Allow to rise in a warm place until double in size, about 1–½ hours.

6. Heat oven to 375°F. Melt remaining butter and brush it onto the rolls. Bake 25–30 minutes until golden brown.

Chocolate Mousse

While not exactly diet food, this mousse contains no egg yolks, making it lighter in both taste and fat than French chocolate mousse.

INGREDIENTS | SERVES 8

1½ tablespoons kirshwasser or cherry brandy

1½ tablespoons dark rum (such as Meyer's)

1 tablespoon plus a few drops vanilla extract

6 ounces dark (bittersweet) chocolate

1½ cups heavy cream

2½ tablespoons confectioners' sugar

6 egg whites, whipped to medium-soft peaks, refrigerated

8 small mint leaves

1. Chill 8 (8-ounce) dessert dishes.

2. Combine cherry brandy, dark rum, 1 tablespoon vanilla extract, and chocolate in a double boiler (or a steel mixing bowl set over a pot of simmering water). Warm, stirring occasionally, until melted and smooth.

3. In a medium bowl, whip together the cream, confectioners' sugar, and a few drops of vanilla until it forms soft peaks when the whisk is lifted from it.

4. Gently fold ⅓ of the whipped cream into the chocolate mixture. Fold the chocolate mixture back into the rest of the whipped cream, mixing only as much as is necessary to incorporate it most of the way (a few streaks of chocolate are okay).

5. Fold the whipped egg whites very gently into the chocolate cream mixture just barely enough to incorporate. Fill the mousse into a pastry bag with a star tip (or a plastic bag with a corner cut out) and pipe it into the chilled dishes.

6. Cover the dishes individually with plastic wrap and chill for at least 6 hours until set. Garnish each dish with a mint leaf.

Old-Fashioned Baked Apples

Serve these delicious apples warm after an autumn day outside. They'll warm you right up. They can even be made in the microwave.

INGREDIENTS | SERVES 4

4 large Rome or Cortland apples
8 whole cloves
2 ounces butter (½ stick)
⅓ cup light brown sugar
½ teaspoon ground cinnamon

Microwave Option

This dish works in the microwave oven, though the flavor develops better in the conventional oven. To microwave, follow steps one and two, then score the apples 1" from the bottom, cover, and cook on high for five minutes per apple.

1. Preheat oven to 350°F.

2. Wash and dry apples thoroughly. Using a small knife, cut a divot from the top of the apples, leaving the stem intact. This "cover" will be replaced when baking. Scoop out the seeds and core with a melon baller or small spoon. Drop 2 cloves into each apple.

3. In a small bowl, knead together the butter and brown sugar, along with the cinnamon, until it is a paste. Divide equally over the scooped apples, leaving enough space to replace the tops.

4. Place apples in a baking dish with ½ cup of water on the bottom. Bake for 1 hour. Sprinkle with cinnamon or powdered sugar before serving.

Cinnamon-Apple Cobbler with Rome Beauty Apples

This dessert is an American favorite, and it makes a beautiful presentation at a picnic.

INGREDIENTS | SERVES 8

Filling:

8 or 9 Rome Beauty apples, peeled, cored, and diced into 1" pieces

Pinch of salt

¼ teaspoon ground nutmeg

1 capful of vanilla extract

1½ teaspoons ground cinnamon

½ cup sugar

¼ cup flour

Juice of ½ lemon

Biscuit Topping:

3 cups flour

½ teaspoon salt

2 teaspoons baking powder

2 large eggs

½ cup sugar

⅔ cup milk

6 ounces melted butter

1. Make the filling: Preheat oven to 375°F. In a large bowl, mix together the apples, pinch of salt, nutmeg, vanilla, cinnamon, ½ cup sugar, ¼ cup flour, and lemon juice. Place in a 6" × 10" baking dish.

2. Make the topping: In a medium bowl, sift together the flour, salt, and baking powder. In a separate bowl, combine the eggs, sugar, milk, and melted butter.

3. Add the wet ingredients to the dry, mixing only until they are well combined. Do not overmix. Batter should have consistency of thick oatmeal. Adjust with milk if necessary.

4. Spread batter over fruit filling as evenly as possible with your hands. Some holes are natural and will make for a more attractive presentation.

5. Bake on bottom shelf of oven for 90 minutes, turning halfway through and checking after 1 hour. Fruit should be bubbling thoroughly and biscuit topping should be nicely browned. Allow to cool at least 15 minutes before serving with vanilla ice cream and a sprig of fresh mint.

Pink McIntosh Applesauce with Cranberry Chutney VN

Don't peel the apples before making this applesauce. Cooking the Macs and Delicious apples with the skins on gives this sauce its distinctive pink color.

INGREDIENTS | SERVES 6

2 cups fresh or frozen cranberries

1¼ cups sugar, divided

¼ cup very finely diced red onion

6 whole cloves

½ cup water, divided

1 cinnamon stick, about 2" long

8 McIntosh and 2 Red Delicious apples, quartered

1. In a small, heavy-bottomed saucepot, combine cranberries, 1 cup sugar, onion, cloves, and ¼ cup water. Simmer 10–15 minutes until all cranberries are broken and have a saucy consistency. Set aside

2. Warm the cinnamon stick, dry, in a heavy-bottomed pot large enough to hold all the apples. Reduce heat to low and add the apples, ¼ cup sugar, and ¼ cup water. Cover tightly.

3. Simmer gently for 40 minutes, then uncover and simmer 10 minutes more.

4. Strain through a food mill or push through a strainer with a flexible spatula. Cool and serve with a dollop of cranberry chutney.

Golden Delicious Apple-Strawberry Crisp

Tailor this to suit your tastes and what's available. Try other berries or different nuts.

INGREDIENTS | SERVES 8

1 cup almonds, toasted and roughly chopped

8 or 9 Golden Delicious apples, peeled, cored, and cut into 1" cubes

3 tablespoons granulated sugar

¼ teaspoon ground cloves

½ teaspoon ground cinnamon

Juice of ½ lemon

1 cup plus 2 tablespoons all-purpose flour

1 cup light brown sugar

⅛ teaspoon salt

4 ounces (1 stick) unsalted butter, cold, cut into pea-sized pieces

1. Toast almonds on a baking sheet lightly in moderate oven at about 300°F. Cool.

2. Increase temperature to 350°F.

3. In a large bowl, toss the apples with granulated sugar, spices, lemon juice, and 2 tablespoons flour. Fill into a 6" × 10" baking dish.

4. Using your hands, rub together 1 cup flour, brown sugar, salt, and butter until mixture clumps. Add toasted nuts and cover the fruit evenly with this topping. Bake for 1 hour until fruit is bubbling and topping is crisp. Serve with vanilla whipped cream or vanilla ice cream.

Toasting Nuts for Fresher Flavor and Crispness

To wake up the natural flavor of nuts, and to ensure that they're crisp and delicious, heat them on the stovetop or in the oven for a few moments. For the stovetop, spread the nuts into a dry skillet and heat over medium heat until their natural oils come to the surface, giving them a sheen. For the oven, spread the nuts into a single layer on a baking sheet and toast for 5–10 minutes at 350°F, until the oils are visible. Cool nuts to just above room temperature before serving.

Banana Nut Bread

*For fun, you can make this recipe into banana nut cupcakes or mini muffins
by baking them for half the time in muffin tins. It freezes well.*

INGREDIENTS | SERVES 10

1¼ cups all-purpose flour

1 teaspoon baking soda

¼ teaspoon baking powder

½ teaspoon cinnamon

½ teaspoon salt

1 cup sugar

2 large eggs

½ cup oil

3 medium overripe bananas, mashed
(1¼ cups)

1 teaspoon vanilla extract

¾ cup coarsely chopped walnuts,
toasted lightly in a dry pan until fragrant

How Large Is a Large Egg?

"Large" eggs connote an actual measure-
ment, not a rough estimate. Buy eggs
labeled "large" when they're specified in
a recipe.

1. Heat oven to 350°F. Butter a 9" × 5" loaf pan.

2. In a mixing bowl, whisk together the flour, baking
   soda, baking powder, cinnamon, and salt.

3. In a separate bowl, whisk together the sugar, eggs, and
   oil; whip vigorously until creamy and light in color,
   about 5 minutes. Add mashed bananas and vanilla
   extract to the egg mixture.

4. Add the flour mixture to the wet ingredients in 3
   additions, mixing only as much as necessary to
   incorporate the ingredients, since overmixing will
   toughen the batter. Stir in the nuts and pour batter into
   prepared pan.

5. Bake in center of oven until the top is springy and a
   toothpick inserted in the center comes out clean,
   about 50–60 minutes. Allow to cool for 10 minutes;
   transfer to a rack to cool completely before slicing.

Spicy Southwestern Cornbread

This smoky cornbread is a warm and delicious treat on its own or served alongside a bowl of your favorite soup.

INGREDIENTS | SERVES 20

4½ cups fine cornmeal

1 cup sugar

2 cups all-purpose flour

4 tablespoons baking powder

1 tablespoon baking soda

4 teaspoons table salt

3½ cups buttermilk

1 cup vegetable oil

1 cup (2 sticks) melted butter

6 large eggs

1½ tablespoons chopped jalapeño peppers

2 tablespoons puréed chipotle in adobo

1. Heat oven to 400°F.

2. In a large mixing bowl, combine the cornmeal, sugar, flour, baking powder, baking soda, and salt. Mix thoroughly with a stiff wire whisk or spoon to combine well and break up any lumps.

3. In a separate mixing bowl, mix the buttermilk, oil, melted butter, eggs, jalapeños, and chipotle; whisk well to combine. Fold the cornmeal mixture into the buttermilk mixture in 3 additions, mixing only as much as necessary to combine ingredients. Pour the batter into two 9" × 5" loaf pans, or one 9" × 13" baking dish. It is not necessary to grease the pans.

4. Bake until the top springs back when pressed and a toothpick comes out clean when inserted into the center. Cook 10 minutes before turning onto a rack to cool completely.

Sour Cream Butter Cake

Frost this cake with homemade Buttercream Frosting (see recipe in this chapter) or a store-bought favorite. The cake is rich and moist, so serve it in very thin slices.

INGREDIENTS | SERVES 12

4 egg yolks

⅔ cup sour cream, divided

1½ teaspoons vanilla

2 cups sifted cake flour

1 cup sugar

½ teaspoon baking powder

½ teaspoon baking soda

½ teaspoon salt

6 ounces (1½ sticks) unsalted butter, softened to room temperature

Buttercream Frosting (see recipe in this chapter)

It Takes a Tender Hand to Make a Tender Cake

Any stirring, kneading, mixing, or working of a batter or dough causes gluten, a natural protein in wheat flour, to develop strands. This makes cakes tough, muffins leathery, and scones basically unfriendly. When a recipe says, "stir or knead only as much as necessary to combine the ingredients," it's telling you that you should avoid developing the gluten in this recipe, lest your product becomes tough as nails.

1. Heat oven to 350°F. Grease a 9" cake pan, dust it with flour, and line the bottom with waxed paper.

2. In a medium bowl, whisk together the yolks, a quarter of the sour cream, and the vanilla.

3. In a large, separate bowl, mix the flour, sugar, baking powder, baking soda, and salt; whisk vigorously to combine.

4. Add the butter and remaining sour cream to the flour mixture and mix well until flour is completely moistened. Add the egg mixture to the flour mixture in 3 separate additions, mixing between each addition. Pour into prepared cake pan.

5. Bake in the middle of the oven until a toothpick inserted in the center comes out clean, usually about 35–40 minutes. Start checking at 25 minutes, since oven temperatures and ingredient characteristics vary and it might be done quicker. Cool 10 minutes, then take out of pan and cool completely on a wire rack.

6. To frost, cut laterally in half and frost both sections, then stack smooth sides and refrigerate to set.

Flourless Chocolate Cake

Luxury incarnate, this voluptuous chocolate cake is a vehicle for fine chocolate, so use the best you can get. Chocolate is high in heart-healthy antioxidants.

INGREDIENTS | SERVES 12

8 large eggs

1 pound semisweet chocolate

8 ounces (2 sticks) unsalted butter, cut into pieces the size of a hazelnut

¼ cup strong brewed coffee

¼ cup cocoa nibs or mini chocolate chips

1. Heat oven to 325°F. Grease an 8" or 9" springform pan and line the bottom with waxed paper. Wrap the outside of the pan in foil to prevent leaks. Prepare a pot of boiling water.

2. Using a handheld or standing electric mixer, beat the eggs until double in volume (about 1 quart), about 5 minutes.

3. Melt the chocolate, butter, and coffee in a double boiler or microwave until very smooth, stirring occasionally. Fold in the whipped eggs in 3 additions, mixing only enough as is necessary to incorporate them. Pour into prepared springform pan.

4. Place springform into a deep roasting pan and place on the lower middle rack of the oven. Pour enough boiling water into the roasting pan to come about halfway up on the sides of the cake. Bake about 25 minutes until the cake rises slightly, has a thin and wispy crust, and reads 140°F on an instant-read thermometer inserted in the center.

5. Transfer springform to a wire rack and cool to room temperature. Refrigerate overnight. Warm sides of springform with a hot, wet towel to loosen, then pop open, cut with a hot, wet knife, and top with cocoa nibs.

Buttercream Frosting

For chocolate buttercream, add 4 ounces of melted chocolate to this recipe at the end. It's excellent with milk chocolate. You can also add fruit liqueur or espresso to flavor the frosting.

INGREDIENTS | MAKES ENOUGH TO FROST 1 (9") CAKE

1½ cups sugar

½ cup water

2 large eggs plus 4 egg yolks

1 pound unsalted butter, softened to room temperature

2 teaspoons vanilla extract

1. In a small saucepan, boil the sugar and water together without stirring until slightly thick and between 234°F and 240°F on a candy thermometer.

2. Whisk together eggs and yolks in a double boiler or steel bowl atop a pot of simmering water. Gradually whisk in the hot sugar syrup; heat, whisking constantly, until the mixture is hot to the touch, thick, and ribbony. Remove bowl from heat and continue whisking until cool, about 5 minutes more.

3. In a mixer or bowl, beat the butter until it is fluffy and light. Gradually beat the whipped butter into the egg mixture, adding it in tablespoonfuls. Add the vanilla and whisk to incorporate. Cool over an ice-water bath until it reaches a comfortable consistency for spreading. Keeps in the refrigerator for up to 1 week.

Blondies

Chewy butterscotch-flavored chocolate-chunk brownies are called blondies, and taste great out of the icebox.

INGREDIENTS | MAKES 36

1½ cups all-purpose flour

½ teaspoon baking powder

½ teaspoon salt

6 ounces (1½ sticks) unsalted butter, at room temperature

1¾ cups brown sugar, packed

2 teaspoons vanilla extract

3 large eggs

6 ounces (about 1 cup) semisweet chocolate chunks or morsels

1. Heat oven to 350°F. Butter a 9" baking pan.

2. In a medium bowl using a stiff wire whisk, whisk together the flour, baking powder, and salt.

3. In another medium bowl, combine the butter, brown sugar, and vanilla and cream together using an electric mixer or by hand until light and fluffy, about 2 minutes. Gradually beat in the eggs, working each 1 in completely before adding the next. Scrape down mixing bowl; add the flour mixture. Beat just long enough to incorporate. Mix in chocolate chunks. Transfer the batter into the prepared baking pan and smooth with a spatula.

4. Bake until a toothpick inserted in the center comes out clean, about 30–35 minutes. Cool at room temperature at least 1 hour. Cut into 36 pieces. Will keep refrigerated for 1 week or in freezer for up to 6 weeks.

Pears Poached in White Wine with Strawberry Sauce

This simply beautiful dessert is perfect in any season. It's light, contains no cholesterol, and finishes an elegant dinner or an everyday lunch with a touch of class.

INGREDIENTS | SERVES 8

1 (750-ml) bottle white wine

Zest of 1 large lemon, shaved off with a vegetable peeler in strips

8 whole cloves

2 whole cinnamon sticks

1 cup sugar, divided

4 whole Bosc pears, peeled (leave stems intact)

1 pint strawberries, hulled and halved

1 teaspoon vanilla

8 sprigs fresh mint

1. Combine the wine, lemon zest, cloves, cinnamon sticks, and ½ cup sugar in a large (4–5 quart) pot and bring to a boil.

2. Reduce heat to a simmer and add the pears, arranging them so they are mostly submerged. Cover tightly and cook slowly for 5 minutes; remove from heat and leave to steep 20 minutes. Chill.

3. In a blender, combine the strawberries, remaining ½ cup sugar, and vanilla. Purée until smooth, adding a few drops of water if necessary to get things started.

4. Spoon the sauce onto dessert plates to form small pools midplate. Serve the pears atop the sauce, garnished with mint sprigs at the stem end.

Chocolate Chip Cookies

This classic and delicious cookie bakes up perfectly.

INGREDIENTS | SERVES 12

2½ cups all-purpose flour
1 teaspoon baking soda
1 teaspoon salt
1 cup (2 sticks) unsalted butter, softened
¾ cup sugar
¾ cup (packed) light brown sugar
1 teaspoon vanilla extract
2 large eggs
2 cups (12-ounce package) semisweet chocolate morsels

1. Heat oven to 375°F.

2. In a mixing bowl, whisk together flour, baking soda, and salt.

3. In a separate bowl, cream together the butter, granulated sugar, brown sugar, and vanilla using a wooden spoon. Add the eggs one at a time, mixing until incorporated before adding the next one.

4. Add the flour in 3 additions, mixing just enough to incorporate after each addition. Stir in the chocolate chips.

5. Drop the dough in tablespoon-sized drops onto ungreased baking sheets. Bake until golden, about 10 minutes. Cool the pans for a few minutes before transferring the cookies to a wire rack to cool completely.

Banana-Pineapple-Yogurt Frosty

For a winning taste, look for a fruit yogurt made from one or a combination of tropical fruits.

INGREDIENTS | SERVES 2

1½ cups nonfat milk or soymilk

1 (6-ounce) container nonfat tropical fruit yogurt

2 medium ripe bananas

1 cup well-drained crushed pineapple

2 teaspoons vanilla extract

2 teaspoons sugar, or to taste

Sprinkle ground nutmeg

1. Combine all the ingredients in the container of a blender and process until smooth.

2. Pour the mixture into a suitable container and chill in the freezer for about 30 minutes or until ice forms around the edges of the container. Stir again and serve.

Almond Cornstarch Fruit Pudding

An old-fashioned cornstarch pudding, this smooth and creamy mixture forms a soothing backdrop to the assertive fruit flavors. A cook's tip: before adding cornstarch to a liquid, always mix cornstarch first with a little liquid to make a paste.

INGREDIENTS | SERVES 4

3 tablespoons cornstarch

2 cups almond-flavored soymilk, divided

2 egg yolks

½ cup sugar

2 teaspoons almond extract

1 teaspoon vanilla extract

Pinch salt

2 tablespoons butter

1 cup blueberries

1 cup sliced strawberries

1. In a medium mixing bowl, combine the cornstarch with 3 tablespoons soymilk. Add the egg yolks and sugar and mix to combine. Stir in ½ cup soymilk to make a paste.

2. Heat the remaining soymilk in a large saucepan over medium-low to medium heat and, stirring gently, slowly pour in the cornstarch mixture. Increase the heat to medium-high and bring the mixture to a boil. Immediately reduce the heat to medium-low and, stirring gently, add the almond and vanilla extracts and the salt and butter.

3. Meanwhile, put the fruit into a 2-quart serving bowl. When the pudding mixture is thickened slightly, pour it over the fruit. Let the pudding cool slightly before serving or chill and serve cold.

Nectarine-Cherry Tart with Oat Crumble Topping

These ingredients come together to yield an old-fashioned taste treat. Instead of heavy cream, you may want to substitute vanilla ice cream.

INGREDIENTS | SERVES 4–6

2 large ripe nectarines, unpeeled and thinly sliced

2 cups fresh or frozen pitted cherries

½ cup firmly packed brown sugar

3 tablespoons instant tapioca

1 tablespoon firm butter, diced

1 teaspoon vanilla extract

1 (9") deep-dish pie crust

1 cup old-fashioned rolled oats

1 cup toasted walnut pieces

½ cup brown sugar

3 tablespoons flour

¼ cup butter

Heavy cream for topping (optional)

1. Preheat the oven to 350°F.

2. In a medium bowl, toss the nectarine slices and cherries together, then add ½ cup brown sugar and tapioca. When this mixture is well combined, add the butter and vanilla extract. Spoon the mixture into the pie crust.

3. To make the topping, combine the oats, walnut pieces, ½ cup brown sugar, flour, and butter in a medium bowl and mix well until the topping is crumbly. Sprinkle over the filling and press down.

4. Bake until the crust and topping are brown, about 30 minutes. Serve warm and drizzle each slice with heavy cream, if using.

Fruited Blondies

Typically, brownies are just chocolate with nuts sometimes mixed into the batter. But this takes the fudgy brownie to a different level with white chocolate and bits of dried fruit.

INGREDIENTS | SERVES 9

½ cup (1 stick) unsalted butter

8 ounces white chocolate

¾ cup firmly packed light brown sugar

1 large egg, lightly beaten

1 teaspoon vanilla extract

1 cup white whole-wheat flour

1 teaspoon baking powder

1 teaspoon salt

⅓ cup dried blueberries, or more as desired

⅓ cup dried cranberries or dried cherries, or more as desired

1. Melt the butter and chocolate together in a double boiler over just-simmering water. When melted, remove from the heat and set aside to cool.

2. Preheat oven to 350°F. Lightly butter an 8" or 9" cake pan.

3. In a medium mixing bowl, beat together the sugar and egg until light and fluffy. Beat in the vanilla.

4. Combine the flour, baking powder, and salt in a separate bowl and beat with the sugar mixture until just incorporated. Stir in the butter-chocolate mixture gently and the 2 different berries until just incorporated. Spoon the batter into the prepared pan.

5. Bake the blondies for about 25 minutes or until the center feels firm and a toothpick inserted in the center comes out clean. Cool on a rack before slicing.

Margo's Rhubarb and Pineapple Tart

This unusual dessert is just fine if served plain, but adding whipped cream or vanilla ice cream elevates it to another dimension.

INGREDIENTS | SERVES 4–6

3 cups chopped fresh or frozen rhubarb

2 cups canned crushed pineapple, well drained

1 cup sugar

2 tablespoons cornstarch

1 sheet frozen puff pastry, thawed

1. Preheat oven to 350°F.

2. Combine the rhubarb, pineapple, sugar, and cornstarch in a large mixing bowl, mixing well.

3. On a lightly floured surface, roll out the sheet of puff pastry just enough to fit into a deep 1½-quart baking dish. Press it into the dish and fill it with the fruit mixture. Fold the corners in toward the center.

4. Bake the tart for about 40 minutes or until the crust has puffed and turned brown. Serve it hot or still warm.

Brazilian-Style Passion Fruit Pudding

For best results, chill the coconut milk before use, and then use only the thickened top cream—do not include the thin coconut water at the bottom of the can. The acidic quality of the fruit thickens the mixture until it becomes firm.

INGREDIENTS | SERVES 6

1 (14-ounce) can coconut milk, well chilled

1 (14-ounce) can sweetened condensed milk

1 (16.8-ounce) bottle passion fruit concentrate

2 cups cubed pound cake

1 cup toasted shredded coconut

Fresh fruits such as cut-up strawberries or blueberries, for garnish

1. Carefully scoop out the thick layer of coconut milk and put it into a bowl. Beat the milk until it thickens and resembles partially whipped heavy cream. Stir in the condensed milk. Fill the condensed milk can with the passion fruit concentrate and pour it into the mixing bowl. Stir well to combine the milks and juice.

2. Line the bottom of a 2-quart dessert bowl with the pound cake. Pour the passion fruit mixture over top and chill until firm.

3. To serve, sprinkle the toasted coconut over the mousse, spoon the mixture into individual bowls, and garnish with fresh fruits as desired.

Chocolate Tofu Pudding

This very easy-to-make pudding tastes like an extravagantly decadent mousse with loads of cream, but its rich texture—and extra protein—comes from tofu. Be sure to use the "cook-and-serve" pudding, not the instant type.

INGREDIENTS | SERVES 4

2 cups nonfat milk or soymilk

1½ cups silken firm tofu

2 (1.3-ounce) boxes sugar-free and fat-free chocolate pudding mixture

1 cup chocolate morsels

1. Combine the milk, tofu, and pudding mixture in a blender and process until smooth. Pour the mixture into a saucepan. Heat slowly over medium-low heat, stirring constantly, until the mixture thickens.

2. Remove from the heat, stir in the chocolate bits, and pour into a heatproof bowl. Chill until ready to serve.

Tropical Cheesecake

This dessert lends itself to variations: Instead of diced papaya, you may substitute diced dried pineapple or mango and use crushed macadamia nuts instead of almonds.

INGREDIENTS | SERVES 8

2 cups crushed gingersnaps

4 tablespoons butter, melted

2 tablespoons freshly grated fresh ginger

2 tablespoons brown sugar

2 pounds cream cheese, at room temperature

2 cups granulated sugar, or to taste

4 large eggs

2 tablespoons cornstarch

2 teaspoons vanilla extract

Pinch of salt

½ cup shredded coconut

½ cup diced dried papaya

½ cup thinly sliced almonds

1. Preheat oven to 325°F.

2. Combine the crushed gingersnaps and the butter in a medium bowl, then press the mixture into the bottom of a 10" springform pan. Sprinkle the grated ginger and brown sugar on top of the crumbs, pressing them into the crust.

3. In a medium bowl, beat the cream cheese and sugar until smooth. Beat in eggs one at a time until well combined. Add cornstarch, vanilla extract, and salt. Stir in the coconut and fruit by hand.

4. Pour half the mixture onto the crust, sprinkle a layer of almonds on top, and pour on the remaining mixture.

5. Bake for at least 1 hour and 20 minutes or until the center is firm; turn off the heat but leave the cheesecake in the oven until it is cool. Then refrigerate it for at least 12 hours before slicing.

Berry-Streusel Tart

This dessert is so easy to make that you may use it often, especially when last-minute friends drop by and want something sweet. You can serve this hot or cold and add ice cream or a whipped topping, as you wish.

INGREDIENTS | SERVES 6

1 (16½-ounce) package sugar cookie dough, divided

½ cup all-purpose flour

3 cups fresh or frozen mixed berries

¼ cup granulated sugar

2 tablespoons cornstarch

1 teaspoon almond extract

1. Preheat oven to 350°F. Lightly butter and flour an 8" × 8" or 9" × 9" round or square cake pan.

2. Slice the cookie dough into 2 portions, using ¾ of the dough for the crust. Press the dough into the bottom of the pan.

3. In a medium bowl, combine the flour and the remaining cookie dough, crumbling the mixture with your fingertips; set aside.

4. In a separate bowl, toss the berries with the granulated sugar, cornstarch, and almond extract and spoon the mixture into the pan. Sprinkle the streusel mixture evenly over top.

5. Bake for about 40 minutes or until the top has turned brown and the center feels firm. Remove from the oven and eat hot or cold.

Triple-Chocolate Cupcakes

A cross between a brownie and a muffin, these elegant chocolate morsels have an intense chocolate flavor heightened by the cocoa powder.

INGREDIENTS | MAKES 16

4 ounces unsweetened chocolate squares

½ pound (2 sticks) unsalted butter

6 large eggs

1 cup granulated sugar

¾ cup cake flour

1½ teaspoons baking powder

2 teaspoons vanilla extract

1 tablespoon cocoa powder

Pinch of salt

1 cup mini chocolate morsels

1. Preheat oven to 350°F. Spray nonstick muffin cups with nonstick cooking spray.

2. In a small saucepan, melt the chocolate and butter together over low heat. When melted, cool to room temperature.

3. Meanwhile, in a large mixing bowl, beat the eggs with the sugar until the mixture turns a pale lemon-yellow. Spoon the cooled chocolate mixture into the sugar-egg mixture and stir until combined. Stir in the cake flour, baking powder, vanilla extract, cocoa powder, and salt and beat for about 30 seconds. Stir in the chocolate morsels. Spoon the mixture into the cups until each is about two-thirds full.

4. Bake 15–18 minutes or until a toothpick inserted in the center comes out clean and the cupcakes feel firm. Cool completely.

Ginger-Tapioca Pudding

A lively ginger syrup adds a hint of the exotic to this old-fashioned favorite. To make the syrup, use about 2" fresh ginger thinly sliced and cooked with ½ cup brown sugar in 1 cup water. Boil this mixture for about 5 minutes, cool, and strain, discarding the ginger.

INGREDIENTS | SERVES 4

½ cup pearl tapioca soaked in 1 cup water for at least 12 hours

1 cup ginger syrup

1½ cups coconut milk

2 large eggs, well beaten

6 coconut macaroons, crumbled

Pearl Tapioca

The old-fashioned tapioca pudding called for using the regular, not instant, pearl tapioca made from the starch of the cassava plant. Larger and harder than the instant tapioca pearls, these require soaking for at least 12 hours, but preferably for up to 24 hours. Otherwise, they never quite soften during cooking. Despite this advance planning, the pudding is really worth the effort.

1. Combine the tapioca, ginger syrup, and coconut milk in a large saucepan. Stir in the eggs and heat over medium-low heat, stirring constantly as the mixture begins to thicken.

2. Meanwhile, sprinkle the crumbled macaroons into the bottom of a 1½-quart dessert dish.

3. When the tapioca pudding has thickened, spoon it into the dessert dish and completely chill until firm.

Mango-Ginger Ice VN

Select ripe mangoes, preferably the flat yellow varieties available seasonally. These have a subtle, sweet flavor that works well with fresh ginger.

INGREDIENTS | SERVES 4

Juice of 3 large limes

1 tablespoon freshly grated fresh ginger

3 ripe mangoes, peeled and sliced

1 teaspoon fresh lime zest

1 cup sugar syrup (see sidebar)

Combine the ingredients in the container of a blender and process until smooth. Chill the mixture and churn according to manufacturer's directions. Scoop the mixture into a container and freeze.

How Do You Make a Simple Sugar Syrup?

To make sugar syrup: Combine 3 cups water and 2 cups granulated sugar in a saucepan and cook over medium-low heat until the sugar dissolves entirely and the mixture turns slightly syrupy. Set aside to cool. Save leftovers for another use.

Ultra Chocolate-Mint Tart

For a totally different take on the filling, use a soy cream cheese instead of the regular one. Whichever you use, this tastes like a ritzy cheesecake.

INGREDIENTS | SERVES 6

1 tablespoon vegetable oil

4 ounces semisweet chocolate squares

1 pound cream cheese, at room temperature

½ cup unsifted confectioners' sugar

2 tablespoons cornstarch

2 large eggs

1 tablespoon unsweetened cocoa

1 tablespoon brandy

1 9" ready-made chocolate cookie crumb crust

½ cup mint-chocolate morsels

Confectioners' sugar for sprinkling

1. Preheat oven to 350°F.

2. Combine the vegetable oil and the chocolate squares in the top of a double boiler and melt the chocolate over just-simmering water. Set aside to cool slightly.

3. Meanwhile, in a large bowl, beat together the cream cheese, sugar, and cornstarch until smooth. Beat in the eggs one at a time. Stir in the cocoa, brandy, and melted chocolate. Spoon the mixture into the crust. Sprinkle the top with the mint-chocolate bits.

4. Bake the tart for about 1 hour or until the center is firm. Remove from the oven and cool. Before serving, sprinkle with confectioners' sugar.

Peanut Butter Cups

A baked version of a popular candy, these biscuits make a delicious dessert, but why not serve them for breakfast as well? Use 3½"-round muffin tins.

INGREDIENTS | SERVES 8

½ cup crunchy peanut butter

1 (8-ounce) package soy cream cheese, at room temperature

¾ cup packed brown sugar

1 large egg, lightly beaten

3 tablespoons cornstarch

½ cup chocolate morsels

1 (16.3-ounce) tube flaky refrigerator biscuits

1. Preheat oven to 375°F. Spray muffin tins with nonstick cooking spray.

2. Combine the peanut butter, cream cheese, and sugar in a mixing bowl and beat until smooth. Add the egg and cornstarch and beat again. Fold the morsels in by hand.

3. Roll out the biscuits one at a time on a lightly floured surface and fit each into a muffin cup so that it forms a "crust." Spoon the peanut butter mixture into each biscuit crust. Reduce the temperature to 350°F.

4. Bake the muffins for 25–30 minutes or until the center feels firm to the touch. Remove from the oven and cool to firm completely.

Appendix A: Resources

Resources for Vegetarian Food Products

www.vegparadise.com
Vegetarians in Paradise presents a comprehensive list of companies processing and marketing natural and vegetarian foods.

www.fantasticfoods.com
Fantastic World Foods is an all-natural, all-vegetarian food manufacturer of such product as soups, entrées, international dishes, and couscous and rice.

www.vegefood.com
Vegefood purports to have the largest online selection of vegetarian food, so chances are that you'll find everything you want in one location.

www.veganstore.com
Selling Pangea vegan foods and a host of all-vegan and cruelty-free housewares, clothing, and office products, plus much more, the Vegan Store has a question-answer section for people asking about all-vegan goods. The Pangea staff is located in Rockville, Maryland, but consumers can order all their products online.

General Vegetarian Resources

www.vrg.org
The Vegetarian Resource Group (VRG) is a source of vegetarian information, vegetarian recipes, and a resource for all aspects of a vegetarian lifestyle, with even a listing of vegetarian travel services and tips on how to order vegetarian when dining out. In addition to its very complete website, the VRG has archived numerous vegetarian-based articles and has published vegan cookbooks as well as a newsletter and a magazine entitled the *Vegetarian Journal.*

http://fnic.nal.usda.gov
Perhaps the most comprehensive collection of information is available from the National Agricultural Library USDA. Here you'll find names of articles, pamphlets, and books covering vegetarian nutrition, plus suggestions on ways to obtain the various materials.

www.vegsoc.org
Formed in England in 1847, the Vegetarian Society of the United Kingdom is the longest-running all-vegetarian group in the world, espousing and supporting an all-vegetarian lifestyle that includes

many levels of activities, from fundraising, lecturing, and providing nutritional advice to creating recipes and teaching cooking. The group also established and runs the annual National Vegetarian Week with concurrent activities.

www.kidshealth.org

Help for parents to learn about how best to feed children for their maximum health.

www.vrg.org/teen

Valuable information and tips specifically aimed at teens.

www.ivu.org

The acknowledged grandfather of the international vegetarian movement, the International Vegetarian Union (IVU) came into being in the early 1900s in Germany during the first vegetarian congress. A nonprofit group, its sole purpose is to promote vegetarianism worldwide, a goal they want to achieve by holding regular congresses, answering questions, dispensing diets and recipes, and maintaining an archive on vegetarian-based information.

Additional Resources

www.moosewoodcooks.com

Upstate New York's Moosewood Restaurant is commonly credited with kicking off the boom of vegetarianism in the United States. The restaurant, which opened in Ithaca in the early 1970s, certainly took vegetarian cooking and ideals and made them palatable and interesting to a new generation of Americans. The website offers hundreds of recipes and information about the restaurant.

www.eatright.org

With more than 68,000 members as of this writing, the American Dietetic Association (ADA) is the world's largest group of dietary professionals. The website covers the fundamentals of a basic vegetarian diet and provides tips on how to eat out vegetarian and ways to shift to a vegetarian way of eating.

www.oldwayspt.org

Founded in the 1980s by Bostonian K. Dun Gifford, the Oldways organization has as its mission simplifying nutritional science and converting food facts into palate-pleasing fare. Gifford and colleague Sara Baer-Sinnott have initiated numerous food-related activities and conferences to promote better health through better diets.

Appendix B: The Vegetarian Cook's Essentials

Equipment for a Vegetarian's Kitchen

While the only tools a cook needs to make most of the dishes in this book are a sharp, solid knife (such as an 8" French or chef's knife) and a good cutting board, the following items will make certain jobs much easier and more professional looking.

Mandolin	A slim metal or plastic board with a planelike blade, a mandolin makes cutting delicate julienne strips and paper-thin slices into child's play.
Greens Spinner	Dressings adhere to dry lettuce leaves, and run off wet ones. An inexpensive lettuce spinner gyrates away excess water, making your salads more intensely flavored.
Wire Whisk	A 10" balloon whisk has fine wires that incorporate air into foods, lightening their texture. This tool is also essential for making dressings and sauces where insoluble ingredients like oil and vinegar are combined.
Standing Electric Mixer	This is an investment for life. Standing mixers cost about $300, but make kneading dough, whipping cream, softening butter, and mixing just about anything so much easier
Food Processor	A food processor makes chopping and mixing faster. Dips and dressings practically make themselves.
Blender	Not to be used in place of a food processor or vice versa, blenders yield smooth, velvety purées that most processors just can't do.
Stovetop Grill Pan	Easier, healthier, and more eco-friendly than charcoal or gas grills, a cast-iron or coated alloy pan with ridged surfaces for indoor grilling is incredibly useful.
Spice Grinder	Any small coffee grinder can be used as a spice grinder. Since the best flavor comes from spices that are toasted as whole seeds in a dry pan, then ground just before use, having one of these devices is a good idea. You can use the same one for coffee if you clean it out really well between uses.

The Basic Pantry

The following items can make your vegetarian cooking the best it can be, and should be around the house at all times:

- ❑ Extra-virgin Olive Oil
- ❑ Dijon-style Mustard
- ❑ Kosher (Coarse) Salt
- ❑ Japanese Rice Vinegar
- ❑ Pickled Jalapeño Peppers
- ❑ Assorted Dried Beans
- ❑ Dried Mushrooms (such as Chinese Black Mushrooms or Shiitakes)
- ❑ Vegetable Bouillon Cubes (in case you can't make stock)
- ❑ Wild Rice
- ❑ Dry Sherry (for use in any dish calling for white wine—it keeps for years)

Standard U.S./Metric Measurement Conversions

VOLUME CONVERSIONS

U.S. Volume Measure	Metric Equivalent
⅛ teaspoon	0.5 milliliter
¼ teaspoon	1 milliliter
½ teaspoon	2 milliliters
1 teaspoon	5 milliliters
½ tablespoon	7 milliliters
1 tablespoon (3 teaspoons)	15 milliliters
2 tablespoons (1 fluid ounce)	30 milliliters
¼ cup (4 tablespoons)	60 milliliters
⅓ cup	90 milliliters
½ cup (4 fluid ounces)	125 milliliters
⅔ cup	160 milliliters
¾ cup (6 fluid ounces)	180 milliliters
1 cup (16 tablespoons)	250 milliliters
1 pint (2 cups)	500 milliliters
1 quart (4 cups)	1 liter (about)

WEIGHT CONVERSIONS

U.S. Weight Measure	Metric Equivalent
½ ounce	15 grams
1 ounce	30 grams
2 ounces	60 grams
3 ounces	85 grams
¼ pound (4 ounces)	115 grams
½ pound (8 ounces)	225 grams
¾ pound (12 ounces)	340 grams
1 pound (16 ounces)	454 grams

OVEN TEMPERATURE CONVERSIONS

Degrees Fahrenheit	Degrees Celsius
200 degrees F	95 degrees C
250 degrees F	120 degrees C
275 degrees F	135 degrees C
300 degrees F	150 degrees C
325 degrees F	160 degrees C
350 degrees F	180 degrees C
375 degrees F	190 degrees C
400 degrees F	205 degrees C
425 degrees F	220 degrees C
450 degrees F	230 degrees C

BAKING PAN SIZES

U.S.	Metric
8 × 1½ inch round baking pan	20 × 4 cm cake tin
9 × 1½ inch round baking pan	23 × 3.5 cm cake tin
11 × 7 × 1½ inch baking pan	28 × 18 × 4 cm baking tin
13 × 9 × 2 inch baking pan	30 × 20 × 5 cm baking tin
2 quart rectangular baking dish	30 × 20 × 3 cm baking tin
15 × 10 × 2 inch baking pan	30 × 25 × 2 cm baking tin (Swiss roll tin)
9 inch pie plate	22 × 4 or 23 × 4 cm pie plate
7 or 8 inch springform pan	18 or 20 cm springform or loose-bottom cake tin
9 × 5 × 3 inch loaf pan	23 × 13 × 7 cm or 2 lb narrow loaf or pâté tin
1½ quart casserole	1.5 liter casserole
2 quart casserole	2 liter casserole

Index